W9-AUN-944

THE CONVICT AND THE COLONEL

THE
CONVICT
AND THE
COLONEL

Richard Price

BEACON PRESS • BOSTON

Beacon Press
25 Beacon Street
Boston, Massachusetts 02108-2892
www.beacon.org

Beacon Press books
are published under the auspices of
the Unitarian Universalist Association of Congregations.

© 1998 by Richard Price
All rights reserved
Printed in the United States of America

Excerpts from "The Schooner *Flight*" and "The Sea Is History"
from *Collected Poems 1948–1984* by Derek Walcott.
Copyright © 1986 by Derek Walcott.
Reprinted by permission of Farrar, Straus & Giroux, Inc.

03 02 01 00 99 98   8 7 6 5 4 3 2 1

Text design by Scott-Martin Kosofsky at The Philidor Company, Boston.

Price, Richard, 1941–
    The convict and the colonel / Richard Price
        p.   cm.
    Includes bibliographical references.
    ISBN 0–8070–4650–7 (cloth)
    ISBN 0–8070–4651–5 (paperback)
    1. Martinique—History. 2. Massacres—Martinique—
History—20th century. 3. Aribot, Médard. I. Title.
F2084.8.P75   1998
972.98'2—DC21
                                        97–29522

To the fishermen of Petite Anse,
old, and especially young,
who continue, against all odds,
to brave the seas, and make a life of it

Contents

"*Photo*" of the Colonel, by Médard Aribot, ca. 1924
Inset: Colonel Maurice de Coppens, early 1900s

"Colonel Coppens—he's the one who sent Méda to forced labor. It was because of that '*photo*.' He made a '*photo*' of the colonel and he showed people. Coppens said, 'Who made that?' and they arrested the man. Hard labor—for life! For a man who had no education, who didn't know a trade, a complete innocent. A man like that, to send him to the penal colony. He hadn't stolen, he hadn't hurt a soul—all he'd done was to make that '*photo*.'"

—ERNEST LARCHER, fisherman, 1983

Prologue

Today, when the spectacle of the past excites the kind of attention
which earlier epochs attached to the new . . .

—RAPHAEL SAMUEL, *Theatres of Memory*

LIKE MANY RESTLESS TRAVELERS during the second half of the twentieth
century, I have experienced the implantation of "modernization"—its
outward signs, its inward contradictions—several different times, each
with its own inflections: first in post–World War II New York City, later in rural
Chiapas and Andalusia, then in the rainforests of Suriname and, intermittently
over a thirty-five-year-long period, on the island of Martinique.

A very early memory. Nose pressed up against a frosty windowpane by my
bed, looking down Broadway at a derailed trolley-car surrounded by gesticulating people, stranded in the swirling nighttime snow. The war was still on, it
would have been 1944. Whenever my grandmother, who lived in that same 115th
Street apartment house, took me out with her, we'd walk hand in hand down that
same stretch of Broadway to Shuck the Butcher's, where thick sawdust formed
little mountains on the floor, we'd go past Yee's Chinese Laundry, the flower
shop, and Salter's bookstore and stop in at Saul the Grocer's, who might give me
a piece of candy, before we went next door to the fruit and vegetable man, whose
name now escapes me but who had brass scales with clock-like hands hanging
from the ceiling. Each time, it was "Good morning, Mrs. Swee" (or, if I was with
my mother, "How are you today, Mrs. Price?"). It seems to me that in the apartment—whether ours or my grandparents'—clothes were always drying on
pull-up racks in the kitchen or, in good weather, on lines operated by pulleys,
strung across to the next building. There was also the itinerant knife-and-scis-
sors sharpener, who sang out his presence, voice echoing between the walls of
apartment houses, and who kept a monkey on a leash. And bottles of milk deliv-
ered at dawn by horse-drawn wagon.

Not long after the crowds celebrating V-J Day (my parents took me down-
town to see the jubilation, which I still remember), or so it seems, a series of

inventions began making their appearance. These harbingers of progress, these icons of modernity, periodically came into my consciousness, usually in someone else's apartment first, then after a while in our own. Each defined a moment, each caused a flurry of excitement and pride of possession: the washing machine, with a wringer on top (my grandmother's, around 1946); the television (nine-inch screen, our own, around 1947); the hi-fi long-playing phonograph (which replaced our wind-up Victrola in the late forties); and then, after the move to our own house in the suburbs (Riverdale) in 1948, yet more significant lifestyle changes—a second car, a basement washer-dryer, a "deep freeze" that made Birds Eye frozen vegetables a staple of dinnertime, and (for my sister and me) a dog. And shopping by car at the A&P—also, as it happens, on Broadway, but miles north of the earlier stores, just across the city line from our new house, in Yonkers—the first supermarket I remember. This march of progress, this material evolution, seemed absolutely normal, very much the order of the day.

In June 1962, from the top of a hill in Martinique, I looked down for the first time on what I saw as a spectacularly beautiful, isolated fishing village—Petite Anse—rimming the blue-green Caribbean. I stayed on to spend the summer there, doing an undergraduate project sponsored by Harvard and the National Science Foundation. There was no electricity or water in the hundred or so small houses, and there were no cars. A sole crank-up telephone served the whole community in case of emergencies. Bread arrived by fishing boat each morning from the *bourg* (with its church and postoffice), which was otherwise three hilly kilometers away by a stony track that had recently been made passable, in good weather, for a once-daily *taxi-pays* (an aging bus that took three or four hours to reach Fort-de-France with its cloth stores and furniture emporiums and administrative offices). My now fading photos show largely green spaces slanting down to the sea, with houses scattered about the countryside—a person could walk from one to another, winding by tethered goats and sheep, without interruption. People were proud that, ever since Emancipation over a century before, not a single outsider to the community, white or black, had owned an inch of Petite Anse land: as far as the eye could see, the land belonged to the families of fishermen. Storebought necessities—rice, sugar, rum, onions, matches—were purchased locally, from tiny shops attached to houses. (Storekeepers replenished their goods by fishing canoe from Fort-de-France.) Most store-buying was on credit, recorded in a notebook and paid up whenever cash was available. Ground provisions came from kitchen gardens or from higglers who headed-in baskets over the hills from the north. Cooking was on charcoal. Chamberpots were dutifully emptied early each morning into the sea. Men fished from three in the morning till noon, mended nets and other equipment in the afternoon, and hit the rumshops by twilight, before retiring soon after. The largest and most modern house in the village was owned by Amédée, the crippled *quimboiseur*, master of the magic that permitted a fisherman to catch more than his neighbor.

Now, thirty-five years later, Petite Anse is officially part of Europe. Electricity, indoor plumbing, roads and streets and streetlights, and everywhere front gates (some electronic), cinderblock walls, and chain-link fences. Houses have more than quadrupled in size, many with rooms underneath for tourists. There are two small hotels, one with a swimming pool. Most adults have driver's licenses and many families own two or even three cars. There are local people who go on Caribbean cruises. The bulk of shopping takes place in giant supermarkets on the outskirts of Fort-de-France, now but forty-five traffic-choked minutes away. Marijuana and even cocaine are beginning to become a problem among the largely unemployed youth. And there are local women who not only drive BMWs and initiate divorce, but who own French poodles, on leashes.

Time, or rather the experience of it that we call memory, is like an old-fashioned Martiniquan concertina—alternately being squeezed and pulled apart, compressing some things, stretching out others, and in the process making music. From my present perspective, the Martinique I first knew represents a midpoint—thirty-some years back from the present, thirty-some years forward from the key events to be described in this book. As I stood on that hill, looking down upon Petite Anse in 1962, the year 1925 was as close to me, in objective time, as is the moment I write today. Yet, experientially, it now seems so distant, nearly "lost"—as the Martiniquan newspaper likes to say of that era—"in the mists of time." Our task here is to expand the instrument, to reopen those folds, to play some of those "old-time" *mazouks* and *béguines*, rife with clarinet riffs.

Today, looking backward, the fishing families of Petite Anse tend to envision an amorphous, atemporal period of "before"—stretching, however implausibly, from slavery days through colonial repression on into the early 1960s. And then there is the "modern" present. "Before," time somehow stopped, relationships between those who had (the *béké* planter class, the mulatto professional class, the white colonial officials) and those who didn't (the working masses, everyone in Petite Anse) seemed set in stone. "Since," bourgeoisification (thanks to floods of money distributed by the French state) has been rampant and every local family has participated. Discussions of "before" bring waves of nostalgia: about family and neighborly relations, about community intimacy, about the small pleasures of life, from homemade coconut confections to families singing creole Christmas carols in candlelit sitting rooms. Now, each new year brings its host of new consumer possibilities. The local world, firmly bound into the global system, changes weekly if not daily; tourism is said to have doubled in the past three years; and while a couple of years ago, three or four sailboats might anchor for the weekend off Anse Chaudière below our house, today [1995]—on a Sunday—I count thirty-five, including Chris-Crafts with jet-skis on board. And nothing surprises anymore—not the boatload of naked (yes, completely nude) tourists that swam ashore to the beach where fishermen were mending their nets last week, not the presence at Christmas dinner of the twenty-year-old son's white girlfriend from Toulouse, not the exhibition *case créole*—a replica of the kind of house many people lived in in 1962— constructed in 1994 on the Place de l'Eglise by the mayor's office as a "cultural exhibition" to show the youth of today the way it used to be. As our friend Emilien commented wistfully the other day: "When you go to Diamant, you don't see any people from Diamant there any more. I wonder where they've gone? All you see," he said, "are foreigners—and restaurants."

THIS BOOK CENTERS on a minor historical event (the Diamant massacre of 1925) and a marginal historical figure (Médard Aribot) to try to unfold meanings of more general significance. These choices are emblematic. Since the same power relations molded these events and people as those that did the better-known incidents of the period, there is the advantage of freshness and discovery afforded by this choice. What I am calling (following local usage) *la guerre du Diamant* (the war of Diamant) is but one of a large number of harsh colonial confrontations during the early twentieth century. (In her detailed chapter on Martiniquan political life between 1910 and 1939, historian Cécile Celma gives it two paragraphs out of forty-three pages of narrative that cover in great detail the better-known excesses of the period, and L. Abénon does not even mention it in his own historical essay on these years.)[1] And Médard Aribot, though he has now become "folklorized" in various ways that preserve his memory (see Part III), remains hardly known at all as a "historical" figure—*France-Antilles Magazine* says, "his life seems closer to a folktale or fantasy . . . no one will ever know the truth," and the editors of the *Cahiers du Patrimoine* add that what we know of him is destined to remain forever at the level of "legend," not history.

Diamant and its neighboring commune Anses d'Arlet—which has been our Martiniquan home since the 1960s—are privileged witnesses to changing Martiniquan realities. The first relatively reliable modern agricultural census of the island, made in the 1930s, discloses that these two communes are the only ones in the south of the island not dominated by sugar cane. The number of Diamantois and Arlesiens permanently employed in the cane fields and distilleries was relatively small. Rather, most men fished (using a variety of techniques, depending on season), did a bit of (largely subsistence) gardening on peasant plots, did occasional artisanal work such as masonry, and engaged in seasonal wage labor in the local sugar industry. People in these communes were far more self-reliant and independent than those, say, who lived in the neighboring communes to the north, Petit-Bourg or Rivière-Salée, where the rhythm of life was dominated by the sugar factories.

What this means is that when Martinique shifted, during the 1960s and 1970s, from a producer economy to a heavily assisted welfare-based consumer economy, the shock was especially pronounced in places like Diamant and Anses d'Arlet, where formerly independent people became more or less passive recipients of state largesse. In contrast, for those who had long lived in the shadow of the sugar mills, one kind of dependence was largely replaced by another. Qualities of independence and initiative that had served southcoast fishermen well during the first part of the century became less relevant as the structure of opportunity and rewards shifted radically.

This Martinique story is, of course, part of a larger one, which some would explain mainly in economic terms (though I hope to show that is only part of the picture). Collini, for example, writes:

The transition from the modernizing aesthetic of the 1940s and 1950s to the "retro" boom of recent decades, the explosion of enthusiasm for all things "period" or "authentic," whether in architecture, design, music, "living museums," or the many varieties of collecting. . . . What distinguishes the pastifying mania of recent decades is that the post-war diffusion of prosperity and higher living standards has put this degree of aesthetic choice within reach of an unprecedented number of people. When the historic burdens of scarcity and labour are initially lightened, the first move is toward convenience and freedom. For a generation whose parents had scrimped and struggled . . . and had endured the rigours of the Depression and the deprivations of wartime austerity . . . the passage to utopia was finished with formica.

Our examination of cognate processes from the eccentric perspective of Martinique may help nuance the larger picture, in which most of us continue to play bit parts.

Fishing canoes (*gonmyé*) in Petite Anse

A King, by Médard Aribot, ca. 1960

[A circle of wooden stakes marking out the cockpit. Dense black crowd, noisy and excited.]

AN EXCITED VOICE: Go for him, Christophe! Get him now, Christophe!

A SECOND EQUALLY EXCITED VOICE: Hold your ground, Pétion! Make him come to you! . . .

AN EXCITED VOICE: Strike, Christophe! Kill him!

A PLEADING VOICE: Pétion, bob and weave, make him chase you. . . .

A VOICE: Alright! Alright! This guy's tougher than Drum Major and Peck-Out-His-Eye!

A VOICE: Momma! What a shot in the old eye!

CROWD: Hurrah! Hurrah!

[THE COMMENTATOR enters and goes stage front]

Let's catch our breath for a moment and tell it like it is. Yes, for some time now, it's been the fashion in this country. It used to be that fighting cocks had names like Drum Major or Peck-Out-His-Eye. But today they're named after political figures—in this corner Christophe, over there Pétion. At first, it didn't much appeal to me but, come to think of it, it's no sillier than many fashions. A King and a President of the Republic are bound to tear each other's eyes out. And if they like to tear out each other's eyes, why not name fighting cocks after them? . . . You might counter that while it's all very simple with fighting cocks, relations between men are more complex. But I'd say, not necessarily. The main thing is to understand the situation and to know the men the cocks were named for. Who is this Christophe? Who is this Pétion? That's what I'm here to tell you.

—"Prologue: The Cock Fight"
in *La Tragédie du Roi Christophe*, by Aimé Césaire

Martinique street scene, 1920s

Election day, main street, Anses d'Arlet, 1962

I. La Guerre du Diamant: 1925

Because the grassroots militants of the Antillean workers' movement were trained more in the Jauressian legal tradition than according to the norms of Marxist-Leninist revolution, legal activities have always been privileged in their political choices.... Not that violence has been absent from Antillean history. But popular violence has never had more than an episodic character, spontaneous and, ultimately, derisory when compared to the permanent, calculated, and highly effective violence of the bourgeoisie.

—ÉDOUARD DE LÉPINE, "Autour des sénatorials," 1977

A Legitimate Aspiration of Martiniquans. Martinique—like Guadeloupe, Guyane, and Réunion, all of which are commonly referred to by the rather inappropriate label "French colonies"—is in truth a *département* of France. Colonized shortly after the Discovery by Normans, Bretons, and Africans, she is today the result of that mixture of races that have trod her tiny soil, a little populace whose epidermic coloration varies from ebony black to alabaster white, but which has the same language, the same interests, the same religious beliefs, the same customs and traditions as those of France. By her historical experience, which, for three centuries, has been one and the same as that of France, by the trials they have experienced together, but above all by her great desire and with all her heart, she now wishes, through complete assimilation, to become an integral part of the great and generous French nation.

—J. LUCRÈCE, *Histoire de la Martinique* (official elementary school textbook, 1932)

IN 1986, Philibert told me, "In those days the Clergy always walked hand in hand with the Nobility. We poorfolks belonged to the Third Estate, all those without money made up the Third Estate."[2] It had seemed a strange way for a semiliterate fisherman to begin recounting an event he'd actually participated in six decades before, alluding to l'Abbé Sieyès and the early days of the French Revolution.

"In those days," Philibert continued,

> the *béké*, the capitalist—he had all the money, he had all the land. And now he wanted the political power. It was the Right who chose their "domestics" to be mayor, men who could hardly read and write, semi-illiterates! It was M. Gabriel Hayot who ran the whole of Martinique. He had the money, he was president of the Conseil Général, he would say "This person is mayor," "That person is *conseiller général*." He'd say, "In this commune, such-and-such a person will be mayor." It was pure dictatorship. He's the one who made Sainte-Rose mayor of Diamant—a carpenter, an illiterate who could scarcely sign his own name. But then, in 1925, old man Giscon threw his hat in the ring. He was better educated than Sainte-Rose, and cleverer. He may not have been a great orator—he didn't speak cor-

Philibert Larcher, 1986

> rect French—but you could understand what he was saying, and he gave his own speeches.
>
> So, it was eight in the morning, May 3rd. We'd gathered in front of the *mairie* [town hall]. The candidates were old man Giscon—a little black fellow, the socialist—and Colonel Coppens, the *béké* who owned the distillery at Dizac. For two days past, the Colonel had been using his ox-cart to have wooden stakes brought in—three meters, five meters tall. Strung with barbed wire he'd gotten in the

Great War, barbed wire with spikes like this, every ten or twenty centimeters! He'd had the whole *mairie* encircled. In front of the building there were rural policemen, customs officials, gendarmes— all armed. Normally, there were four gendarmes in Diamant, and they were there too. So we asked the chief, a Corsican named Battistini, "M. le Brigadier, why is the *mairie* still closed and we can't get in to vote?" No response, so we milled around for a while. Then suddenly he said under his breath, "All you have to do is bust in the door!"[3]

The doors of the *mairie* were wooden shutters. Well, we pushed them in and entered. Once inside, we saw that they'd changed the table, they'd put in a table made of heavy wood, four centimeters thick. And they'd nailed down the ballot box. You couldn't move it, you couldn't take it away. It was bigger than the door, it was too big to pass through the window. We'd been had! When the crowd entered the *mairie*, we were met by the men of Colonel Coppens.

"Not a voter in sight." Troops guarding a *mairie*, municipal elections, May 1925

They had come in through the rear. We'd come in through the front. They were waiting with clubs—right and left, the blows began falling.

I interrupted to ask if the club-wielders were gendarmes. "No," Philibert continued,

they were the Colonel's hired help, his own thugs, the men who worked in the distillery, right on his property. Now I saw all this. And I saw a fellow called Eugène Désanges[4] with a revolver. There was an old fellow—he was seventy—who called out to him, "You're a thief! We've caught you with your hand in the cookie jar!" Because we saw that the ballot box was already full! The box had been stuffed. Ballots top to bottom—all with the name of Coppens. So, the old man shouted, "You're a pack of thieves!" And the other one struck him a blow on the head and the old man fell, *vip!*, face to the ground. Bloodbath! The gendarme was there, just strolling around the *mairie*. I said, "Look at that man. He struck that other one. He's in a pool of blood!" The gendarme just kept walking, hands in his pockets. Me, I was twenty-five—no, twenty-two, twenty-three years old. So I grabbed the gendarme by his shoulder strap, "Look, that guy with the revolver just struck that other man. Arrest him! Arrest him!" The man with the gun went outside and picked up a stone. He came at me *poh!* *Pip!* I went down and didn't wake up for twenty-four hours. Look.

Philibert bent and pointed to his head, where the scar was still clear.

Now everyone was fighting—inside the *mairie* it was *pa! pa! pa! pa!* I was being crushed underfoot by the crowd. Well, someone went and telephoned Anses d'Arlet to report that I'd been killed. "They've gotten Larcher. There's been a bloodbath." Des Étages—the man they murdered later in Ducos—he came over from Anses d'Arlet, where he was supervising the election, and took me in a car to the hospital in St-Esprit. Doctor Magallon took care of me and nursed me back to health.[5]

At this point, Philibert probably wouldn't mind if we paused for some context, some filling-in from the kinds of books and papers he so respected. Aimé Césaire's soaring words on classic colonialism—written for another occasion—provide some tools that help us begin to grasp the realities of Martinique in the 1920s.

> No one colonizes innocently, nor can a nation colonize without one day suffering the consequences. . . .
>
> Security? Culture? The rule of law? In the meantime, I look around and wherever there are colonizers and colonized face-to-face, I see force, brutality, cruelty, sadism, conflict, and, in a parody of education, the hasty manufacture of a few thousand subordinate functionaries, "boys," artisans, office clerks, and interpreters necessary for the smooth operation of business.
>
> I spoke of contact.
>
> Between colonizer and colonized there is room only for forced labor, intimidation, pressure, the police, taxation, theft, rape, compulsory crops, contempt, mistrust, arrogance, self-complacency, swinishness, brainless elites, degraded masses.
>
> No human contact, only relations of domination and submission which turn the colonizer into a schoolroom supervisor, an army sergeant, a prison guard, a slave driver, and the native into an instrument of production.
>
> It's my turn to state an equation: *colonization = thingification.*
>
> I hear the storm. They talk to me about progress, about "achievements," diseases cured, improved standards of living.
>
> *I* am talking about societies drained of their essence, cultures trampled underfoot, institutions undermined, lands confiscated, religions killed off, magnificent artistic creations destroyed, extraordinary *possibilities* wiped out.

It was indeed the height of empire, a turning point between the emergence from slavery and the present, an "ambiguous" period balanced between the depths of colonial repression and the hope for a more dignified future, "the period out of which," as historian Cécile Celma puts it, "emerged the Martiniquan of today."[6] With "universal" suffrage (for men only), elections had become the focus of intense interest. To the working masses who made up the great bulk of the population, the ballot box held out the promise of a better day. To the rising mulatto bourgeoisie, from which was drawn the class of politicians, it represented direct power. To the large *béké* planters and their ally the colonial governor, who ran the island from behind the scenes, elections represented moments of danger, and no efforts were spared to maintain control.

The *békés*, as de Lépine reminds us, were at the time the sole industrialists of the island and their sugar/rum factories the only factories. Land and industry were theirs and theirs alone. The "ten families" of *békés* who dominated the island constituted less than 5 percent of landowners but owned more than 75 percent of the land. Sugar and rum comprised 90 percent of Martinique's exports and this industry employed more than two-thirds of the island's labor force. Vast *béké* fortunes had been built during World War I, as the export price of sugar increased by a factor of five and that of rum by ten, ushering in a grand era of

Ruins of the distillery (which functioned into the 1950s) and the eighteenth-century *château* of the Hayot family, Anses d'Arlet. Above, 1963. Facing page, 1996

conspicuous consumption—the latest American motor cars (Fords, Studebakers), ostentatious villas on the Route de Didier high above the capital—and no family benefited more than the Hayots.

During the 1920s (and the surrounding decades), brute force—whether exercised by the *békés* (and winked at by colonial authorities) or exercised directly by the *forces de l'ordre* in the name of state security—was repeatedly used to keep the working population cowed. When on 5 February 1923, Conseiller Général Eugène Aubéry—owner of the giant sugar factory of Lareinty and perhaps the second richest man in the island[7]—heard that his socialist adversary Lagrosillière was holding an electoral meeting at Morne-Pitault above the Lamentin plain, he loaded several dozen armed men in trucks, drove up to the house where the meeting was underway, and opened fire, wounding eight and killing, by error, his own assistant at Lareinty. It was only a matter of months before the incident was permanently shelved by the judiciary. A few days later it was the turn of the colonial authorities themselves. In a bloody confrontation at the sugar mill of Bassignac (Trinité), heavily armed gendarmes under the command

of Brigadier Nouvel, as well as relatives, friends, and employees of the *béké* sugar mill owners, fired at the backs of fleeing sugar workers, who had been on strike, leaving two dead and three wounded.

Politics had a face-to-face reality and rivals often squared off directly. In 1921, in the courtyard of the Palais Bourbon in Paris, the two rival *parlémentaires* from Martinique, Lémery and Lagrosillière, tussled publicly, the latter telegramming Fort-de-France triumphantly: "Slapped, kicked in the behind, spat in face of Lémery publicly courtyard Chamber of Deputies to avenge democracy and persecuted

Lémery and Lagrosillière

friends."[8] And similar behavior was not uncommon in the chamber of the Conseil Général in Martinique: Lagrosillière had exchanged harsh words with another pillar of the Right, the *béké* Colonel de Coppens, a relative and close friend of Aubéry, accusing the "capitalists" of having tried to buy him off with cash, which led to a formal duel between Lagrosillière and the Colonel.[9]

Two political parties faced off during the mid-twenties in Martinique. The Bloc Républicain (l'Union, the Parti de l'Usine) was led by Sénateur Henry Lémery, who had the support of the Church, the *grands békés* (who owned the sugar industry), the mulatto bourgeoisie, and the colonial administration—and who, as former undersecretary of state for Transportation and the Merchant Marine, was also well-connected in Paris.[10] They were opposed by the Fédération Socialiste, led by ex-Député Joseph Lagrosillière ("Lagros"), whose grandmother had been a slave and who drew his support from the working masses.

The colonial governor was Henri Marius Richard (whose father had also been governor of Martinique). Born in 1879 in Algeria, he had taken a diploma in the Annamite language and had served as administrator in Indochina and Dakar. In 1922, on the eve of his departure to take up his post in Martinique, Richard was described by the *chef du service* in glowing terms: "In the several capacities he has occupied during the past years, Administrator-in-Chief RICHARD has always shown himself to be a truly outstanding civil servant, not only highly cultured but recognized for his ability to carry things through." On arrival, he announced his political neutrality and respect for the laws. "I am in Martinique solely as an administrator. Those under my charge will soon find that political squabbles will in no way influence me nor will I ever involve myself in them." And as a true man of the empire, he noted with enthusiasm, "There was a time, perhaps, when one could speak of a France bounded by the North

Sea, the Atlantic, and the Mediterranean. But today, France is one vast land stretching out to Africa, Madagascar, Indochina, and the Antilles."

By early 1924, Governor Richard had developed a precise perspective on what he called "Martiniquan politics," and the idea that his adversaries hoped to gain power through the ballot almost seems to have shocked him: "There are two parties here," he wrote the minister of the colonies.

Governor Richard

> The first, which is "neo-Schoelcherist," blindly follows M. le député Lagrosillière. It is highly organized and well-disciplined. The second is less a party than a conglomerate of fairly heterogeneous interests (shopkeepers, planters, factory owners, etc.), grouped around M. Lémery and devoted to quelling the rising tide of a thinly disguised Communism, not to say Bolshevism. The goal of the neo-Schoelcherists is simple: to win, by hard struggle, all electoral seats and take over all elected assemblies in the Colony. . . . The ravages wrought by this strategy are immense.

At times, Richard now displayed open disdain toward Martiniquan audiences. In François, June 1924, he is quoted as having warned: "I will leave Martinique when I am good and ready. I will be tough, very tough, on my political adversaries and, at the same time, intend to reward those who share my political opinions." And shortly thereafter, he pinned the medal of the *Légion d'honneur* on Eugène Aubéry. The governor had become "the man of the *békés* and the reactionary sugarmill owners." He had by this time also helped "arrange" the election of rightist *sénateurs* and *députés*, with the financial support of large *béké* families.[11]

By early 1925, France had a new government (the "Cartel of the Left") and a new minister of the colonies, André Hesse. Richard, who didn't have the confidence of the newcomers, seems at this time to have been doing his best simply to hang on. The ministry had been getting an earful from diverse sources. Louis Séjourné, losing socialist candidate in the Sainte-Marie elections of May 1924, had cabled the minister to

> protest with indignation . . . the scandalous frauds that have
> deprived me of a sure majority in the elections, as well as the incred-
> ible attitude of Governor Richard, who actively participated in the
> campaign against me, has shown disdain for all your instructions
> and dispatches, has expelled our delegates from the voting bureaus,
> and filled the voting places with gendarmes in order to terrorize the
> electorate and arrive at a result which is a heinous caricature of uni-
> versal suffrage. I protest in the name of the broad majority of a
> population whose attachment for the Mother Country has been
> profoundly damaged.

And Hesse took it upon himself to send Richard a cable warning him to maintain complete neutrality and to avoid even the appearance of taking political sides. Meanwhile, Hesse was relying on Inspector General Pégourier, whom he had sent out from Paris specifically to report on the May 1925 municipal elections, to tell him the truth about what was happening. Hesse reiterated in a cable on 21 May: "I therefore ask you to follow very closely electoral events on the ground and report back in great detail. I especially want you to confirm that army and gendarmerie are used only to maintain order and that no military or police deployment be made that could be interpreted as aiding one or another political party."

We are faced with stark contrasts. The mass of poor people believed in elections, excited by the possibility that voting might change their condition. The oligarchy and the governor, hiding behind legalisms of one sort or another, were hard at work trying to disguise their ongoing subversion of legal rights and the maintenance of the status quo. Racialist perspectives helped rationalize both *béké* and French-administrative actions. One of the more "progressive" *béké* industrialists of the period, a man who had traveled widely outside Martinique,

"... to rot ... in ramshackle rumshops." Photo by Denise Colomb, 1948

told a reporter, "I am delighted that the black laborer, emancipated by the great Schoelcher, has become a citizen just like you and me. But since his capacities are generally quite limited, and he cannot expect to become a factory owner, engineer, or prefect, it is better for him to continue wielding his cutlass in the canefields . . . rather than to rot, clad in rags, in ramshackle rumshops and engage in trivial and ignorant discussions of electoral politics." And many *békés* and others in power clearly did question whether the black working class had the necessary capacities to fulfill the special privileges granted to residents of *les vieilles colonies*. In Paris, Raymond Poincaré's reaction to a 1923 socialist request that electoral irregularities in Martinique be investigated was that "The only real question that needs to be addressed in the Antilles concerns the elimination of universal suffrage." The very even-handed Inspector General Pégourier advanced his argument that the average citizen of the commune of Diamant was by nature brutish, by writing that "He is, indeed, so *sauvage* that the inhabitants of this place are referred to by the nickname of 'Africans.'" And *Le Matin* asked on 20 August 1925, "Must we conclude that France showed an imprudent generosity when it suddenly transformed the poor blacks in our *vieilles colonies*, who had been slaves only yesterday, into voters endowed with all the privileges that it took us, *métropolitains*, so many centuries to win?"

Though official voting laws were the same as in France, electoral abuses had become so frequent and notorious that during the early 1920s, socialist *députés* had proposed special laws in the National Assembly, designed to regularize colonial voting lists, voting cards, and the selection of officials to preside at each polling place. The standard laws required there to be a list of registered voters in each commune, for each voter to have a "voting card" (an official I.D.), and for voting to take place in the *mairie*, presided over by a "voting bureau" (a temporarily set-up group of authorities, normally including the mayor and members of each participating party). Apparently, it had become customary in Martinique to distribute the "voting cards" only on the election day itself and often only to the political allies of the mayor, and to choose as "supervisors" of the voting bureau only his friends. Governor Richard, when queried about these proposed reforms, indicated assent but insisted that, in addition, "all voting must be overseen by the mayor, assisted by two gendarmes" and affirmed that "it is indispensable that the counting of votes be done by two gendarmes."

During one eight-month period in 1923-1924, eighteen separate elections were held in Martinique (including those for *député* and *sénateur*) and "almost all," according to the governor, "were later appealed through official channels" because of allegations of fraud. The situation was clearly getting out of hand. Just before the municipal elections of May 1925, at the same time the Minister sent out Pégourier's special mission, the French Socialist Party, ever alert to potential repression in the colonies, sent out the editor-in-chief of *Paris-Soir*, Ludovic[Louis]-Oscar Frossard, to report back.

Only days before the balloting, the governor ordered summary arrests. Frossard cabled that Lagrosillière and Séjourné, the socialist leaders, had both been detained: Lagrosillière "is accused of so-called 'inciting to riot' during a political speech. This ridiculous and heinous judicial harassment is a scandal.... During the upcoming municipal elections, we must see that universal suffrage is truly free—no gendarmes guarding the ballot boxes and with supervision carried out by the official representatives of each party." Frossard's colleague Charles Lussy added: "The only crime committed by MM. Séjourné and Lagrosillière was to lead the electoral campaign against the friends and allies of the governor. This raises a question: Does universal suffrage still exist in Martinique, or are the Colonies beyond the reach of the law?" And he concludes by underscoring some key Martiniquan realities: "Do not forget that in this colony, where there's all this talk of 'inciting to riot,' there are some thirty big industrialists who have thousands of workers who earn four francs a day. And a loaf of bread costs two francs fifty!"

In a later dispatch, Frossard gave some particulars on local electoral practice, underlining abuses of power:

> If the voting were done honestly, the socialists would win crushing victories in at least 25 of 32 communes. Some 75% of all voters are in their camp. But ballot-box burglary falsifies all results. Here, you're not *elected*, you're *designated*. Having the voters on your side means little if the gendarmes are on the other. To elect a *député*, 100 gendarmes are worth more than 30,000 voters. The 30,000 vote, the 100 gendarmes announce the winner—orders of the governor. This is a fact that no one denies.... Even Governor Richard told me, "There is no truly honest election in this country." ... How do you cheat? First, you fabricate false voting lists ... adding in the dead—this procedure is called "the cemetery".... On election day, you take over the polling place and the voting bureau, expelling the representatives of the opposing party. As for the vote count, no need to worry. Here is a Lagrosillière ballot: the vote counter coolly reads

out "Delmont" and the die's been cast. You protest. You ask the gendarmes to attest to the *flagrant délit*. The gendarmes pay not the slightest attention. . . . In the communes run by the socialists, the gendarmes take away the ballot boxes and stuff them before the count. . . . In Martinique, you can only be elected if M. Richard wishes.

In this political/economic/social context, Philibert Larcher's allusions to the *ancien régime* and the Revolution begin to reverberate more fully.

A one-hundred-franc note, apparently from the late 1940s. At left, the Count of Bourdonnais, eighteenth-century governor in the French Indian Ocean

DIAMANT, like every Martiniquan commune, had its specificities: some two thousand people, divided between a seaside *bourg*—"two rows of little red-roofed houses on either side of a long street along the seacoast," with its church, cemetery, primary school, rumshops, Sunday market, *mairie*, and gendarmerie—and scattered hamlets, including "Morne l'Afrique" where a shipload of indentured "Congos" had settled in the 1860s, stretching over the hills to the north.[12] Most men fished, joined their wives in maintaining peasant gardens, and, in the season, cut cane for *l'usine*, the distillery just outside of town at Dizac. (The existence of a fishing economy, no matter how small-scale, lent Diamantois a significant degree of independence—relative to the rural proletariat of inland communes, who were almost completely dependent on the sugar industry, they could eke out a living at least in part on their own.[13]) Many women worked as higglers, carrying off fish in the morning in baskets on their heads and returning in the afternoon with vegetables from the agricultural communes to the north and east. Here and there along the long unbroken beach, facing spectacular Diamond Rock, a wealthy professional from Fort-de-France would rent a vacation home for the season.

The municipal elections of 3 May 1925, which took place in all the communes of Martinique, forced Diamantois to take sides: the locally born socialist

Main street, Diamant, site of the 1925 "war" (1986)

Ruins of the colonel's distillery at Dizac (1986)

Hilarion Giscon versus the *béké* owner of *l'usine*, Colonel de Coppens. With election fever running particularly high, the governor expected trouble in several communes, including Diamant. On 17 April, he cabled the minister of the colonies for reinforcements, requesting a warship with "at least 100 men," which would stay for a month—but there was insufficient time to put this plan into action.[14] Nonetheless, the governor already had at his disposition a detachment of 86 gendarmes, a company of the colonial infantry (138 men), and a battery of artillery (143 men). Richard had decided to take no chances: each *mairie* would be surrounded by barbed wire and ringed with troops, strictly controlling access to the voting booths.

Richard was operating in an atmosphere charged with paranoia. Five days before the election, the police chief of the commune of Carbet informed him that the socialist mayor, M. Donatien, was "one of the most active members of the extremist committees organized by ex-*député* Lagrosillière" and that he was planning to recruit various "terrorists" who would occupy the *mairie* on election day to assure that only their supporters could vote. "I in no way exaggerate," continued the police chief, "in predicting the gravest disorders, given the state of overexcitement that MM. Lagrosillière and Consort have encouraged by their criminal exhortations, which incite their partisans to revolution. . . . To help avoid this, it would be very useful to have some mounted police who would be able to disperse the crowd."

Outside of Diamant on 3 May, in elections marked by numerous "incidents," something over half the *mairies* were declared won by rightists, the remainder by the left, with most contests then appealed on the basis of suspected fraud. The voting in the commune of Carbet, which was stopped by orders of the governor, received particular notoriety because Richard and his allies thought they could "demonstrate" once and for all what they claimed to be the general methods of the socialists. There, the socialist mayor had constructed a ballot box so large it couldn't be taken through the doors or windows of the *mairie*, in case the governor's men wanted to remove it for "official" counting (in the gendarmerie or in Fort-de-France). Hearing what was going on, the governor had the election halted, the mayor suspended, and the *urne* (ballot box) dismantled and brought to the capital, where he had various photos taken to show the way the socialists planned to cheat by slipping ballots through cracks between the planks. The governor meticulously annotated each photo by hand, before sending them on to the minister of the colonies in Paris: "The whole police brigade of Fort-de-France [9 men] fits comfortably inside the Carbet *urne*," "As the voters cast their ballots, the president could slip other ballots into the *urne*," "Ballots could easily be slipped in through the slit shown in this photograph," "This photograph shows how easily ballots could be slipped into the *urne*."[15] Other sources make clear that on the same day in the commune of Ducos, large sums of money were publicly distributed by the *békés*—one hundred francs per vote, more than seventy thousand francs total. And other frauds were perpetrated elsewhere.

In Diamant itself, on the eve of the May 3rd election, Lagrosillière visited for a meeting in order to galvanize the socialist faithful and to counsel sang-froid—above all, that people not fall into the trap the governor had laid by militarizing the whole procedure.[16] (The socialists had been holding similar meetings throughout the island, knowing they now held a majority among voters.) In Diamant, the socialist majority felt ready to reverse the rightist mayor, Eleuthère Sainte-Rose—the yes-man of Colonel Coppens and the *békés*—and to take political control of the commune. According to law, it was Sainte-Rose who presided over the "voting bureau." And when Philibert and his companions found the ballot box stuffed with three hundred ballots designating Coppens,

"The whole police brigade of Fort-de-France fits comfortably inside the Carbet *urne*"

before the voting had even been declared open, it was Sainte-Rose who was held responsible.

Philibert's account can be supplemented by that of Mathieu Battestini, brigade chief of the gendarmes stationed in Diamant, who described the events of the day in a handwritten report to Governor Richard, dated that very afternoon.

> Acting in accordance with the orders of M. le Gouverneur of Martinique, issued 1 May 1925, designed to insure the maintenance of order in the commune of Diamant on the occasion of the municipal elections of 3 May 1925, we attest that on the said day at eight o'clock, one shutter of the door to the polling place being open, someone called out from inside, "The polls are open." At that moment, some forty voters, who had been in the street outside the polling place, rushed to get inside, yelling, "Open the door," and at the same time pushing the shutter that was still closed. As this would not yield, they broke it in as well as the two windows that bordered the door on each side, and they surged into the polling place. . . .
>
> At about 8:01 . . . we entered the polling place where about thirty people were milling about. Some said, "The voting can now begin."

"As the voters cast their ballots, the president could slip other ballots into the *urne*."

Others yelled out, "No! Open up the ballot box." And others were fighting with clubs. One of these, a certain Philibert Larcher, received a blow to the head and fell unconscious. He was quickly taken to his house. The secretary of the *mairie*, Crossard, as well as two others who took flight, were slightly wounded in the head. A gunshot was fired from outside and the bullet pierced a wall of the front room. Upon our arrival, several people escaped through the rear door of the polling place. Some fifteen stayed, saying they refused to leave until the voting bureau was properly operating. The president of the bureau then asked that everyone leave the room so he could prepare the voting, and all did so. Shortly thereafter, the president, Mayor Ste. Rose of Diamant, opened the ballot box, removed a number of ballots from said box, and tossed them through an open door into a room contiguous with the polling place. He then asked the voters to reenter and at nine o'clock the voting began. When some members of the voting bureau requested that the ballots be counted, the president displayed three packets of one hundred each and asked a policeman to buy some ordinary envelopes, in a store, to replace those that had already been used, but he did not find a sufficient number.

At approximately 11:30, our Commandant de Section, briefly apprized of these facts, instructed us by telephone to ask the president of the voting bureau whether he wanted us to provide special security to insure order for the rest of the day but the president told us that, given the high state of agitation of the populace, it would be better to postpone elections till the following Sunday. . . .

A full investigation will be undertaken into the cause of these various disturbances. [Signed Mathieu Battestini, brigade chief, and two of his mounted police, Laurent Jaegge and Marcel Rouquette]

In the wake of these incidents, Governor Richard canceled the vote and suspended the mayor, rescheduling for 24 May the balloting here and in the three other communes where there had been similar "irregularities." Meanwhile, Inspector General Pégourier sent off a cable to the minister of the colonies, saying: "Irregularities committed by both parties render announced election results suspect. However, all in all elections satisfactory, given no blood was spilled, as excited state of voters might have suggested would occur."

The working masses had once again seen their hopes dashed. Though the socialists held a large majority among voters, they were declared winners of only ten of twenty-six *mairies*. Socialist leaders renewed their efforts in the four remaining communes, where the vote was now set for three weeks hence, and rumors of upcoming fraud and violence were rife. In Diamant, two of the candidates on the socialist list, Hilarion Giscon and Emmanuel Roc, sent a letter of concern to the inspector general, explaining "in a spirit of justice and equity" that while they represented the "largest political party in the commune," the man whom the governor had appointed to preside over the upcoming election as substitute for the suspended mayor was "a schoolteacher who has repeatedly and flamboyantly expressed his political views in public. And already the few—very few—partisans of the mayor's list who are here have been going around boasting that, thanks to the complicity of this president, the ballot box will be taken to Fort-de-France where the results will be falsified to give an overwhelming victory to the mayor's list."

Governor Richard, in a confidential letter of 13 May addressed to the minister of colonies, gave his own summary of the events of 3 May, stressing the subversive nature of "the party that calls itself 'socialist' but which is, in effect, nothing but M. Lagrosillière's personal fiefdom." And in a subsequent "top secret" letter to the minister, Richard expanded, in a more personal vein:

> I have but one regret—that I did not have M. Lagrosillière arrested the day after his last arrival in Martinique when, in a public meeting, he was already inciting his listeners to murder and mayhem. The courts did not dare—such fear does he inspire in them—to take this precautionary measure. . . .
>
> A search warrant was used yesterday at M. Lagrosillière's house. Here is the list of the books that comprise his personal library:
>
> 1°) *The Communist Manifesto*, translated by Charles Audler;
> 2°) *The Communist Manifesto*, by Karl Marx and F. Engels;
> 3°) *The Proletarian Revolution and the Turncoat Kautsky*
>   [by V.I. Lenin];

4°) *"Left-Wing" Communism, an Infantile Disorder*
   [by V.I. Lenin];
5°) *Terrorism and Communism*, by the aforementioned Kautsky;
6°) *On the Road to Insurrection*, by N. Léline [sic. for V.I. Lenin];
7°) *The Communist International at Work*;
8°) *The Dictatorship of the Proletariat* [by Karl Kautsky];
9°) *How Our Colonies Get Treated*, by Boisneuf, sold privately
   by the author.

Is this latest proof really necessary to demonstrate the close links between Lagrosillière and the terrorist mentality of the Communist party?

At the same time, the rightist newspaper, *La Riposte*, published a letter "to the voters of Diamant," dated 16 May, which reveals some of the personalist nature of local electoral battles:

Citizens: Were you not disgusted on 3 May, whichever party you may support, to see the assault on the *mairie* by some thirty crazies armed with clubs, who pillaged this building that personifies the commune and whose sanctity, throughout our political struggles, has always been respected? Diamant has already experienced its share of troubles. Today a new danger looms. M. Emmanuel Roc is bent at all costs on returning to the *mairie*, which, for eighteen years, he considered his private preserve. Who would be capable of enumerating the number of bottles of Quinquina and St. Raphael that he consumed in the company of his three or four mistresses!—whom he supported with public funds, while the church, the school, the *mairie*, the office of the justice of the peace, and the presbytery were falling into ruin!

Meanwhile, the socialist newspaper, *l'Aurore*, in a front-page editorial devoted to the 3 May elections in Diamant, expressed some particularly prescient polemics:

Once again Governor Richard has made a travesty of universal suffrage in Martinique. Once again, through the violence of his gendarmes and reckless soldiers, this representative of the government of the Republic among us has substituted his personal wishes for the will of the people.

This negrophobic potentate had decided at all costs to proclaim the reactionary lists elected, and for that he had the brigades of gendarmes, he had the soldiers of the colonial artillery and infantry, he had the local customs men, and he had the rural police. All these valiant men, whose mission is to defend society, found themselves transformed by force of circumstance into electoral bandits and ballot box burglars.

And the crime was committed! . . .

Throughout all this, our own friends remained calm. They did not give Monsieur Richard the pretext he was seeking for a fusillade.

The stage was set for what Diamant fishermen still call *la guerre du Diamant*—and what French officialdom (including the national archives) refers to as *l'affaire du Diamant*—an event forever etched in bi-partite form, the Left on one side, the Right on the other.

"The polls are open," 1925[17]

Philibert making a fishpot, 1986

La Gauche

[PHILIBERT LARCHER, RECORDED 28 MAY 1986[18]] *After two weeks in the hospital, I came back home so I could vote on the 24th. My head was still bandaged. Me and my friends, we were all set to vote. There was a black man called Cadrot who was principal of the school in Petit-Bourg—or was it*

Fisherman's house (1920s?)

Ducos? Anyway, they had sent him here to preside over the voting. So, he said, "Each party will have its representatives," he said this and he said that and so on and so forth—it was all going smoothly. And then he also said that when the time came for counting the ballots, they would have everyone go outside in front of the mairie *except for four people from my side and four people from your side and do the count. Everyone agreed. It all went along smoothly. Everyone was voting: vote, vote, vote, vote. (It was only men who voted in those days, women didn't vote. There were more than 300 registered voters and scarcely 50 were for Coppens.)*

La Droite

[GENDARMERIE NATIONALE: 24 MAY 1925, 18h30] The undersigned, Justin Nouvel[19] and Antoine Delfour, brigade chiefs, and Jacques Brihl, Joseph Piotelet, Fernand Duffaud, and Georges Thomassin, mounted police, all residing in Diamant . . . certify that at 7:30 this morning we went to the *mairie* where at 8 o'clock the president of the voting bureau passed on to us the formal request that we:

    1°) maintain order in and around the voting place throughout the day, and

    2°) when the balloting is finished, seal the ballot box and transmit it to the governor. . . .

Colonel Maurice de Coppens

At 8h30, the bureau was opened without incident, presided over by M. Cadrot, president, and by two assessors from each party.

It was around eleven o'clock or noon when I saw Coppens strolling down the street. I was just going by the post-office on my way to ask my buddies from St.-Esprit what news they had of the elections there. He said to me [in Creole], "You're singing, you're talking, but we've already taken care of Des Étages and Zizine." "Liar! Fucking toad! Coward! Asshole!" That's how I replied to Coppens. I was tough. But besides, I didn't really believe what he said. He told me, "Des Étages and Zizine have already been taken care of. Your friends in Ducos, they're dead. And your own turn won't be long in coming." That's what he said! At first I thought he was joking. I couldn't believe it. Total savagery. After all, we were in the time of the Republic. I didn't imagine it could ever come to that!

[TELEGRAM FROM GISCON TO INSPECTOR PÉGOURIER, sent 14:20 from Diamant, while voting was still in progress]: *"Have honor to inform you bureau constituted illegally. . . . Delivery voting cards denied our party beginning 9 o'clock. Outgoing mayor and candidate Coppens distributing cards in middle of street. Have just seen citizens BORROMÉE, FAUSTIN, and REMY CARDE shoving about fifteen ballots into box.*[20] *VERONIQUE Félix surprised*

At 12h45, in the presence of 5 or 6 voters, several men plus the representatives of the candidates pushed their way toward the ballot box and began a shoving match. We intervened and, after having freed up the ballot box, seized a packet of ten ballots from the hands of Georges Montout and Stanislas Chéry, the first representing Sainte-Rose [the rightists], the second Giscon [the socialists], which they were fighting over. Stanislas Chéry told us that he had grabbed them from the hands of Félix Véronique as this latter was trying to force them into the ballot box. This latter, also present in the room, denied this and declared that when he had approached the ballot box to vote, he was holding only one ballot, which he showed us. Georges Montout claimed to have seen them in the hands of Stanislas Chéry. The president asked us formally to clear the room, except for the candidates. We did this and calm was reestablished. The voting continued. . . .

with 18 ballots seized by gendarmerie, MONTOUT Georges, who is not on voting lists, allowed to stay in the room despite protests.

[Signed] GISCON

The bust of Colonel Coppens

[Philibert again:] *Well, around two o'clock—no, maybe four o'clock in the afternoon, it was time to count the votes. They got ready to take the ballot box from the* mairie *to the gendarmerie for the count. Everywhere, there were truckloads of soldiers, soldiers, soldiers. As soon as they'd gotten it to the gendarmerie, where we couldn't get at it, they would do their business [he makes stuffing motion]. We didn't want that, we—*

At ten o'clock and at four o'clock, we booked two men for possession of an illegal weapon: 1°) Sainte-Aimé, Eloi (for carrying an awl), and 2°) Ignace, Raphael (for having a slingshot hidden in his clothes)....

A 15:00, the populace, which had been calm till then, massed in front of the *mairie*, in an open field to the north of the building. Making menacing gestures, they repeatedly shouted, "You're all thieves. Tonight we're going to kill you." Then they marched around and around the *mairie* carrying a wooden statue representing the bust of an officer, saying, "It's him we want! And we'll get him tonight!" On this statue, there were military decorations painted in yellow, with designs showing buttons, badges, stripes, and medals. Without a shadow of a doubt, the crowd was alluding to Colonel de Coppens. (Incidentally, he had told us numerous times that they were out to get him and would surely try to kill him.)[21]

This ruckus continued until five o'clock, at which time the members of the voting bureau prepared to seal the ballot box so it could be brought to the gendarmerie. At that point, all of those who had been standing outside the *mairie*, some 500 all together, picked up arms— clubs they had hidden in the brush or inside houses along the street.[22] At six, once the ballot box had been sealed, candidate Giscon, who had been shuttling back and forth between the *mairie* and the crowd for some time, entered the voting

the people—we didn't want to let them take the box from the mairie. *We tried to grab the box from the soldiers. There was scuffling. Everywhere gendarmes, soldiers—maybe fifty gendarmes in all. The crowd tried to seize the box. But finally, they got it into the gendarmerie. Since the morning, in front of the* mairie *there had been gendarmes, soldiers, customs men, rural police, all controlling entrance to the place. They didn't have guns like today's; they had Lebels—large ones that the customs men had long been using, with a bayonet long like this and broad like that. And the people in the crowd struggled with those who had the guns.*

Coppens was in the presbytery. With the priest, L'Abbé Person. That's when the shooting began. Afterwards, he came down to the mairie *with a big smile on his face to say, "Hold your fire!" But there was a little Guadeloupean called Milaque, a soldier.[23] He and I had been chatting off and on together since morning. He told me about the* député *from Guadeloupe, Boisneuf. And this fellow, he was also a socialist. So we compared notes. I had a brother who was a bit of a trouble-maker. The Guadeloupean told me that Coppens had told him to wait for an opportunity to take care of that fellow. He told me that. About my older brother. "Ever since morning, he's been telling me to kill that fellow." But he didn't want to. He was the one with the machine-gun. In front of the* mairie. *And then, after the scuffle, they carried the ballot box into the gendarmerie. And Gendarme Nouvel said, "Fire!" (The socialists were to the east, Cop-*

room and told the president, "If you had done the vote count here, my friends would have stayed calm, but since you're sending the ballot box to Fort-de-France, I can no longer be responsible for what might happen." He then disappeared and was not seen again.

At 6:10 p.m., just as we were leaving the *mairie* carrying the ballot box to bring it to the gendarmerie, the crowd began shouting, "Let's get the box!" and tried to wrest it from us, shouting threats and throwing stones, bottles, and conch shells at us.[24] As we moved between the *mairie* and the gendarmerie — about 150 meters—we told the crowd nearly a dozen times to calm down and disperse, or else we'd have to use our guns. They paid no attention to our warnings at all. About 50 meters from the barracks, several of us were hit by stones and blows from clubs, so we turned to face the crowd and kept moving, walking backwards now, until we got to the gendarmerie.

Just as we were carrying the box into the barracks, where the family of the chief and those of two gendarmes lived, we heard someone cry out, "Brigadier, watch out, they're going to shoot you," and then we heard several shots.

Chief Nouvel, commander of the detachment, having fallen from a rock to the head, and several others of us having been hit by various projectiles, we—in the absence of judicial or administrative authorities—made use of our arms.[25]

pens's men to the west.) Right into the crowd . . . . they fired brbrbrbrbrbrbr, people were killed, falling all over the place. I was on a balcony, I saw people running, falling. "Are you crazy or what?" I said. I'd never seen anything like it.

After this skirmish, some ten bodies of civilians, three of which were lifeless, lay not far from the barracks. The wounded were immediately taken to neighboring houses and to the *mairie*, where the corpses were also left.

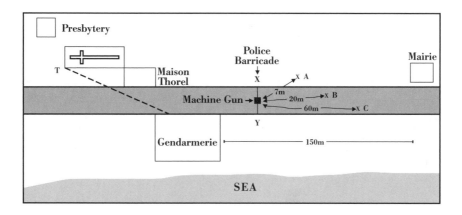

Then it was completely still for a time. And suddenly I heard [high, shrill:] "weeee, weeee, weeee, wuuuu, wuuuu, wuuuu" [bullets screaming]. I didn't see a single rifle fired. I was on a balcony one hundred meters away. It was the machine-gun they were firing. The gendarmes had given the order to fire on "certain categories." The head of the troops was the gendarme called Duffaud, the son-in-law of Doctor Guinette, who used to be the rightist mayor of Rivière-Pilote. He gave the order to shoot only "certain categories." So they shot at those. I saw people . . . [sound of groaning, people expiring]. Everyone else ran to hide.

Machine-gun in front of *mairie*[26]

The soldiers arrived in force, guns at the ready. They called out, "Shut your houses, close them up! No one allowed in the streets!" So we took off. And then after a bit, Colonel Coppens—he'd heard the machine-gun—came down toward the mairie *to say, "Hold your fire." But the Guadeloupean had been watching for him. Pa! He got him. Coppens fell, and the others in his group took off, palapalapalapala—he hit seven or eight of them. Meanwhile, we'd taken to the woods, since they'd said to close the place down. It was a—what do they call it?—a curfew. We heard they'd wounded Coppens and—*[RP: Did the Guadeloupean shoot Coppens on purpose?] *Yes!! Ever since the morning, he'd been asking me what he looked like. I said, "Okay—Coppens is a small* béké

Considering the state of mind of the populace, we had men patrolling through the town all night long, breaking up any gatherings. The barracks was guarded by sentinels. We were able to protect the ballot box, which will be transported later on to Fort-de-France to be given to M. le Gouverneur. [Signed Nouvel and the five other gendarmes]

[TELEGRAM: GENDARMERIE DIAMANT TO GOV RICHARD, 6 PM 24 MAY 1925] Brigade Chief Nouvel wounded troops responded civilian deaths request fifty men reinforcement—urgent.

[CODED CABLE, GOV RICHARD TO MINISTER OF THE COLONIES, 24 MAY 1925] Priority Top Secret. Regret to announce

créole, *with blue eyes"* — *just like yours* [he added looking straight at me]— *"and he's got this yellow mustache and he's kind of skinny. He wears a* sept-toiles *suit, a khaki outfit." (On election day, in any case, other than the military he was the only white. Everyone else was my color. That's the way it was in those days.) The Guadeloupean did it on purpose, shooting at Coppens and his men. You know, Guadeloupeans are the blackest*—pli nèg, pli nwa—*like shoepolish. Well, they'd ordered him to shoot at the blacks, at his* collègues, *and he did it. And then, out of vengeance, he shot at that whole pack of* milats! [laughs] *He did it to avenge his* collègues. *Guadeloupeans aren't like us, you know. They're not like Martiniquans. They're more vengeful, more* sauvage, *too…*

[GENOR NAUD, who was six years old at the time and lived on the outskirts of Diamant at Anse Caffard, describing 24 May 1925 in 1986] *It was late afternoon, when I heard people shouting, running from Diamant, going in all directions. They said, "They're busting up Diamant!" There were folks from Anses d'Arlet—they ran right through Anse Caffard. They were going every which way—some ran straight over Morne Larcher! Around six in the evening, my father showed up covered with blood, red all over. We realized he'd been wounded. He told us he'd been hit as soon as it started, that he'd tried to hide behind a large quenette tree. But once the thing really got going, he dove right into the sea. And even though he'd been in the sea, he came home covered with*

Colonel Coppens *conseiller général* killed in Diamant during election. Following information pending confirmation events as follows: 17 hours president municipal commission transferred ballot box to gendarmes for later counting by Judicial Appeals. When detachment gendarmes arrived gendarmerie where box to be stored, assaulted by armed crowd that fired on them. Also, many shots fired from house across gendarmerie one gravely wounding gendarme other hitting Coppens in stomach. Coppens died moments later. Gendarmes responded. Seems several dead and wounded. RICHARD.

blood. There were so many people. The
wounded were crying out. It was the Congos
who'd been fighting there. . . . In Coppens's
day, stick-fighting was the thing. Although
they used the machine-gun, we fought with
sticks and clubs. But it was the machine-gun
that killed all those Congos. . . . They were
against Colonel Coppens. Those savages,
those brutes [he laughs], they were yelling,
"The Labitaille Congos will win the election!" They'd swept down from the hills of
Labitaille with their sticks and Coppens was
already there with his men. By the afternoon, it was stick-fighting time! And then he
commanded his soldiers, "Open fire!"

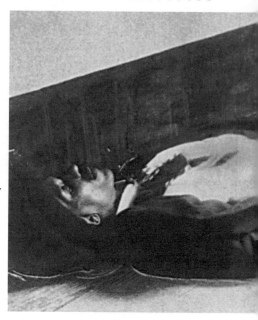

[SPECIAL—BY CABLE TO *PARIS-SOIR*, 25
MAY, under the headline: "Bloody Elections in Martinique. Barbed Wire and
Machine-Guns: The War? No, a Polling
Place!"] *Frossard's warnings tragically prescient. Partial elections with deployment
large armed force, machine-guns in four
communes where socialist victory was certain.*

In Ducos friends Des Étages and Zizine
conseillers généraux *killed, struck in back
by gendarmes' machine-gun in corridor of*
mairie *after they had been photographing
barbed wire encircling* mairie.

[CABLE TO SÉNATEUR LÉMERY (in Paris)
FROM THE PRESIDENT OF THE COMMIS-
SION COLONIALE AND THE VICE-PRESI-
DENT OF THE CONSEIL GÉNÉRAL (in
Martinique)] Dramatic bloody events
Saturday Sunday Majority Conseil
Général and Republican Municipalities
demand immediate intervention to get
intelligence and assure security STOP
. . . Sunday at Ducos while voting pro-
ceeding calmly DES ÉTAGES fired two
revolver shots at gendarme STOP
Threatened with arrest DES ÉTAGES
tried to fire again gendarme reacted and
DES ÉTAGES and ZIZINE standing
behind him killed by single bullet STOP
. . .

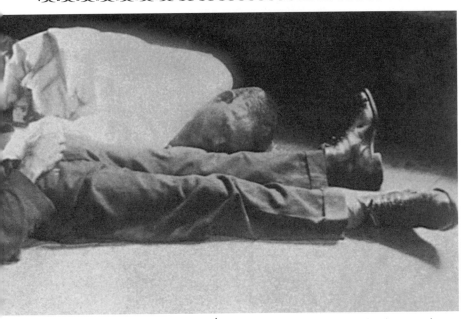

Charles Zizine and Louis Des Étages, lying where they were shot by a gendarme

In Ajoupa-Bouillon, voters demanding voting cards thrown out of mairie / [there seems to be a cut in transmission—switch to report on Diamant, where] *gendarmerie which was not under threat used arms despite exhortations caution, killing passerby on Diamant road.*

Latest information: eight dead including Colonel Coppens, conseiller général, *from the other party, killed by a blast from the machine-gun, and thirteen wounded. All victims unarmed.* [Signed George Forgues, editor, *Presse Coloniale*][27]

[CODED CABLE FROM INSPECTOR GENERAL PÉGOURIER TO MINISTER HESSE, 27 MAY 1925] *10—Primo: Diamant: According to ongoing investigations, non-socialist* Sunday Diamant Coppens brutally assassinated. After close of balloting Coppens in presbytery child comes says needed in *mairie* STOP Without suspicion leaves gets two blasts from shotguns fired by two people STOP Hit shoulder and stomach Colonel dies soon after STOP Same time gendarmes assaulted stones and guns chief detachment hit stone in face fell unconscious STOP Overwhelmed detachment fired killing or wounding some twenty STOP All carefully prepared by month-long communist campaign led Lagrosillière Frossard Séjourné Labat and others STOP Campaign *Paris-Soir* articles reproduced in local press incite population STOP Coppens assassination apparently premeditated during *witnesses claim demonstrators opened fire. Troops and especially machine-gunner seem to have lacked sang-froid. Death of Coppens apparently caused by shots from detachment. The blow from stone received by chief of detachment seems to have occurred after detachment opened fire. . . .*

Tertio: Until now the only charges against Lagrosillière consist of an anonymous accusation that during dinner Friday in Diamant he said, "It will be necessary to spill blood to get the governor recalled." . . .

Quarto: Population calm.

PEGOURIER

meeting held Diamant Friday night by Lagrosillière, schoolteacher Blanchard, tax-collector Menivier STOP[28] General protest revolutionary and anarchist actions encouraged by accusations *Paris-Soir, Résistance,* and *Aurore* against Minister STOP Intolerable for Minister leave French territory at mercy band of assassins paralyze governor's action menace security population . . . STOP Population left on own to defend self STOP Serious situation requires urgent energetic measures to consolidate power of governor who has peoples' full confidence. [Signed Sainte-Luce, Président Commission Coloniale, Saint Félix, Vice-Président Conseil Général]

[INSPECTOR OF COLONIES PÉGOURIER TO MINISTER OF THE COLONIES HESSE, REPORT ON THE RECENT EVENTS FOR WHICH MARTINIQUE SERVED AS THE THEATER, DATED 28 MAY 1925] *The confrontation in Diamant May 24 was much more serious, in terms of its consequences, than those in the other communes. I remind you that the election could not be completed on 3 May because the mayor, M. Eleuthère Sainte-Rose, was accused of having slipped a large number of ballots into the box. Since that time, those in the opposing camp—the socialists—have been particularly excitable. . . .*

But it is not these kinds of incidents [the shoving matches, attempts to stuff the ballot box], without lasting consequence and extremely frequent in this colony, which pro-

[SÉNATEUR LÉMERY, IN *LE PETIT PARISIEN,* 26 MAY 1925] I must say I expected this. For a long time now, I have been warning the government that there would be troubles in the colony, and I requested that the troop of gendarmes—who alone are capable of maintaining order—be augmented. The facts that have just been brought to my attention prove I was correct. . . . I consider that the gendarmes in Diamant who fired on the agitators were in a state of legitimate self-defense. The government must take every precaution not to undermine the authority of the governor, M. Richard, who is a solid, prudent, and fair administrator who deserves its full confidence.

duced the irritation of the populace. The true cause must be attributed to the decision of the president of the voting bureau not to count the ballots in the mairie but instead to have the ballot box sent to the capital to be counted by Judicial Appeals. . . . The atmosphere of suspicion that reigns in Martinique regarding elections is such that the populace has absolutely no confidence in this procedure and political passions suggest to one of the parties that it represents a means, however apparently legal, to practice fraud to its detriment.

The effervescence of the populace could only increase, then, when the news got out. And it was only with the greatest difficulty that the detachment of gendarmes, hounded by a hostile crowd brandishing sticks and threatening them with stones, could traverse the several hundred meters that separated the mairie and the gendarmerie, where the ballot box finally arrived at 6 o'clock.

It was shortly thereafter that the tragic events which cost the life of ten people occurred. The crowd continued to assault the gendarmes with stones and it seems possible that they would have invaded the building to take possession of the ballot box. It was at this moment, under circumstances still unclear and which the judiciary will undoubtedly illuminate, that the troops, and especially the machine-gunner, opened fire, sweeping the street in the direction of the mairie. If the initial reports that I have received prove correct, the fusillade killed more victims among bystanders than among the hostile crowd. This is because Colonel de

[CODED CABLE FROM GOV RICHARD TO MINISTER OF THE COLONIES, 27 MAY 1925]: 110—Confidential. Primo: Everything continues calm. Secundo: Funerals of all victims occurred yesterday without incident. Tertio: A certain Saint Aimé, suspected assassin of Colonel Coppens, arrested. I should report that 3 May, Saint Aimé having publicly announced intention to kill Coppens, justice of the peace cited him and sent accusation to attorney general Fort-de-France. Instead of taking immediate action this latter scheduled hearing for 4 June leaving time for Saint Aimé to accomplish on 24 May what he could not on 3 May. . . . Quarto: I hereby dismiss police commissioner Battestini of Diamant who has never reported properly to me and who last week shared an automobile with Lagrosillière between Diamant and Fort-de-France after the meeting signaled in my cable number 105. RICHARD.

[LETTER FROM "V.(?) BROCHARD" TO MINISTER OF THE COLONIES, DATED 25 MAY 1925] I take this opportunity to pass on to you whatever information I happen to have on the unfortunate victims in Martinique, of whom the newspapers wrote this morning. I know all the island's conseillers généraux. M. de Coppens belonged to an old family which had settled in the island long ago. A brave and honorable man, he was the true aristocrat of the land. I once saw him dressing down for more than an hour the Conseil

COPPENS *(conseiller général and candidate in the municipal elections) had given the order to his partisans to accompany the ballot box in order to lend support, in case the gendarmes needed it.*

This fact is expressly confirmed by the witness THOMASSINE. *Following instructions from the colonel, his partisans walked in front of the crowd in order to form a buffer between it and the ballot box. It was over their heads that the projectiles which fell on the gendarmes were thrown.*

The sketch map reproduced here allows a fuller picture of the site. [See page 29.] *The troops had blocked the street at X–Y, with the machine-gun at Z. At points A, B, and C were the demonstrators, and it appears from initial reports that the first two were friends. The street was immediately cleared except for the dead and wounded who lay on the ground. The demonstrators took off to the right and the left of the street and, either expressly to get them or simply by lack of sang-froid, the machine-gunner followed them with his fire as did the gendarmes and the military, who seem at that moment to have fired in all directions.*

It was at this time that one of the saddest events of this tragic day occurred. When the fusillade erupted, Colonel COPPENS *was on the street in front of the house of* THOREL, *along with his chauffeur* HUBERT *and one of his partisans,* BORRHOMEE. *He entered the house, which belonged to one of his political friends, as this latter has testified. (The deposition of* THOREL *is, thus, beyond suspicion).*[29]

Général, in which he—all by himself—formed the opposition. Indeed, this ended with an official duel between him and Lagrosillière (it was the second).

Des Étages was a mixed-blood, but a man who was always courteous and proper in his personal relations . . .

Zizine was a black, without much public accomplishment.

M. de Coppens was a kingpin for M. Lémery, Des Étages for Lagrosillière.

[GOV RICHARD TO MINISTER OF THE COLONIES, REPORT ON 24 MAY ELECTIONS, DATED 30 MAY 1925] TOP SECRET. I wish to furnish you with the facts as they have come to me from the various trials going on or from sources of incontrovertible authenticity. . . . In Diamant, in the wake of the events of 3 May, I suspended the mayor and appointed a voting bureau headed by a school principal. As the population of Diamant includes some extremely dangerous elements (I must tell you that there is one part of the commune called "Little Africa" because of the savage character of its inhabitants), my choice for the presidency of the bureau was an energetic civil servant whose impartiality is above suspicion and who seemed fully capable of handling these ill-fitted and, unfortunately, highly gullible voters, who make easy prey for agitators.[30]

These latter did not fail to live up to expectations. M. Lagrosillière himself showed up two days before the elections

Here is how he put it on the 26th of May: "The colonel, Borrhomée and Hubert came in the house. The shots were so close together that they had to have been fired by a machine-gun. I was hit by one bullet. At the same time, I heard Coppens cry out, 'Ah! I'm dying!' As for Borrhomée and Hubert, they were lying on the ground, dead. The bullets had passed through the walls and hit us. The colonel died about ten minutes after he was hit."

The autopsy performed the day after the drama revealed a singular particularity. While there is no doubt that Borrhomée and Hubert were killed by small-caliber bullets fired from a military weapon, the case of Colonel COPPENS divided the medical specialists, of whom there were five, including two from the army. Four of them, including the military ones, concluded that, given the nature of the wound, the victim could not have been killed by a bullet coming from an army weapon, since the entry wound as well as the interior lesions were significantly larger than those usually seen in such a case. . . . On the other hand, the fifth specialist, a civilian doctor named MAGALLON, in an extremely detailed dissenting report, concluded that such a wound could well have been produced by the combined effects of several military bullets. In any event, all of his colleagues agreed with him that the wound was not compatible with the hypothesis of a shotgun blast.

Given the circumstances that caused the death, it is indeed difficult to imagine how the victim could have been wounded inside

and dined with his partisans, some of whom have since been arrested for inciting rebellion on 24 May. I would add that he rode back to Fort-de-France that same evening with the Commissioner of Police whose dismissal I already announced to you.

The day was calm. About three o'clock demonstrators massed before the *mairie*. A number of people threatened the gendarmes and paraded around with a statue representing an officer, crying out, "He's the one we want, and we're going to get him tonight." Clearly, it was poor Colonel de Coppens they had in mind. He himself knew it and had said that surely they would kill him.

At five o'clock, the voting bureau decided, because of the growing excitement, not to count the votes in the *mairie* but to have the sealed ballot box taken to the gendarmerie and thence to Judicial Appeals in Fort-de-France.

One might have thought the matter finished, since normally such precautions are favorably received by the voters, who find that counting by Judicial Appeals provides all sufficient guarantees.

But, unfortunately, this was not the case in Diamant. The crowd, incited by several leaders who tried to make them believe the ballot box would be falsified, wanted to seize it. While the gendarmes were carrying it to the barracks, they were assaulted by several hundred individuals—including many strangers to the commune—determined to bring them

the house (even a wooden house) other than by a military weapon.

The question is of the greatest importance. As is only natural, political passions have begun to appropriate the facts and turn them to their advantage. If the death of Colonel de Coppens was caused by a military bullet, the day would bring little glory to the adversaries of M. Lagrosillière, who count not a single victim among their own ranks—other than those owing to the hatred of the troops—while the socialists suffered numerous dead and wounded. One must expect that very great efforts will be made to prove that the death of Coppens was due to his adversaries, and it will take considerable firmness on the part of the judiciary—in particular, the judge in this case—to resist the pressures that will be put on him in this regard.

I hasten to add that according to the best information I have received, the probity and competence of M. OLLIER, the young magistrate in charge of the case—like that of M. BAUDU, the Attorney General—place him above all suspicion. I should add that I tell you this, Monsieur le Ministre, only because I would in no way be surprised if a campaign of calumny were launched against these judges, as has already been begun against me.

In any case, it is clear from the deposition of M. THOMASSIN Laurent, political friend of COPPENS, which I have already mentioned, that the crowd had not fired a single shot before the fusillade began. It may turn out that gendarme NOUVEL

harm. I would stress that word had been spread among these fanatics that the gendarmerie had no more cartridges and could easily be massacred.

Brigadier Nouvel, chief of the detachment, was hit by a rock and fell unconscious. Since there was a man who had been pointing a rifle at Nouvel and several blasts of gunfire had been heard, the troops made use of their arms.

In this milling crowd, squeezed into a narrow street, the fusillade caused numerous casualties. Eight dead, fifteen wounded—such was the result of this bloody skirmish.

After the close of voting, Colonel de Coppens had calmly gone up to the presbytery, thinking everything finished. He was chatting with the parish priest and some friends just before he left. According to reliable sources, someone (who has neither been identified nor found since) came to say he was wanted at the *mairie*.[31] This was clearly a pretext since there was no longer anyone in that building. He'd scarcely left when he was hit with a shot. Mortally wounded, he took refuge in the house of one of his friends, where he died about an hour later.

Rumors were spread—with transparent motives—that he was killed by a bullet fired by a soldier or gendarme. The autopsy conducted by five doctors, including the Director of Public Health, absolutely rules out this version. Two doctors say that the wound could not have been caused by a military weapon.

had some responsibility in this affair, but the judicial investigation has not progressed sufficiently for me to give an informed opinion. However, it does seem clear that this gendarme, who was hit by a rock in the face, was wounded only after the firing that he had ordered had commenced. The only precision given by the troops regarding threats of shooting by the crowd is that there was a demonstrator standing at point "T" (see map) who was pointing a gun at the gendarmes who were in front of the mairie *[gendarmerie?]. A man was arrested for this reason, but it would be premature to conclude anything about the facts.*

I should add that Colonel de COPPENS was little liked by a portion of the population of Diamant—which is, by the way, uncivilized to the point that the inhabitants are known by the nickname of "Africans." It seems that the victim had been the target of death threats and that during the voting the crowd, in order to insult him, carried around an effigy meant to represent him. I would not presume to explain the reasons for this unpopularity. But it does not seem to be in doubt and, in the end, it would not have been surprising during the course of the day had COPPENS fallen victim to a demonstrator.

As of the time of this writing, the number of victims of the 24th May has reached 21, of whom 10 were killed or succumbed to their wounds. . . .[32]

Two others believe it unlikely that the wound was caused by a military weapon. The final doctor draws no conclusions. It would certainly seem, then, that Colonel de Coppens was killed by a slug fired from a shotgun. There are, by the way, a certain number of these guns in the region, which the inhabitants use to shoot large fish.

The reason the reports of the gendarmerie are silent about the death of Coppens is that at the very moment he was assassinated, they were fighting for their lives—at a certain distance from the place where he fell—against their aggressors. The threats of which he had been the object for the past several days, the failed attempt on his life on 3 May, the hatred which he inspired among certain bandits in the region who had boasted of "taking care of him" because they did not want a "white" as mayor—all this leads me to conclude, along with all of Martinique, that M. de Coppens was assassinated. He was a gallant man with an admirable loyalty, bravery, and conscience.

As soon as I learned of these events, I dispatched a steam launch to Diamant with as many soldiers and gendarmes as I could round up in Fort-de-France, that is, about a dozen. A doctor accompanied them. Thanks to these reinforcements, the night was calm and tranquility has been maintained ever since. It has, however, been necessary for the little garrison of Diamant to take a number of precau-

The Dead

- de Coppens, Maurice, industrialist, b. 1872
- Borrhomée, Paul Firmin, fisherman, b. 1890
- Mathieu, Joseph, Lubin (Hubert), mechanic, b. 1894
- Libanus, Jean, Germain (Hurard), cultivator, b. 1896
- Saint-Aimé, Simon Evariste, cultivator, b. 1895
- Pierron, Michel, mason, b. 1897
- Galo, Casimir (Neveu), cultivator, b. 1893
- Joilan, Henri (Hector), cultivator, b. 1901
- Matau, Hector, Boniface, cultivator, b. 1897
- Sounocadi, Charles, Gustave, cultivator, b. 1873

The Wounded

- Damazie, Michel, policeman, b. 1886
- Thorel, Gabriel, fisherman, b. 1867
- Borhomée, Julien (Orléus), fisherman, b. 1886
- Marie-Angélique Eleuther (Louis), fisherman, b. 1878
- Thomassine, Laurent (St-Ange), fisherman, b. 1868
- Jourdain, Ambroise, Félix, cultivator, b. 1898
- Claka,[33] Jean (Isidore), cultivator, b. 1885
- Briand, Paul, not from Diamant
- Adolphe, Duverly, cultivator, b. 1894
- Ste-Catherine, Jean François, cultivator, b. 1874
- Namosi, Pascal, Justin, cultivator, b. 1893

tions to head-off a possible offensive by a certain portion of the populace.[34]

Six individuals identified by the gendarmerie as having incited the population to rebellion were locked up. A seventh named Saint-Aimé was arrested and may well be the assassin of Colonel de Coppens.[35] . . . I feel I must tell you, Monsieur le Ministre, . . . that M. Olier, the judge in charge of these matters, is not only a total mediocrity without any serious experience, but that he brings to his work a slowness that many say is carefully calculated. I should not hide from you that it is a notorious fact that he has very close relations with a certain Labat, first lieutenant of Lagrosillière, whose own judicial past leaves much to be desired. . . .

The events of 24 May had been carefully orchestrated by M. Lagrosillière and his partisans. The campaign of violence which preceded it sowed the seeds for the fatal drama. . . .

What were Lagrosillière's ambitions? First, to carry out a Bolshevist or Communist plot worked out in Moscow. (The Department has long known of this plan, which directs his activities and, probably, pays his support.) Second, to seize by force the *mairies*, which are a first step toward gaining control of the Conseil Général, control that he and his friends absolutely need in order to survive. Third, to get me recalled from my post. . . .

Without the gendarmerie, which substituted for the inadequacy of its man-

[*L'Aurore*, Fort-de-France, 6 June 1925, p. 1] *RICHARD II AT THE HELM. THE MASSACRE AT DIAMANT.*

"You've got gendarmes, customs men, and soldiers and you still can't take care of business!" said Richard to Coppens on May 3, after the voters discovered in the ballot box—before a single person had voted—300 ballots! At that moment there were already three wounded, including one who was critically wounded right in the middle of the mairie by Lessanges, who was not even prosecuted!

The blood of the people matters little to Richard, who won't tolerate blacks who dare to lay claim to the freedom to vote which he has suppressed.

It was outgoing mayor Sainte-Rose who was the felon on 3 May, but it's the people whom the cynical bandit wants to bring to heel by all the "legal" means at his disposal—carbines and machine-guns.

For the second round of elections (24 May) no means were spared to deliver the mairie to Coppens. . . The dispatching of 15 gendarmes and an equal number of soldiers with machine-guns and ammunition. As well as the dispatching, as commander of the troops, brigadier Nouvel, that dangerous recidivist who can count to his credit the fusillade at Bassignac, where he had his troops, without warning, fire into the crowd!. . .

Voting cards were not distributed to partisans of the socialist list while piles of cards were placed in several houses in town for use

power an admirable bravery, the day of 24 May would have far more horrible than one could imagine. What would have been left of the good people of this land, especially the whites? I simply cannot say. Believe me, Monsieur le Ministre, I do not exaggerate at all.

[*La Riposte*, Fort-de-France, 3 June 1925] Here are the results of that painful day:

Our dead:
⟩ Colonel de Coppens . . .

Their dead:
⟩ Pierron, Michel . . .

Our wounded:
⟩ Thorel, Gabriel . . .

Their wounded:
⟩ Cléka, Jean Isidore . . .

[Gov Richard to Minister of the Colonies, coded cable dated 3 June 1925]: Personal and confidential. Doctor who examined [words missing] wounded in Diamant attests that various wounds without any doubt caused by explosion bomb STOP This confirms intelligence that crates of explosives were sent 24 May Fort-de-France to Donatien, ex-mayor Carbet STOP Despite careful search, crates not yet located STOP It can be assumed that explosives were similarly sent Diamant. RICHARD

by those ready to commit fraud on the 24th.

The day of the vote, Cadrot constituted his voting bureau according to his fancy after a ridiculous "examination" in which handwriting played the central role.

Our majority in Diamant is so large that despite the various frauds and the distribution of voting cards to outsiders, brought in by truck, we were well on our way to victory.

At noon, Cadrot carried out his plan. He left for lunch and transferred the presidency not, as the law requires, to the oldest member of the voting bureau but to Lucien Régis, one of the candidates of the Lémery party. A certain Paul Montrassier was soon seen trying to slip 16 ballots into the box, which were then seized by Chéry and given to the gendarmerie.

Despite protests . . . these people continued their shameless frauds; others, including a certain Ti-Félix, were caught with multiple ballots.

Nonetheless, Coppens—still unsure he would win, since our own voters had turned out in numbers—decided with Cadrot to seal the ballot box.

Since Richard's arrival, that's been the "classic" solution. The box is taken to a police barracks where it can be stuffed at ease, and then, after counting at Judicial Appeals, the voters learn that, in spite of themselves, they voted for Richard and Co.

Who would have thought that in a tiny town like Diamant, where the vote count wouldn't take two hours, and with all the armed forces at the disposition of Cadrot, in

[INSPECTOR GENERAL LE CONTE TO Minister of the Colonies, Report dated 19 August 1925, excerpt] Even had Brigadier NOUVEL given the order to fire before having been wounded, he would be beyond reproach from a legal standpoint. In truth, however, the facts suggest that no single person ordered the fusillade. Rather, seeing their chief being pointed at by a demonstrator with a rifle, seeing him wounded in the head and losing great quantities of blood, the troops—threatened, harassed, and struck throughout the 150-meter-long passage from the mairie to the gendarmerie, and seeing the crowd of rioters readying itself to invade the building that housed their wives and children—these troops had spontaneous recourse to their arms! My strong opinion, M. le Ministre . . . is that these troops—from the moment that their chief was hit—were in a state of legitimate self-defense.

[INSPECTOR OF COLONIES TO MINISTER OF THE COLONIES, DATED 28 MAY 1925, excerpt] The law in fact requires members of the voting bureau to be able to read and write, and the candidate presented by Giscon for this position was in fact unable to write his date of birth correctly. (Instead of "1904," he wrote "194.") Thus his disqualification was fully proper.

[LA RIPOSTE, FORT DE FRANCE, 3 JUNE 1925, p. 1] AFTER THE DRAMA OF

*a building surrounded by barbed wire . . .
that he would find it necessary to seal the
ballot box?*

*The box had already been brought into
the gendarmerie when an altercation took
place between Nouvel and a voter. The
brigadier received, he claims, a blow to the
face. There remains not a trace of it.*

*But immediately, carbines and the
machine-gun began firing, both down the
main street and toward the seaside, that is,
behind the barracks. 8 dead and 12 wounded.*

*The firing stopped only when Coppens's
overseer, Mathieu Hubert, called out that
Coppens was wounded and that he, too, was
in need of our prayers.*

*The killers have concocted the most fan-
tastical stories to mask their responsibility.
Riot, they say, since the gendarmes were hit
by projectiles (conch shells, bottles of sand).
But the facts speak for themselves.*

*How many gendarmes or soldiers
wounded? Not a one.*

*Nouvel's scratch cannot justify ten
deaths. And all hit in the back!. . . Not a button out of place on the uniforms of the gendarmes and soldiers.*

*This was no riot, but a premeditated
murder. The corporal with the machine-gun
had been saying since morning, as he
cleaned his weapon, "This evening you'll see
it in action."*

*As for Coppens, he died like the others
from one or several Lebel bullets, notwith-
standing the lies of the military doctors
under orders from Richard. . . .*

DIAMANT. The Autopsy: It was con-
ducted throughout the whole of Monday.
That of Colonel de Coppens took place at
Dizac. Five doctors were involved: the
Director of Public Health, Head Doctor
First Class Arnoux. Second Class Major
Beaujan, and doctors Lacoste, Suffrin,
and Magallon.

Their report is conclusive. The victim
was killed by a projectile from a shotgun.
Their findings—direction of the shot,
position of the victim, nature and form of
the entry wound, terrible tears in the exit
wound—all combine with their personal
opinions to prove that Colonel de Coppens was brutally assassinated.

Doctor Magallon agreed with the
body of the report but had certain reservations. Are these reservations as fanciful
as the political speech he pronounced at
the grave of Zizine and Des Étages?[36] In
any case, he was playing his role. For him
to admit that the colonel was killed by a
shotgun would force him to recognize
premeditation, an ambush, an assassination committed by a lackey of Lagrosillière himself, aided by his Red Guards....

He wanted none of that. How could he
condemn his own political boss? That?
Never! Better to be a perjurer, to say that
he simply didn't see and be silent about
what he did, in fact, see....

And Magallon's private thesis—you'll
never believe this one!—it's that two bullets from the machine-gun hit Colonel de
Coppens almost simultaneously, entering
by the same hole, ripping up his

[*Tribune Libre*, Fort-de-France, 30 May 1925] *During the funeral procession for Colonel de Coppens, the corpse—which was being transported to François for burial— was insulted as it passed through Rivière-Salée. Indeed, stones were thrown at it.*

[*L'Aurore*, Fort-de-France, 6 June 1925, p. 3] *Wednesday 11:20 a.m. Two of the victims have still not been buried. The boxes serving as coffins were so badly nailed together that dogs have been seen pulling at the shoulder of one of the badly decomposed bodies. . . . The little town of Diamant remains occupied by the military.*

[*Paris-Soir*, 14 June 1925] Headlines: The Machine-Gun and the Gendarme. Martinique under the Terror . . . Machine-Guns in front of the Ballot Box ... Ten Dead, Fourteen Wounded from the Crowd, Not a Single Gendarme Hurt.

intestines, and exiting by the same gaping hole. All this to explain the width of the exit wound from which the burst intestines hung. . . .

Is it possible to imagine a dumber and less likely hypothesis?

[Gov Richard to Minister Hesse, cable dated 13 July 1925] Having suffered for some months from violent rheumatic pains and having a badly crippled arm, I had been planning to request return to France end June. Because of recent developments I thought it my duty to remain at post and postpone request. Now, calm is completely restored. Doctors say it is urgent that I receive special treatment in France. I would be grateful if you could request a sick leave for me at this time.

[Minister Hesse to Gov Richard, cable dated 18 July 1925] As serious incidents during last elections caused violent polemics in press and questioning in Parliament I now counsel extreme prudence on the eve of new elections STOP ... If gendarmes and army indispensable to maintain order avoid public deployment and recommend moderation and prudence . . . STOP Avoid also use of barbed wire and machine-guns in front of *mairies* which may give wrong impression STOP.

[L.O. FROSSARD. "OPEN LETTER TO M. ANDRÉ HESSE," MINISTER OF THE COLONIES, *PARIS-SOIR*, 22 JUNE 1925]: *The general situation is well known to you: five or six manufacturers of rum enrich themselves by the millions with the labor of two hundred thousand fine people, peaceful and hard-working. A worker earns six francs per day cutting cane under the tropical sun from seven in the morning till three in the afternoon, and three francs a day when he weeds.*[37] *A house-maid receives thirty francs of wages per month plus fifteen cents a day for food—because she is not given food. Wages for a store clerk in Fort-de-France are between thirty and forty francs a month. And bread, Monsieur le Ministre, costs 2 francs 40 the kilo.*

The owners of the sugar factories are not content to be absolute rulers in their domains—they also want political power. And it's here that the governor steps in. Martinique has universal suffrage. The good old Negro, born to be exploited, is a voter. Every four years, he gets his little piece of sovereignty. Do not think him unworthy of the rights that the metropole has conferred on him. He votes with care. Between the exploiters and those who defend his interests, he knows how to choose. If he accepts starvation wages a bit too easily, if he submits to his condition without really accepting it, at least he uses his ballot to good purpose. He has a class instinct, as the factory owners have painfully learned. When the pressures of circumstances force an honest election, the factory owners are beaten handily. But luck-

[GOV RICHARD TO MINISTER HESSE, CABLE DATED 22 JULY 1925] Have always recommended moderation and prudence to gendarmerie. . . . In Diamant armed forces fired only at very last moment, when chief of brigade had already fallen unconscious, when several gendarmes had already been wounded, when shots had already been fired at them, and the barracks which housed the families of gendarmes had already been invaded by the crowd bent on spreading destruction.[38]

I never used barbed wire since the responsibility for protecting the *mairies* remains fully with the mayors, whose prerogatives I have always respected. To my knowledge, only the mayors of Trinité and Ajoupa-Bouillon utilized barbed wire, which, in any case, is commonly employed in the colony to fence gardens and most houses.

[GOV RICHARD TO MINISTER, COMMENTS ON M. LAPERGE'S REPORT ON ELECTIONS, DATED 15 AUGUST 1925] As long as the strictest discipline is not maintained in the colony, as long as the judiciary is non-functional, as long as civil servants are anarchists and rebels, as long as the local press continues to commit its well-known excesses, and finally, as long as the governor is disarmed, there is nothing to be done. In an exceptional country, exceptional laws are required. . . . Radical measures are necessary in the short term. Tomorrow it may well be too late.[39]

ily the governor is there. He *"corrects"* the mistakes of universal suffrage. In place of voters, he substitutes gendarmes. With a hundred gendarmes armed to the teeth, one gets guaranteed results. The voters cast their ballots. The gendarmes count the ballots. The governor proclaims the winner. And the factory owners triumph. . . . I believe it necessary, even though insufficient, to effect the immediate recall of Governor Richard. When a high functionary shows himself guilty of abuses of power, when he bears on his shoulders responsibility for events as tragic as those in Ducos and Diamant, he deserves to be smitten immediately with administrative sanctions and brought to justice. There are twelve cadavers standing between Governor Richard and the people of Martinique.

[*PARIS-SOIR*, 24 JUNE 1925] HEADLINE: *From Burglary to Murder.*

[*LE COURRIER DU PARLEMENT*, PARIS, 6 SEPTEMBER 1925] *HOW UNIVERSAL SUFFRAGE IS "MANAGED" IN MARTINIQUE. Three unimpeachable photographic documents—it is now Minister André Hesse's turn to speak out.*

[ATTORNEY GENERAL BEAUDU, MARTINIQUE, TO MINISTER OF THE COLONIES, EXCERPTS FROM REPORT ON EVENTS OF 24 MAY, DATED 9 AUGUST 1925] Confidential. Perhaps you are surprised that justice takes its course so slowly in these cases and that those who have the understandable impatience that the truth be told are concerned. But I would remind you that the magistrates must deal with their normal caseload in addition to all this and that, also, in the tropics—and particularly in the present season—it is not possible to furnish as intense and continuous efforts as if one were in France. . . .

In Diamant . . . 12 gendarmes and petty officers of the colonial infantry, including a corporal with a machine-gun, were present to protect the *mairie* from possible aggression, which seemed likely, given the ebullient state of the population since the abortive elections of 3 May. . . .

Despite the simultaneity of the death of Colonel de Coppens and the fusillade by the soldiers and gendarmes, it does not now appear that it was due to these latter and particularly not to the machine-gunner. Four of the five examining doctors concluded that the projectile could not have come from a military weapon. In which case, an assassination seems likely and all evidence points to a certain Eloi Saint-Aimé, who had already threatened M. de Coppens. . . . It has, however, not been possible to indict him on these grounds, the evidence being insufficient to support such a serious charge. On the other hand, we have him well out of harm's way, having locked him up and charged him with taking part in the rioting and the violence against Police Chief Nouvel.

It has not proven possible to link the ten individuals currently in detention, who are charged with rebellion and violence, to the death of Colonel de Coppens. These latter were identified by the gendarmes as having taken a more or less active part in the rebellion. They are: Chéry, called Cototo (who has just been released because of his advanced age); Sénart (Placide) called Reynal; Larcher (Louis); Makessa (Clément); Makessa (Mikael); Mayoulika (Paul); Norbert (Casimir), called Clairvillien; M'Bassé (Henri), called Charles Henri; Saint Aimé (Eloi); and Roc (Emmanuel).

In front of the *mairie*, election day, 24 May 1925[40]

[PHILIBERT LARCHER, 5/28/86] *It was pure politics. Dirty politics. Barbarism. Barbarism. Every last one of those people paid dearly. One was killed in prison. All died badly. Dirty politics. . . . All of them came to a bad end.*

[INA CÉSAIRE'S *MÉMOIRES D'ISLES* HAS AN OLD WOMAN REMINISCE] *That morning, they'd killed the Leymeriste, the big* béké *who owned the distillery at Diamant. . . . They'd put gendarmes and the army in front of the* mairie. *In those days, there were no black gendarmes. There'd been a tremendous deployment of police to control the masses, as for every election back then. Folks felt rebellious but had such fear of guns! And the day after the elections, we heard on the [state-run] radio in town: "The elections took place without incident." Without incident!*

[GOV'S OFFICE TO MINISTER, CABLE DATED 31 AUGUST 1925, ON THE SENTENCING OF THE TEN DIAMANT "AGITATORS"] Seven were given 6 months for rebellion, Saint-Aimé and Lunyoulika received 8 months for violence and rebellion, Roc received one year for conspiracy to violence and rebellion.[41]

[INSPECTOR GENERAL LE CONTE, AT END OF MISSION TO ASSESS POLITICAL STATUS OF MARTINIQUE, JANUARY 1926] In conclusion, our investigations counsel rejecting each of the extreme solutions—complete assimilation or autonomy—and adopting either maintenance of the status-quo or purely administrative reorganization.

[GOV RICHARD TO MINISTER OF THE COLONIES, CABLE DATED 24 MAY 1925] Municipal election results for 24 May: Primo: In Ajoupa Bouillon the list of Lorand "Bloc Républicain" elected. Secundo: In Carbet the list of Térullien "Bloc Républicain" elected. No incidents reported in either commune. Tertio: Ballot boxes from Ducos and Diamant consigned to gendarmerie for counting by Judicial Appeals. RICHARD

[GOV RICHARD TO MINISTER OF THE COLONIES, CODED CABLE DATED 28 MAY 1925] III—Following my 103 Judicial Appeals today completed the ballot counts for Ducos and Diamant. In both communes the list of the "Bloc Républicain" [the Right] was elected.

Election-day reinforcements, May 1925

MARTINIQUE

"House of the Fisherman—or of the Convict" (postcard, ca. 1983)

II. "My Own Secret":
The Life and Work of Médard Aribot

I met History once, but he ain't recognize me,
a parchment Creole, with warts
like an old sea-bottle, crawling like a crab
through the holes of shadow cast by the net
of a grille balcony; cream linen, cream hat.
I confront him and shout, "Sir, is Shabine!
They say I'se your grandson. You remember Grandma,
your black cook, at all?" The bitch hawk and spat.
A spit like that worth any number of words.
But that's all them bastards have left us: words.

—DEREK WALCOTT, "The Schooner *Flight*"

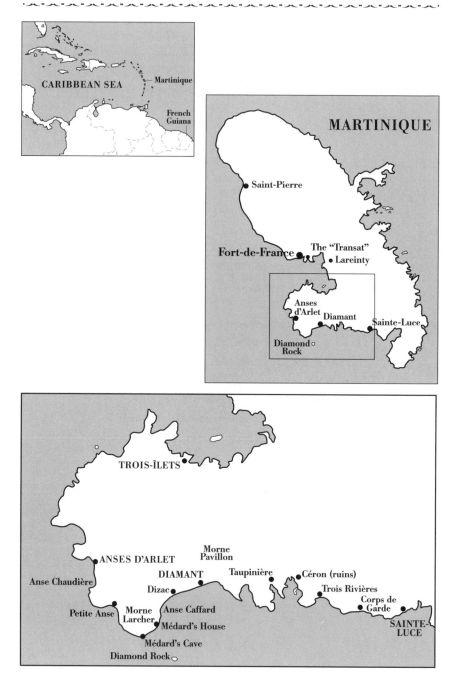

JULY 1983. We were rattling up the dirt track to Morne l'Afrique, high above the bay of Diamant, squeezed into the front seat of Julien's dilapidated pickup truck, its doors tied shut by lengths of rope—Julien, his wife Tina, Sally, and me. A kind of joyous Sunday outing, in search of traces of Médard, people who might have known him, people who might be willing to share their reminiscences. We pull up even with a very old man, walking up the steep slope leaning on a staff. "Good afternoon," greets Tina out the window in Creole. "Good afternoon, Madame," he answers, graciously tipping his *bakoua*. "We're looking for the place where Méda used to live, you know the man who—" "Madame, no one ever got to the bottom of that fellow! What a tremendous secret he had! . . . His house is further up the hill, at Bompí, but it's hard to find, you'll have to ask." We thank him, and Julien grinds the old Peugeot into first gear for the climb.

Farther along, by the side of the road, we come upon an elderly man lifting a sack of charcoal onto his head. Had he known Médard? we ask, again out the window. "He was a genius—a genius without the diploma," he replies without hesitation. Could he tell us where Médard had lived? "I'll bring you there, it's on the path I'm taking myself." So, we pull over to the side and, on Julien's insistence, cut staffs against snakes and follow the man down a path toward the setting sun.

The scenery takes our breath away. The whole bay of Diamant is spread out at our feet, the white foam of breakers washing the distant beach, and Diamond Rock floating in a sea of turquoise. To the right rises the deep green slope of Morne Larcher, a worn volcanic cone and the highest peak on the island's south. We slip and slide down the narrow path, trying to keep the old man in sight, converting our snake-killers into walking sticks on the steep terrain. Finally, he yells up at us

Julien and Tina, 1983

and points in the direction of the only house in a little side valley. We shout our thanks.

The tiny house sits at the edge of a deep ravine amidst lush vegetation—bananas, papayas, lime trees, callalou plants. It's in a verdant cul-de-sac, backed against the hill, and facing, across the ravine, the sweep of the bay and Diamond Rock. We call out greetings and a man emerges—shirtless, flour-sack pants held up by a rope, cutlass in hand, as "country" a character as we've ever met in our twenty-year-long acquaintance with Martinique. He's gruff and suspicious but not openly hostile, and says—when we ask about Médard—that he's his brother-in-law and lives here alone with his dog (who looks and sounds fierce but is tied to a post near the separate, banana-leaf-covered kitchen). When Tina asks, and explains, he says we can look at the house and take pictures, if we don't stay long. She continues to chat him up as we do our anthropological thing, sketching, taking notes, and shooting photos. Julien, who lives right by the sea with Tina and their four kids, stands by the house, admiring the expansive view. As we go up the rickety stairs and into the front room, we're startled by the body of a long, thick *fer de lance* snake the occupant had killed and hung from a rafter.

We knew it had been Médard's last house, that it was from here he'd been carried, ill, up the path, and brought to the hospital in Trois Ilets, where he'd died soon after, some ten years earlier. It was hard for us to take in all the architectural detail. The structure, made from *bois campêche*, and particularly the complex

decorations, had already deteriorated seriously. There was gingerbread everywhere, some in the form of Christmas-trees, and, atop the galvanized roof, a wooden weathervane in the form of the French tri-color. We could see that the whole house had once been painted in stripes.

Back in the truck, on the way down the hill, Julien remarks that it's not surprising this place is called "l'Afrique," since the people are so black. Every time we stop along the road to ask passersby about Médard, mere mention of his name brings a smile to their face.

"The tiny house sits at the edge of a deep ravine"

I'd first heard of Médard around 1978, during one of our periodic trips to visit Petite Anse. Since the early seventies, when a serious fishing accident had forced our friend Emilien to change his way of life and open a rumshop/general store (and sometime restaurant)—"Le Rayon" (The Sunbeam)—with his wife Merlande, we'd stayed with them whenever we visited. During our 1962/1963 fieldwork, when I spent much of my time with Emilien and his fishing partners, we had lived with Merlande's parents—she and Emilien were still courting at the time. Now, the old folks were gone and when we passed through for a few days—often on our way to or from Suriname—Merlande would send off their son to a relative's so we could sleep in his narrow bed, in the same room as their own. The room was built right onto the store, connected by a small door, next to the shore and the fishing boats. At night, after Merlande had knelt by their bed to say her prayers, we would fall asleep listening to the Caribbean waves lapping the beach.

Charlemagne (Emilien) Larcher, in front of The Sunbeam, 1983

Emilien was always making improvements to the store—laying tiles on the concrete floor one year, installing a freezer for ice-cream pops the next, building new shelving for canned goods the following year. And then, on one of our visits around 1978, we noticed—among the rum bottles, high up above the narrow counter that served as bar—a painted wooden statue we'd never seen. Emilien said it was "a general" and that they'd gotten it from Merlande's godfather, Monsieur Ador, who had died that year. Ador's house, which I'd known since the

"... among the rum bottles ... a painted wooden statue"

Ador's house, 1962

early sixties, still stood right next to where Emilien had built his store. I'd never been inside, but Emilien told me the old man had kept the general on a little table, with a couple of carafes. The general had been made, Emilien told us, by Médard. He seemed surprised we hadn't known him—since he'd died only a few years before. Together, we realized that during our main stays in Petite Anse in the early sixties, the coastal road connecting the hamlet to Diamant had not yet been built, and boat and road travel to the outside had always been in the opposite direction via Anses d'Arlet, which was why we knew relatively little of Diamant and its characters, including Médard.

The sculpture intrigued us and during the following days we took the general down from his perch, described him in our notes, and photographed him from various angles.[1] Watching us working one day, Emilien remarked, "When I was young, they told me, 'There was a general who came here. Méda drew him exactly. It was too true-to-life.' That's why they put him in prison, that's why they sent him to the *bagne* [penal colony]."

"we . . . photographed him
from various angles"

I began to ask around about this Médard, and one thing kind of led to another. While in Suriname, working with Saramaka Maroons (the descendants of escaped slaves), I had become interested in historical consciousness, the often-heroic ways these Afro-Americans envisioned their collective past. Caribbean writers and thinkers from the islands, however, tended to argue that rural folk—the kind of people I was particularly interested in now—suffered instead from a kind of historical amnesia, that there was little tradition of the kind of lively resistance to slavery that I had found among Maroons. Most Caribbean intellectuals—Glissant, Lamming, Naipaul, Patterson, Walcott, and many others—insisted that colonial education had effectively wiped out the type of historical memory that gives a people the strong and proud sense of self I had found among the Saramaka. But as I began to hear people talk about Médard, I thought I'd found a handle on a different kind of history, a subterranean vein that deserved mining. Off and on for a number of years, I followed Médard's traces where they took me, in search of this alternative vision of the past.

I eventually obtained a copy of Médard's birth certificate (as Walcott puts it, "The French are very good at these sort of thing; every other frog is a Descartes"), and determined that he'd been born in 1901 at Sainte-Luce, and that his legal name was Médard Aribot, after his mother, Marie-Thérèse Aribot.[2] His surviving age-mates—those who knew Médard in his youth—told me he had grown up mainly in Diamant, living in a cave by the sea and spending his time fishing from the rocks and catching crabs in the mangroves. He would walk along the shore to Sainte-Luce to visit his mother, who lived amidst the ruins of a seventeenth-century sugar estate called Céron, but he seemed closer to his father's people, who stayed up in the hills above Diamant, where Médard at times kept a small garden. "He was always alone," his agemates insisted, "and he never once set foot in a schoolhouse."

Emilien's mother's sister, Tante Na,[3] a former higgler who lived within a few hundred meters of Médard's cave, stressed his gentleness: "He was a sweet fellow who never bothered with other peoples' business. Always polite, he'd say, '*Bonjour*,' but nothing else. He was half-hidden, walking *sous les bois* (in the bush). He lived all by himself, in the woods near the sea, in his cave. As he got older, children would make fun of him—he was always dirty and unkempt, his pants were made of flour sacks held up with a rope. He wore no shirt and always carried a sack over his shoulder. I never once saw him laugh." Philibert Larcher offered, "He was gentle as a lamb, as simple as could be—but highly intelligent. He lived off the land, finding shellfish in the mangroves, fishing off the shore. A completely harmless fellow. When we were conscripted into the army together, right after the Great War, they'd shout out, 'Arimbó! Stand at attention! Do this! Do that!' But he wouldn't understand, he couldn't follow. He was a lamb, a sheep, very gentle—but thick-skulled—so finally they released him." And then Philibert made a comparison that I was to hear occasionally from others of his generation when I asked about Médard: "They told us in school that Joan of Arc was a kind of lamb, too, that voices told her, *'Vous allez sauver la France!'* and that she went to King Louis XV and asked him to let her save France. She was mad and people made fun of her, too, if I'm not mistaken, but she won the war for them and she saved France."

Dinette Louisy, who ran a little grocery store and bar at Taupinière, at the foot of Morne l'Afrique (Morne Pavillon), told me a bit more about Médard's origins: "We called him 'Méda Kunú' because his father was a *nèg-kongo*. You know," and she rattled off the rest like a litany, "all those Buku, Ngelá, Zumbé, Ombá, Kaléka, Makéssa, Síba, Mbásse, Méleyo, Kámbisi, Mabiála, Djúdin, Kabási, Luímata, Nguála, Mútusami, Mavéngo, Mungála, Kikáta, Maiyúlika, Vóba, Pinbá, Morénda, Meltjió, Mavúm, Sumaké—like Medá Kunú—they're all Morne Pavillon folks. The Congos came in a ship and they left them here, where they made families. Méda's father was from there."[4] Philibert, who was probably closer to Médard than anyone else I spoke with, confirmed that Médard's father was actually born in Africa. "Méda's father," he told me, "carried the name Kunú, but his mother was Arimbo. The old man recognized his other sons but he was very sick in the hospital and, the last one, Méda, he simply wasn't able to before. . . . You know, the father was a disembarked African, not an African from here. He was an African from the other side!" And this makes sense: some five thousand of the ten thousand "Congos" who debarked in Martinique around 1860—most of whom were teenagers at the time—were still alive at the turn of the century, when Médard was born.[5]

Among the old folks Médard and his peers knew as children, slavery was a living and vivid memory. Philibert recalled some generalized stories:

They stole all those people. The *békés* and Europeans went with great ships to Africa. The Africans were dying of hunger. So, they gave them a bit of rice, some *blaff*, arranged a dance—*temtemtemtem*—gave them something to eat. And then they put them in the ship and raised anchor. Some jumped into the sea during the night—they didn't want to leave. When the whites saw that, they put the others below, stowed them in the hold like freight. They unloaded them at Schoelcher. And then the *békés* bought them like merchandise. The big *békés* would take this many, there would be that many for Monsieur Hayot, so many for this one, so many for that one. They sold them exactly like they sell fertilizer.

And he continued with more specific stories of the sort that many of the older people in the region have in their repertoire, in one or another version.

I myself saw the man called Robert, an imported African. He'd been a slave at Dizac. His job was to watch over the sheep, and then one day a sheep disappeared. The master came and said, "It's you who ate the sheep," and he said, "No, master, it's not true," and he beat him. Every day this would happen—he beat him in the morning and he beat him in the evening. Then they arrested him, brought him to the smithy, held his hand down on the anvil, and chopped off the ends of his fingers. And then they took a red-hot iron and stanched the bleeding with it. He said, "Ah, Monsieur. I've shit on myself, I've shit on myself. A man like me! I've shit on myself and pissed on myself!"

Whether or not Philibert actually saw this ex-slave and others whose stories he told, he could have. Born in 1902, he would have known octogenarians who'd been twenty at Abolition in 1848. In telling me slave-time stories, Philibert always tried to specify what he'd seen and what he'd merely heard. For people of his generation, slavery was not an abstraction but a measure against which to judge how far things had changed, in some ways for the better and in other ways not.

Old man Mabial, I knew him too. I saw him like that, with just the stub of a finger. His master had cut it off. I saw it myself and that's what he told me. But I also heard that for certain Africans who wouldn't obey, they made a large barrel, drove nails into it, and forced the person to get inside. Then they'd haul it up to the top of the mountain and let 'er roll. Those black Africans told me that—I didn't see it. People say that. I've always heard it.[6]

Throughout the Americas in slave-times, theft was a highly charged and ambiguous act. The central contradiction of slavery—that human beings were defined as capital goods—inflected other notions of property as well. "Masters," as Douglas Hall has written, "were torn by conflict between these two views of their property"—though slaves were legally property, masters were constantly calling upon them to act in human ways. And enslaved men and women dealt with these legalisms according to their own logic. Jamaica serves as a setting for one famous version: A slave caught stealing sugar repeatedly denies that he stole, insisting that he has merely "taken" it. "'As sugar belongs to massa, and myself belongs to massa, it all de same ting—dat make me tell massa me don't tief; me only take it!' 'What do you call thieving, then?' 'When me broke into broder house and ground, and take away him ting, den me tief, massa.'"[7]

In Martinique, such notions of property did not die with Abolition. Older rural people, respectable folk—though now increasingly with embarrassment, as the process of *francisation* takes its course—continue to think in similar terms: "stealing," when it's from massa, is a whitefolks' way of looking at the matter. Ernest Larcher, a retired fisherman in his early sixties, laughed as he reminisced about the 1930s and 40s, when he'd fish with his father and his little brother, Emilien:

> Our family, too, we had people who would steal sugarcane for us. We used to set our nets off Trois-Rivières. There was a guy there called René Mouchémoun [René Snotnose]. Mouchémoun was a man who always had a stuffed nose, a great big cold. And every time he went "Kerchoo!! Kerchoo!!," it was if he'd blown out [*mouché*] a whole person [*moun*]. He would steal sugarcane from the *usine* at Trois-Rivières. In the evening, we'd set our nets just off Trois-Rivières, that's where we worked. He'd bring us a big bundle of cane. Because the overseer had his eye on us, we couldn't get at the

cane ourselves. But the other guy was there, he'd spy on the overseer and watch for the right moment and get the cane to bring us. We'd give him some fish, we'd give him a little something.

Over and over, in speaking about the recent past, people stressed that it was stealing from poor people, from other rural folk, that was criminal. Taking from a sugar factory, or from any *béké* or whitefolks' enterprise, was seen rather as getting one's due—even though, in the period in question, most people didn't actually engage in such acts and, at most, were happy secondhand beneficiaries of them.

Such ideas about theft provide a further entrée into our knowledge of Médard. For part of the fame of the man rests on his singular skills in accumulating merchandise of the most varied kinds. From an early age, Médard took (and then stored or sold or gave away) all sorts of basic goods. And without exactly being viewed as a Robin Hood, he seems to have chosen his sources with remarkable consistency—fancy shops in town, La Compagnie Générale Transatlantique (the French shipping line that held the monopoly of transport, known familiarly as the "Transat"), the major sugar factories of the island, and even police barracks and the home of the district attorney.

Génor Naud, then sixty-six, told me his earliest memories of Médard.[8]

> I remember him from Anse Caffard when I was just a boy. It was when Méda was living in his cave. I was the one who discovered him. One day, around three in the afternoon, I looked down and saw someone bathing in the sea. I wouldn't have noticed but my father had a big garden there, he kept a whole troop of animals in that place. I was standing on a rock, guarding the animals. I'd always done that and I'd never seen him before. And he'd never laid hands on a single animal. So, I took off and went and told my father. I said, "I saw this man bathing in the sea, I saw this man bathing completely naked in the sea!" My father came down with me to see who it was. But as soon as Méda saw us, he disappeared. We hadn't yet caught a glimpse of him. We didn't know where he went. The next afternoon, the same thing. I saw him searching for *brigauds* [shellfish] at the water's edge. I told my father and he circled around this time and

walked along the shore. He said, "What do you think you're doing here?" He replied [mimicking a high little voice], "Ahh, Thierry, it's me, Méda!" My father knew him. My father had known him from way before. My father said, "What are you doing around here?" "This is where I live. I've been here for quite a while. Ever since I left prison, this is where I've lived." My father said, "I've come here I don't know how many times and I've never seen you. All that time I was making my garden, I never once saw you." He said, "Ahh, I was here. And I saw you! A day hasn't gone by when I haven't seen you in your garden." And then he said to my father, "Come over here. Let me show you around." My father was pretty scared. He was afraid because he knew the man had been in prison, he didn't know what he might do to him. But he kept standing there, saying, "Monsieur, c'mon, I want to show you things, come look around." It was a place in the rocks you could enter, there was a sort of doorway. "Come on inside, I'll show you. Let's just stretch out our necks a bit, and you'll see! Anything you might need for your kids, anything you see here, I'll give it to you." My father said, "What's that you're telling me?" Méda pleaded, "Don't leave, take this." And he held out salt fish, he gave him salt meat, he said, "I'd give you a sack of imported flour [farine france], but you wouldn't be able to carry it. So, I'll give you half a sack and you can come back later for the rest. This is my place, this is where I live. But if anyone ever comes around asking for me, never tell them I'm here."

Médard, I've been able to figure out from police records, was at that very moment on the lam, after a 1929 prison break. Dinette Louisy told me she'd heard he had long tunnels—passageways dug in the earth—for smoke to escape from his cave in different places, so people up above wouldn't know where he was. But even while he was being careful to avoid the police, he was restocking his cave with merchandise. Génor describes what he himself saw when he was invited into the treasure house.[9]

Underneath that cliff there was a cave as long as from here to Emilien's [several hundred meters]—big enough to hold houses. There

The entrance to Médard's cave, 1996

were several stories. As you climbed up through the rocks, you went up to the next story. Every room was filled with a different kind of merchandise, eh! It was amazing. He'd stacked stones to make ceilings, with merchandise up above. Everything that's in a big store was there. What you see in Emilien's grocery—all that was there. Sacks of potatoes, sacks of rice, sacks of lentils, sacks of beans, sacks of imported flour, crates of saltfish. What he had there in that cave was enough to feed people for five or six months without ever leaving. Not to mention the drinks. Every single kind of drink you can imagine, every kind. And where Méda found all those things, no one knew. Each room was chock full. There was stuff that would just spoil in there, it was so much. Salt meat barrels weighing 150 kilos, 200 kilos apiece!

All this Médard obtained and transported by night, never once—according to people who knew him well—walking on a road. He was remarkably, almost superhumanly, strong. "Méda was strong, eh!" said Ernest Larcher. "Everybody wondered how he could have the strength to carry those things on his head like that, where he got that strength. He must have had some secret source of strength. He'd steal things that weighed a hundred kilos! He'd go over to the sugarmill and steal a sack of sugar. He'd steal a whole sack of imported potatoes. A whole barrel of saltmeat!"

Médard also took orders from his neighbors. "Whatever you asked him to take," Génor reported, "it would arrive on your doorstep at three or four the next morning. He'd carry it all by himself, all alone! As soon as you woke up, you'd see the barrel in front of your door. He'd say, 'Open up, where do you want the barrel?' and he'd put it there and disappear. He wouldn't ask for money. The next morning he'd be back with more. Exactly where he got it all, no one knows—but it came from Fort-de-France, from Lamentin. Nobody helped him, he carried it all alone. *Formidable*, eh! He must have had a spirit, some kind of [supernatural] thing. I don't know. But, I assure you, he never harmed a soul. He never hurt anyone. And he certainly never laid hands on a single thing owned by a poor person."

Médard seems to have taken things whenever he needed or wanted them—but only from those who were rich and powerful. Clairville Naud, who kept his sheep and goats near where Médard lived at Anse Caffard and considered him a friend, asked me one day, "Have you ever heard of Colonel Coppens? Well, it's because of that *monsieur* that Médard first saw the inside of a prison cell! Médard would steal, he'd steal. The colonel, he owned Dizac—the canefields and distillery. He's the one who reported him, who said he'd stolen there. And that was the very first time they locked him up." Indeed, Médard's penal record shows a first conviction in 1923 for "theft from the fields." He served two months in the prison of Fort-de-France before returning to his cave.

Besides his nighttime sorties through the woods—ranging far and wide over the island but particularly, according to his contemporaries, taking goods from the heavily guarded warehouses of "La Transat"—Médard was spending some of his time creating artworks. As people who knew him always say, "He only worked at night—without tools, without machines—it was all with a little tiny bit of a knife." Génor described visiting Médard's cave of an evening. "You'd come there and he'd immediately put down what he was working on so you couldn't

Entrance to the "Transat," early twentieth century (postcard)

see it. The work that he was doing, he'd never let you see it. It was always at night, by candlelight. All night long, he'd work on his thing. And in the morning he'd let you see it finished. But he'd never show you while he was making it."

Among his favorite early subjects were the great ships he'd see passing out at sea, steamboats carrying cargo and warships laden with cannon. Sometimes, Médard could be seen in Fort-de-France, carrying one of his ships on his head, going from bar to bar, from shop to shop, offering the piece for sale. Génor said, "He'd be walking around town with one of those ships, people would marvel at the ship—but no one would recognize Méda. He'd be going around with the ship on his head and people would be asking for Méda, and he'd just keep on walking with the ship on his head."

Médard was also making musical instruments, particularly pianos, sometimes with a hole that you could look through and watch dancers swirling as he tinkled the keys. He also modeled an extraordinarily realistic Diamond Rock, bought by the post-Coppens proprietor of Dizac. "It was exactly the Rock—if you saw it, you'd be amazed," said Armand Ribier (born 1913). "I was just a kid when I saw

". . . the great ships he'd see passing out at sea"[10]

that. He could look at you for a moment and make an exact copy in a piece of wood."

It would have been around this time, after his first stint in prison for stealing from Colonel de Coppens's canefields at Dizac, that Médard made his "*photo*" of the colonel—the very sculpture that was borne aloft by the crowd during the 1925 massacre, which later landed in the tiny house of Médard's friend, Monsieur Ador, in Petite Anse, and that then passed after his death to our friends Emilien and Merlande. Julien Privat, who knew Médard only in his later years, tells of his persistent fascination with pomp and circumstance: "Though he was a loner, he'd come at night and stare for hours through the window of the *mairie* whenever there was a *bal*. He loved to watch dancers, people all dressed up. And parades—whenever there was a military parade, he'd be there, watching." Amélius Naud, who, like his brothers Clairville and Génor, tended flocks near Médard's cave, added a precious detail: Médard, by this time, had rigged up an upside-down iron pot suspended from a rope in front of the entrance to his cave and he dramatically struck the hours on it with a piece of metal—"noon, two o'clock, six o'clock. Just like the chimes of a large clock." (Needless to say, Médard's "noon" or "two o'clock" was very much of his own determination,

"Whenever there was a military parade, he'd be there, watching." Bastille Day, on the steps of the church, Anses d'Arlet, 1962.

though the ceremony he parodied was one of the central symbols of the sugar mill, as well as of the military ships he'd seen in harbor.)

Génor told me, "At that time, Méda was making every kind of nonsense! But Colonel Coppens was one of the first. I believe it was right after he got out of his 'first prison.'" Which places the "general's" creation in 1924–1925, so that Médard's more politically militant friends—to whom he'd have shown it off— would have had the image fresh in their minds and ready to use on that fateful election day.

MÉDARD CONTINUED his habitual ways. In early 1926, he did a three-month prison stint for "theft of harvests"—presumably bundles of sugarcane from one of the factories he frequented. But his first really serious brush with the law— what we might call grand larceny—was yet to come. As Génor tells it,

> He would take things no one else could take. In those days, he'd go from here all the way to Saint-Pierre [the other end of the island]. Once he went to Saint-Pierre and took a gigantic bolt of cloth. It was a kind of cloth that they had sent out for the first time, it had arrived fresh from France. A light-colored cloth they called a *nyan-king*,[11] it was used only to make trousers. There was another kind you made the jacket to go with it from. The very first bolt of that cloth that arrived in that store, that's the one he took. He took it and carried it back to Diamant, where he began to sell it to people by the trouser-length. And then people began saying, "Cloth's been stolen in Saint-Pierre." The gendarmes started investigating, asking questions, snooping around. Finally, they arrested a man who had a pair of those pants. They asked where he'd gotten them. It wasn't local cloth, it had barely arrived in the stores. In fact, that store hadn't yet sold a single meter. So they really went at the guy, interrogated him, locked him up, investigated—until he finally said, "It was Méda." They began to keep him under surveillance. But it took them a good three years before they caught him. Meanwhile, he was selling his cloth and whatnot. But once they caught him, they really put him away. It was the first time he was caught for a big theft. The thick-

ness of that bolt of cloth—it took four men to carry it—but he managed to carry it here all by himself.

Médard's penal record shows that it was in December of 1927 that the gendarmes finally caught up with him. He served six months in prison and paid a substantial fine of twenty-five francs, finally getting out in June of 1928. But his sentence had another twist: presumably because the owners of the distilleries at Dizac, and perhaps Trois-Rivières, found him a continual nuisance, the court slapped on an order of five years' banishment from Diamant. Médard was forced to move from the area.

Officially, Médard now resided in Saint-Pierre. One of Philibert's nephews, seventy-six at the time I interviewed him there (and in the early stages of Alzheimer's disease), said he himself had moved from Diamant to Saint-Pierre just before Médard—around 1926—and remembered him well. Médard didn't live at "Anse Médard," as I had imagined, looking at a place by that name on the map, but rather toward Le Prêcheur, "where all those caves are." So, Médard hadn't changed his favored kind of domicile. "The police," the nephew added, "always had him under surveillance. He had to be very cautious." Nevertheless, Médard seems to have spent relatively little time in his new home and preferred his better established cave at Diamant.

In 1929, despite the prohibition on his presence, Médard was arrested for theft in the heart of Diamant—and it was not just any theft. The late mayor, Armand Ribier, told me:

> It was all rather mysterious. The gendarmes had lost some rabbits. They claimed that Méda had stolen the rabbits. Now, it would be pretty unusual for someone to steal from the police, don't you think? Maybe it was people who worked in the gendarmerie, I don't know— I really don't know how it happened. But when he found out that the gendarmes suspected him, he headed right into his cave, over near Anse Caffard, facing the Rock. Eventually, he was betrayed by two or three people and the gendarmes caught up with him. In those days, the gendarmes in Diamant were mounted police. There were two horses, two gendarmes, and they caught him. They walked him along. The ones from Diamant would march him to Rivière-Salée.

The ones from Rivière-Salée would bring him to Ducos, and so on. All the way to Fort-de-France. And Méda kept denying that he'd committed this theft. Now when you leave Diamant, going in the direction of the Novotel, there's a turn in the road—there are two houses there on the left, an old one and a newer one a little bit behind. Well, when the gendarmes got to that place, I don't know how it happened, but one of the gendarme's horses startled and the gendarme was thrown. They couldn't continue. That was strange indeed. Afterwards, he had to leave Diamant for Saint-Pierre—but what did he have in Saint-Pierre? This is a man who'd never killed, never raped. . . .

According to police records, Médard was sentenced to three months and a day of prison and his five-years' expulsion from Diamant was extended. He was also deprived of his civil rights—the right to vote and other things that he could scarcely have cared about—for five years. But he didn't serve out his term.

On 22 May 1929, Médard escaped—the records don't specify how—and he remained on the lam in his Diamant cave for the next several months. This time, the gendarmes were really onto his case. But he managed to continue to take things at night without being seen and to deliver them to his neighbors—because, people hint, of his special powers. Génor recalls that Médard would show up at your house before dawn when he made his deliveries.

One time, he came to make a delivery to a woman's house in the early morning. "Open the door, make room!" he said. (If she didn't come outside, there wouldn't be room to move the barrel in.) The woman said, "No!" When Méda called out, it was four o'clock in the morning. She startled, she was afraid. Méda said, "Don't be scared, it's those things you wanted I've brought for you." The woman said, "What kind of joke is this? It's been ages since I asked you about those things. I wasn't being serious." And then the woman opened the door a crack and looked at the stuff. "Méda, where did you get all that?" He said, "Don't worry, you don't have to be afraid. Just open the door for me and let me take care of things." The woman opened the door but she was pretty frightened. Méda brought everything inside and then went out and shut the door. Three or four days later, Méda came back, he was sitting at the woman's table and three gendarmes from Rivière-Pilote showed up asking for "Médard," for a certain Médard. The three gendarmes were sitting there at a table drinking and asking her for Médard. Méda was sitting right there! They continued drinking. The woman told them, "I don't know Méda, I don't know any such person." The gendarmes said, "Everybody knows Médard. How can it be you don't know him? The way Médard is always passing by here—and you say you don't know him?" Méda is sitting there the whole time, right next to them. They drank some more, they got up, they rode off. They left Méda sitting right there. That man was powerful, eh!

When the gendarmes did catch up with Médard, a few months later, he served thirty days—half for the prison break, half for violating his expulsion order.

Six months later, once again, the gendarmes picked up Médard in Diamant and he served another thirty days for being where he wasn't supposed to be. Then, in 1931, he served a full six months for an unspecified theft, and for staying in Diamant. By this time, his pattern seems pretty clear: giving to the poor, stealing from the rich, saying little to anybody, and creating pieces of art (ships, "*photos*" of people, musical instruments) that filled everyone who saw them—from local fishermen and canecutters to urban businessmen and civil servants—with genuine wonder. And all the time living in caves and dressed in rags—barefoot, floursack pants held up with a rope, broad torso bare.

It was in 1932, for reasons that allow considerable room for interpretation, that Médard ran afoul of one of France's strangest and most draconian laws, designed to rid the streets of metropolitan cities of petty crimes and criminals—the infamous *Loi du 27 Mai 1885*. Philibert's version fits best with that in police records:

> You know, he was sweet as a lamb, Méda. He wasn't a real thief. But there came a moment when he had no clothes. Well, my cousin, Marius Larcher—he was district attorney in the capital—he had taken a little house right next to where the *mairie* is now, he was renting it,

on vacation in Diamant. Méda came along and took a pair of pants from the clothesline in the courtyard and someone saw and told Marius Larcher and he filed a complaint and they put Méda in jail. And from there, the *bagne*! (Maybe it wasn't pants but a blanket he'd taken to sleep on, because sometimes he'd sleep in the woods, he'd hang out in the mangroves over near Anse Céron, he sold crabs and things. But in any case it was people from here who betrayed him.) The gendarme was going on with his investigation and someone said, "It was Méda!" The idea of sending someone to the *bagne* for that! It's pure politics. Barbary, savagery!

Génor reminisced about how the gendarmes finally caught up with Médard:

I hadn't seen him for some time—he'd been hiding out. Then one day, a couple of guys were coming back from the city where they'd sold fish and their *canot* passed right by the shore there. From the sea they saw someone hiding. One said, "That's Méda over there!" The other said, "No way, how could it be Méda? He's hiding out." The first, "I'm telling you, that's Méda there!" And he shouted out, "Méda, what are you doing here?" Méda startled. Then he called back, "I'm doing all right." So the first one sent the second to the gendarmerie. He got to Diamant just as the sun was going down. *Iii- éép, maman!* The gendarmes swept down and encircled the cave. They grabbed him, held him, and locked him up. He hadn't known they were coming. It was around six in the evening when they took Méda out of there. People came running as if there was an election![12] Everyone came down. They were all saying, "They've caught Méda!" Everyone came to watch, but then they started getting angry. People began to get aggressive, saying they shouldn't be taking Méda away. The next morning, the gendarmes showed up at his cave and began emptying out all the merchandise. Diamant people came in droves and started carrying off the goods for themselves. People were really angry that they were taking off Méda like that. He could have died where they took him. That man had never hurt a soul. He never did a thing to anyone. They should have let him take care of his own business. They should have left him alone in his misery. He stayed fifteen or twenty years in Cayenne!

Girard Sénart, born in 1923, shared his own memories of Médard's arrest, describing what he witnessed on the main street of town:

> When they came to take him away, I was just a little schoolkid, six—no, maybe ten years old. They went to get him at Fond Diamant, at his cave. And then I saw him passing by, with a big package on his head—and with shackles on his wrists and ankles.

And old M. Eustache, one of Médard's contemporaries from the hills above Diamant—after commenting that "Méda was a true magician" and that "He made statues that were simply too true"—reconstructed the departure scene yet more graphically: "When they arrested him to go to the *bagne*, clad in leg-irons, he carried that statue of Colonel Coppens on his head right into the gendarmerie." As Armand Ribier, shaking his head at the image of Médard being led away to the *bagne* in chains, reiterated:

> Those were the days of the colony. If someone said, "Méda stole such and such a thing," they'd simply send out an arrest warrant and bring him in. He was completely harmless, a man who was never violent. It was shameful. We're not going to see a man like that again soon!

It would be twenty years before Médard again set foot in Diamant. Let us try to retrace some of his steps as he was led away, first to his year-long sentence in the prison of Fort-de-France, then to his two-decade-long exile from his native land.

Detail of one of Médard's ships

Entrance to the *quartier-disciplinaire*, Camp de la Transportation, through which Médard so often passed. (Photo by Rodolphe Hammadi, 1994, © CNMHS/SPADEM.)

IT IS ENORMOUSLY difficult to write about French Guiana or the *bagne* without getting ensnared in stereotype and cliché.[13] Here, I shall try to keep our focus firmly on Médard, reconstructing something of his meanderings through this most total of all institutions.

A few words must be said first, however, about France's Law of 27 May 1885—the one that served as justification for Médard's banishment to the *bagne*. Often described as a "bizarre" proposal that punished petty delinquents worse than major offenders, the law of permanent banishment was envisioned less under the rubric of punishment than of public hygiene, an efficient means to cleanse French society of its undesirable elements. During the 1880s, as historian Gordon Wright tells us,

> For the first time, official crime statistics were being widely publicized in the popular press, and they helped to fuel public passions. Most major crimes, it was argued, were committed by persons who had begun as vagrants, beggars, or petty thieves. . . . Parliament was bombarded with petitions from local councils and citizens' groups; in 1880 the Freemasons of France submitted a monster petition carrying 60,000 signatures. . . . [Transportation of criminals to Guyane] could be compared to channelling the sewage of Paris onto a sandy suburban plain, which was enriched by this effluvium.

In 1885 the law was finally passed, specifying that, after a recidivist petty criminal had completed his sentence in the prisons of France—in other words, after he had served out his "punishment"—he would then, in the interests of preserving the security of the honest folk of the Republic, be banished for life. And since such habitual malefactors could not be expected to support themselves honestly during their banishment in the colonies, "they would be kept under penal supervision and put to work as if they were *bagnards* [criminals sentenced to life at hard labor]." The following excerpts from the several-page text of the law seem relevant for our story and speak directly to the care the French state took to classify its citizens, even those already living in the colonies and as apparently uninterested in such matters as Médard.

LAW OF 27 MAY 1885

N° 15,503—Law regarding recidivists (repeat offenders)

Article 1. *La relégation* (permanent banishment) will consist of the imprisonment for life, on the soil of French colonies or possessions, of those convicts whom the present law is designed to keep outside of France. The places of banishment and other details of confinement will be determined by rules of public administration to be promulgated later. . . .

Article 4. To be banished: those repeat offenders who, in whatever order and within any period of ten years (not counting time in prison), have received the sentences enumerated in the following paragraphs:

1° – two sentences of hard labor or long-term imprisonment (unless subject to paragraphs 1 and 2 of article 6 of the law of 30 May 1854);

2° – one sentence of the type specified in the preceding paragraph plus two sentences, either for felonies or sentences of more than three months of imprisonment for:

> theft
> fraud
> breach of trust
> indecent behavior
> debauching a minor
> vagrancy and begging (as defined in articles 277 and 279 of the penal code);

3° – four sentences, either to imprisonment for felonies or for imprisonment of more than three months, for any of the offenses in the previous paragraph;

4° – seven sentences, at least two of which are specified in the above two paragraphs, and of which the others are either vagrancy or violation of a prohibition on residence signaled in Article 19 of the present law [regarding residence in the regions of Paris and Lyons] as long as two of the other sentences were for more than three months of imprisonment.

The law of *relégation* quickly led to situations that ran counter to a common-sense notion of justice. Pierre writes that, "Even more than in trials ending in sentences of hard labor, it is in sentences of *relégation* that the whole horror of the judicial and penal systems became apparent," and he outlines, among other cases, that of a man who, in his youth, had been sentenced to several derisory prison terms, "the most serious being four months for drunkenness and theft in Bordeaux in 1868," who was then arrested in 1888—twenty years later—for having tapped into a cask of wine on the docks. "Brought before the court in Bordeaux, he pled guilty to the charge and was condemned to four months of prison—followed by *la relégation* [banishment for life]." He died in Guyane six months later.

Here are the relevant portions of a document that I extracted with the greatest difficulty and extraordinary luck from the French archives—the record of Médard's own conviction under this law, which gave him an effective life sentence of banishment at hard labor in the *bagne* of Guyane.[14]

Section V (detail) from Médard's Order of Permanent Banishment

RÉPUBLIQUE FRANÇAISE
LIBERTÉ-ÉGALITÉ-FRATERNITÉ
COLONY OF *la Martinique*

PERMANENT BANISHMENT

Law of 27 May 1885
Regarding the Banishment of Recidivists
(AS APPLIED IN THE COLONIES)
INDIVIDUAL RECORD

Extract of Criminal Proceedings
MARTINIQUE—COURT OF APPEALS

...that the so-named *Aribot, Médard*...was found guilty of the crime of *theft and insubordination* according to articles *379-401-209-212-278 of the Penal Code, 57, 58 of the Penal Code, 365 "C9."* and sentenced to *one year* of imprisonment, *and permanent banishment....*

[signed]: **Clerk of the Court of Appeals**
24 June 1933

PERMANENT BANISHMENT—DOCUMENT 1—COLONY OF *la Martinique*

I°—PERSONAL DATA

1° Family name, given names, nicknames: *Aribot, Médard, nicknamed "Pélage"*
2° Date and place of birth: *born 9 June 1901 in Sainte-Luce (Martinique)*
3° Place of last residence: *Saint-Pierre (Martinique)*
4° Parents: *Aribot, Marie Thérèse, his mother, deceased*
5° Unmarried, married, or widowed: *unmarried*
6° Children: *none*
7° Parents or friends who care about the convict
    and might come to his assistance: *none*

II°—PHYSICAL DESCRIPTION

height *1 meter 750 mill.*	Mouth *average, thick lips*
hair and eyebrows *black*	Chin *round*
forehead *normal*	Beard *black*
eyes *brown*	Face *oval*
nose *large*	Color *black*

SPECIAL MARKS *right foot Missing second toe*

V°—PROFESSIONAL APTITUDES AND RESOURCES

1° Assets and Resources acquired
   when he was free: Savings *owns nothing*

2° Professions practiced when he was free. . . .
   Mentioning those to which the convict might be
   assigned during his permanent
   banishment: *Knows a little about carpentry*
   Could be used for above-mentioned work

3° Professions practiced while in the prison system:
   Breaking rocks.
   Street-cleaning detail.

4° Possible uses of the convict: *All the hard labor of banishment—*
   logging, forest clearing, road-building, earth moving

5° Education: *Illiterate*

6° Religion: *Catholic*

VI°— CONDUCT WHILE FREE AND WHEN IN PRISON

1° Conduct when free: *Poor. 8 convictions.*

2° Conduct in prison and during *Good conduct in prison.*
   preceding detentions: *Submissive.*

3° Moral condition
   Likelihood of rehabilitation: *Little chance of rehabilitation*

NOTIFICATION FROM THE COMMISSION
OF COLONIAL CLASSIFICATION

(SESSION OF *16 November 1933*)

THE COMMISSION According to the law of 27 May 1885 regarding the permanent banishment of recidivists; according to the decree of 26 November 1885 bearing on the rules of public administration regarding the execution of the law stipulating permanent banishment; according to the order "loc 1" of *29 July 1887 regarding permanent banishment;* According to *the recommendations of the Chief of the Judicial System, the Warden of the Prison, and the General Secretary* Considering that the so-named *Aribot Médard a.k.a. Pélage* age *32* son of . . . .

and of *Aribot Marie-Thérèse* profession *without*
marital status *unmarried* convicted *3 April 1933*
by *the Appeals Court of Martinique* to *1 year of prison*
and permanent banishment for *theft and insubordination*
in accord with paragraphs *2 and 3* of article 4 of the
law of 27 May 1885, having previously
had *seven* convictions for *theft*

*Classed for permanent banishment in the
category of relégation collective*

[signed]: **The President of the Commission**
[signed also by]: **The Governor of the Colony**
[and by]: **The Minister of the Colonies**

III°– PENAL RECORD

1° Date of conviction: *3 April 1933*

2° Jurisdiction: *Court of Appeals of Martinique*

3° Type and length of sentence: *1 year prison followed by permanent banishment*

4° Type of crime: *theft and insubordination*

5° Date of Release: *1 November 1933*

6° Record of previous convictions:

DATE OF CONVICTIONS	JURIS- DICTION	CRIMES	SENTENCES –RELEASE DATES	OBSERVATIONS
2 Dec 1927	Criminal Court of Fort-de-France	theft	6 mos prison, 25 f. fine –1 June 1928	5 year expulsion (from commune of Diamant)
19 Apr 1929	idem	theft	3 mos & 1 day prison –27 Oct 1929	5 years expulsion (from commune of Diamant) & 5 years depriva- tion of civil rights as specified in art 42 of penal code
13 July 1931	idem	theft & violation of expulsion order	6 mos prison –13 Jan 1932	
3 Apr 1933	Appeals Court of Martinique	theft and insubor- dination[15]	1 year prison & permanent banishment –1 Nov 1933	on order of a judge of Court of Appeals dtd 17 Feb 1933

II° – Convictions Not Counted Toward Permanent Banishment

DATE OF CONVICTIONS	JURIS- DICTION	CRIMES	SENTENCES —RELEASE DATES	OBSERVATIONS
4 Oct 1923	Criminal Court of Fort-de-France	praedial larceny	2 mos prison —2 Dec 1923	
14 Jan 1926	idem	theft of garden produce	3 mos prison —2 May 1926	
24 Aug 1929	idem	violation of expulsion order & escape by prison break	15 days prison for 1st offense, 15 days prison for 2nd offense —26 Sept 1929	
14 Nov 1930	idem	violation of expulsion order	1 month prison —13 Dec 1930	

Médard's classification as a *relégué collectif* placed him in what was, arguably, the most unfortunate category of prisoners in the whole French Guiana penal colony. According to the inversion of "straight" values that reigned in this enclosed world, the most serious criminals (the *transportés*)—murderers, arsonists, big-time bank robbers—enjoyed the highest prestige, while political prisoners (the *déportés*) had a status apart, being consigned to Devil's Island off the coast.[16] But recidivists (the *relégués collectifs*), who were mainly petty thieves, minor sexual offenders, vagrants, and the like, were considered by guards and fellow-prisoners to be the lowest of the low—*pieds de biche* ("crowbar men"), as they were commonly called.[17] Michelot concludes: "Despised by both *transportés* and guards, the *relégués* were consistently characterized as swindlers, thieves, cowards, and liars. . . . Charles Hut, a former *bagnard*, said, 'For the other convicts, the *relégués* were almost pariahs.'" Another former convict, René Belbenoit, wrote that "Most of the [*relégué*] men are perverts. . . . Several of the inmates dress as women. . . . Many are syphilitic . . . [It is] an existence of utter degradation. . . . Even the convicts have more freedom and better food than the *relégués*." And the investigative journalist Albert Londres wrote that "the *relégués* are the shame of the *bagne*. What sort of flea-bitten trash is it who steal three chickens here, a hundred francs from a drawer, a painting from a gallery? It would be hard to find a seedier bunch. Around these parts, respect requires at the least having committed armed robbery." But the *relégués* were also an unusually tough bunch. A former prison doctor wrote, "They're more fearsome than the other prisoners because they have no regard for anyone, including one another. They display a raw wickedness, fueled by all sorts of abnormal jealousies." An official French publication aimed at an American audience explained that *relégués* were "vicious and hardened criminals" compared to *transportés*, "many of whom were first offenders." "*Relégués*," writes Alex Miles, "could be put in solitary confinement and were more likely to be abused by the guards than *transportés*." On the eve of Médard's arrival in the *bagne*, in the early 1930s, the mortality rate was even higher among the *relégués* than the *transportés*; indeed, Belbenoit claimed that during this period, 55 percent of *relégués* died in their first year.

It was not common for a Martiniquan (or Guadeloupean) to be sent to the *bagne*, especially as a *relégué*. During the 1920s and 1930s, a handful of convicts were shipped out from these island colonies, but they normally included only the most serious type of hardened criminals.[18] It is worth noting, nonetheless, that more than a third of all prisoners condemned to the *bagne* were non-Europeans—a quite astounding figure, given the original justifications for the practice of transportation and banishment. As Pierre writes,

> Severe in its sentences, intransigent in its repression, the Third Republic's ruling class applied a penal politics in its colonies that strongly encouraged the assimilation of other ethnic groups to its own judicial ideas. In Algeria, in Black Africa, in Indochina, judges exercised a great severity, paying little attention to local judicial traditions. . . . Theft from the European population was always punished with several years of hard labor.

But it would seem that *relégation* (as opposed to *transportation*) was little practiced by the colonial judiciary—except in Algeria, which had a substantial population of Frenchmen. (During the whole history of the *bagne*, only 901 of the 15,995 *relégués* [= 5.6 percent] came from colonies other than Algeria—that is, from the Black African colonies, Indochina, or the allegedly more "civilized" Old Colonies of Martinique, Guadeloupe, Guyane, and Réunion.[19]) This makes a certain sense, in that, in the logic of social hygiene, the "cleansing" of a colony where Frenchmen did not live was almost a contradiction. As Peter Redfield writes, "Rather than simply laboring for the nation, here [in Guyane] the colony also serves to solve an internal problem for the nation, that of delinquency. While the metropole still defines it, here the colony also marks the lower limit of the national society as well as its extensions, holding criminals and colonials in one place." Overall, Africans and their descendants made up only a small proportion of prisoners in the *bagne*: from 1886 to 1938, Europeans represented 63 percent, Arabs 25 percent, Asians 5 percent, and Blacks 7 percent.

During the inter-war years, well over 99 percent of all prisoners arriving in Guyane—whether *transportés*, *déportés* or *relégués*—came on the infamous "deathship," the *La Martinière*, a German freighter refurbished for the purpose by the Ministry of Colonies, which administered the *bagne*.[20] The twice-yearly voyage began at the fortress-prison of Saint-Martin de Ré, which lay off La Rochelle, and, one trip in two, touched shore at Algiers to pick up additional prisoners. Once at sea, up on deck, fifty guards patrolling day and night with large caliber pistols. Below, nearly seven hundred prisoners, divided among eight giant cages, each holding sixty to eighty men, fitted out with hammocks and a stinking central latrine and crisscrossed by steam pipes that could be opened at the first hint of rebellion. Seasickness was endemic, among guards as well as prisoners, as the old steamship lurched its way toward the tropic seas. Captain Rosier, the last commander of the *La Martinière*, wrote of

> the zoo-smell that normally arose from the hold but which was nothing compared to what one smelled in bad weather, when it was necessary to batten down the hatches, and the rolling and pitching made the convicts, still unused to the sea, even sicker. Gripping the bars of their cages, slipping about in their own wastes, emptying their stomachs wherever they could, shaken by violent retching, which nothing could calm. It was a terrible spectacle, which even the most hardened heart could not easily bear.

On board the La Martinière: *the prisoners in their cage*, by Francis Lagrange

Incorrigibles were placed in special "hot cells" constructed of sheet iron just over the boilers, so small that one could not straighten up in them; these prisoners were given only a quart of water a day to drink and, when freed, were "a mass of blood and blisters." Each morning during the two- to three-week voyage, the other prisoners were permitted twenty minutes above deck and, at precisely two o'clock, a communal shower of seawater, as firehoses were aimed into the cages.[21]

The biannual arrival of the *La Martinière* caused a flurry of excitement in the administrative center of the penal colony, Saint-Laurent-du-Maroni—known during the early twentieth century as "Petit Paris" for the charm and cleanliness of its convict-swept streets and convict-tended flower beds.[22] As the long line of unfortunates filed by, all Saint-Laurent would turn out to watch: wardens' wives in their Sunday best, colonial officers standing at attention in their dress whites and pith helmets, Chinese shopkeepers, Arab turnkeys, gold prospectors originally from Saint Lucia and Dominica, free Saramaka and Ndjuka "Bush Negroes" from Suriname, and other curious onlookers. "We debarked at Saint-Laurent at three in the afternoon, in a silence fueled by resignation and shame," wrote one former convict. "We were a vanquished troop, ready to be dispatched quickly, like cattle. We were dying of heat in our heavy clothing. But through

Debarking on the Maroni from the La Martinière, by Francis Lagrange

the dripping sweat that blinded me, I could see—under their white and green parasols—officers who joked with elegant young women who were pointing fingers toward us. They were looking for 'celebrity' convicts."

It was a colorful scene, laden with emotion, as the prisoners were marched off the ship and through the brick gate, where they were officially reminded of the verse "Abandon All Hope Ye Who Enter Here!" Though Médard himself probably arrived less spectacularly (either on the *Biskra*, which plied the waters between Fort-de-France and Saint-Laurent, or on the twice-monthly steam launch that connected Saint-Laurent to Cayenne, where a freighter from Martinique could have deposited him), the *La Martinière*'s arrival was the kind of scene that especially intrigued him. (And it is not entirely out of the question that he was sent on the twice-monthly packet to the metropole to join the prison convoy at La Rochelle and thence made the voyage to Guyane on the *La Martinière* itself.) In any case, sometime during his twenty-year stay in the colony, Médard built his own *La Martinière*, which Kenneth Bilby was able to locate in 1984, lying half-forgotten under a table in the office of the former chief of the prison hospital.[23]

"Médard built his own *La Martinière*."

Whatever its initial conception, by the time of Médard's arrival the *bagne* had become a machine to break and use men, and had taken on a life of its own. Only 25 percent of convicts survived for twenty years, earning the place its best known nickname, *la guillotine sèche* (the dry guillotine). Doctor Louis Rousseau, who ended his term as chief prison doctor in 1932 on the eve of Médard's arrival, concluded that

> The *bagne* is a charnel house, a mass grave, running from syphilis to tuberculosis, with all the tropical parasites one can imagine (carrying malaria, ankylosis, amoebic dysentery, leprosy, etc.), all destined to work hand in hand with an administration whose task it is to diminish the number of prisoners consigned to its care. The fiercest proponents of "elimination" can rest satisfied. In Guyane, both *transportés* and *relégués* survive on the average five years—no more.

Prisoners were subjected to a highly rationalized system of dehumanization.

> In the *bagne*, everything was dictated by texts, with a staggering meticulousness. Every aspect of the daily life of *transportés* and *relégués* was precisely described and programmed. . . . As one tries to comprehend the accumulated mass of texts, rules, and decrees, one enters an almost surrealistic universe in which everything is prescribed and foreseen. The manual for guards . . . specifies "the knife commonly called 'pocket-knife' is permitted for prisoners as long as the blade is folding, ending in a right angle without convexity or a point, and is sharpened on one side only." . . . And the rules for punishment go on for pages: giving bread to a man in punishment = 30 days in prison; giving tobacco to a man in punishment = 60 days in prison; complaining about the quantity or quality of food = 30–60 days in prison; wearing a non-prison-issue hat = 15 days in prison; talking back to a guard = 8–30 days in prison; not completing the daily work quota = complete privation of food.

Arrival in the penal colony was marked by well-practiced rites designed to strip off whatever traces of civilian identity still lingered for each prisoner. Soon after setting foot on land, on 22 March 1934, the man who had been known even

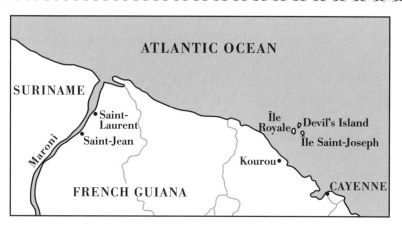

The geography of the *bagne*

in the colonial prison of Fort-de-France as Médard Aribot became—in principle, forever—simply Number 15,930, the fifteen thousand nine-hundred thirtieth *relégué* logged in since the French Guiana *bagne* began.[24] From the Saint-Laurent registration office, where verbal formalities were completed, Médard was taken next door to the Anthropometry Bureau, "a vast room . . . with desks for different specialists, a height gauge, a scale, a camera mounted on a tripod, and a table with ink pads for fingerprinting." As one author described the generic scene:

> The dreadful day when he had stood stripped in the office where authorities registered finger prints and made inventories of men's bodies, recording every distinguishing mark, every wart or mole, every birth blotch and every tattooed design, making measurements, and adding these things to one's name and age and birthplace, and to the individual crime histories and sentences sent over by the French courts—all indexed and cross-indexed to facilitate emergency reference.

Also photographed, both full face and profile, with and then without the distinctive wide-brimmed hat that all *relégués* were issued. (*Relégués* were also supposed to be distinguished from other *bagnards*—who wore grey uniforms with red stripes—by their all-blue outfits, but at least one eyewitness claims that during Médard's time in the *bagne*, they, too, wore pinstripes.) The spaces for Médard's "anthropometric description" on his Permanent Prison Record (*registre matricule*) are titled: Height, Cranial Vault, Chest, Head (length, width), Armspan, Height of Arch of the Foot, Upper-Arm Length, Palate Height[?], Right Ear (length, width), Left Foot, Left Middle Finger, Little Finger, Nose (back, base, size, particularities), Forehead (inclination, height, width), Description of Right Ear, Eye Color, Beard, Hair, Apparent Age, Other Special Characteristics, Special Marks, Observations Relative to these Measurements— Data recorded the [date], Checked the [date]. But for reasons unclear to me, the blanks are not filled in on the copy I have seen. However another, apparently less technical, section of Médard's Permanent Prison Record, labeled simply "Description" (*signalement*)— which includes much of the same material (and corresponds to the "physical description" portion of Médard's Fort-de-France records)—is duly filled out in handwriting, meticulously noting, among various other details, the missing second toe on Médard's right foot.[25] "This new dossier [the *registre matricule*] that was constituted for each convict," writes Michelot, "had a cardinal importance. During the whole life of the prisoner in Guyane, it followed and kept precise track of him," serving as the slate on which each infraction was inscribed and each reclassification of his status recorded.

After the completion of registration formalities at the Saint-Laurent administration center—which, in his case, took four days—Médard was transported, either by barge or by train, the seventeen kilometers up the Maroni to Saint-Jean, the sprawling jungle camp where some twenty-five hundred *relégués* were housed, known ironically as "Little Switzerland" or "New Rome" (because of its hilliness) or more dryly as "the city of thieves" or "the *bagne*'s oubliette." Suriname journalist D.G.A. Findlay made the narrow-gauge train trip during Médard's era and described the scenery as the decrepit flatcars-with-benches-nailed-on followed the already-ancient locomotive across the iron bridge spanning the Crique Balaté, which formed the border between the penal colony proper and the vast domain of the *relégation*.

> We first passed Camp Saint Louis, across from the island of that name reserved for lepers. Then Saint-Maurice, which at one time had a distillery that used convict-grown cane but which had fallen

into disrepair and now housed a few (liberated?) Arab convicts trying to eke out a living by farming. Next, the train passed the dreaded Camp Le Tigre, where human "tigers" [*relégués*] are sent to work for a few months before they expire. After that, we passed Nouveau Camp, where convicts [*relégués*] with elephantiasis and similar diseases live.[26] Soon, we crossed a *pousse*—a kind of trolley propelled by two poles on which the military guards ride. And finally the arrival in "Little Switzerland," the town of *relégués*. To wean men from theft and to rehabilitate them, they're sent to Saint-Jean. But in fact, they simply go from bad to worse. Once in Saint-Jean, the *relégués* learn every trick of the trade. The place is also famous for its "theater." In Saint-Jean, there are actors for every role. A "pretty maid" appears on stage—you have to pretend not to see "her" tattoos and wrestler's biceps. But then these prisoners have learned not to be too demanding.

"Soon, we crossed a *pousse*." *La pousse*, by Francis Lagrange

The prisoner population of Saint-Jean, composed solely of *relégués*, was housed in communal barracks mounted on stilts, each holding fifty or sixty men. (During Médard's time, men slept on the floor for their first couple of years, until enough prisoners had died for a bed to be free.) In the same large clearing were workshops, a slaughterhouse, and an infirmary, as well as administrative offices and bungalows for the personnel—and the dreaded punishment cells. ("Saint-Jean possessed the most fully developed disciplinary premises [of the whole penal colony]," writes one specialist.) On a hillside overlooking the river were the villas of the camp commander and chief warden. In addition to the complement of armed prison guards, a garrison of 120 Senegalese riflemen (described by one *relégué* as "a mob of black lunatics lusting to kill") watched over the place.

Money could buy almost anything in the *bagne*, and one of the better-known aspects of daily life is that each prisoner had his *plan*—a capped cylinder, usually of metal, some ten centimeters long and four or five in diameter, which held coins and paper money, a knife, file, or needle—"worn" in the rectum. It was apparently the only way to put aside money, though we know nothing about Médard's adaptations to the practice. During those periods when he was not in cellular confinement for breaking one or another regulation, it seems likely that he participated in the *relégué* privilege of being allowed, every Monday, to take the little train down to Saint-Laurent and sell things in the market—basketry, chairs, and tables are the usual items mentioned for *relégués*. For, after Médard's liberation at the end of the war, we know he made and sold diverse handicrafts to tourists. So, in his "free" time during late afternoons at Saint-Jean, or perhaps at night as when he was home in his cave at Diamant, he was probably busy making ships, toys, and other wooden objects for sale.

Many contemporaries claim that in Saint-Jean, immorality and violence held sway even more than among the hard-labor criminals downriver at Saint-Laurent. A former guard's account, said to apply to the barracks in which *relégués* were shut at night, describes some of this activity:

> At the end of the corridor was the W-C, known as the "Love Suite."
> Once lights were turned off at nine o'clock, the building began its
> night life. Blankets were strung between the two bars that held up

the hammocks in such a way that the guards couldn't see in and, around the little oil lamps or candles, the games began. Rowdy hands of "La Marseillaise" [a card game] went on well into the night, sometimes till dawn. From time to time, players would slip off to the Love Suite for awhile and then return. Things might get pretty hot, with contraband rum helping out, and there were often fights. Knives would appear and, in the morning when the doors were opened and the guards came in, a man would be pinned to his hammock, bathed in a sea of blood. No one had seen a thing.

We can only imagine, on the basis of the scraps of evidence at hand, how Médard would have navigated life in these unfamiliar and perilous conditions. Always the loner, he had the benefits of his size and strength, which would presumably have spared him certain of the indignities forced upon many newcomer *relégués*. We can be fairly sure that as a connoisseur of dress balls and other fancy occasions, he would have been fascinated by the more dramatic and theatrical

Settling a Score, by Francis Lagrange

aspects of *relégué* amusements. "In 1936 at Saint-Jean-du-Maroni, the officials of the *bagne* permitted the formation of a transvestite ballet troupe, whose star dancer was a certain Coronella. People killed for 'her.'"[27] And among the *relégués*, other famous "queens" of the day flaunted their charms publicly: "la Marquise," "Mistinguet," "la Tigresse," "la Panthère," and "la Duchesse." It is also reported that during the thirties at Saint-Jean a former theatrical director, the *relégué* Mayol, organized a performance of *The 28 Days of Clairette*, a vaudeville operetta in four acts. Surely, Médard would have been an avid spectator at these and similar evening diversions.

Work routine varied, depending in part on the prisoner's relations with guards and with each other. But it seems clear that the *relégation collective* could be truly backbreaking for those whom the guards sought to "punish," either for their own amusement or from other motives. Médard's prison record, as well as his reported post-*bagne* remarks, make it clear that he was often a victim of such circumstance.

One factor was certainly racism. At certain times in the history of the institution, prisoners were actually segregated by "race," with Europeans placed in one large room and in another "a multicolored mixture of all nations and races—Arabs, Chinese, Indians, Senegalese, and Blacks of all sorts." Early in the century, the administration set up the Camp des Malgaches, where they gathered together black prisoners, who were reputed to be especially fit for forest-clearing and other hard labor. Michelot noted dryly that "racism was a part of life in the *bagne*," but he didn't report, as did Pierre, that the early-twentieth-century specifications for daily food rations were officially differentiated by race: "the European race . . . , the Arab race . . . , the Annamite race . . . , and the Black race, who did not have the right to eat fresh meat." Although it is generally agreed that after certain reforms in 1925, the degree of sadism and repression in the *bagne* went up and down, until the camps were finally closed after the war, Médard clearly suffered terribly during his years spent under collective discipline. As one of his *relégué* contemporaries testified, "There were times when things were really tough, when we were so hungry we ate raw breadfruit off the ground, or banana peels, whatever we could scavenge."

Médard—because of his strength, his color, and his unbending attitude—would almost certainly have been recruited for the toughest work in the forests.

A former *relégué* told Michelot, "The timber workers would leave at three or four o'clock in the morning—those who had a daily quota of hardwood to cut. . . . Around eleven, soup would be prepared and, whenever they returned from work, they'd take their tin plate and eat." Another ex-convict described how "In the forest camps, Antillean prisoners who were better adapted to the climate managed to cut the onerous daily quota of hardwood—a meter cubed—in only half a day. 'So I simply paid a Martiniquan two francs a day to cut my share.'" Médard, as we know, could do the work of several lesser men—if he wanted to.

Médard clearly did not take to his new surroundings and began to resist, apparently more bullishly than with forethought and ruse, from early in his stay. The records suggest that the prison authorities tried repeatedly to break his will, but without success. Six weeks after his arrival in Saint-Jean, Médard was "noted" for his first punishable act—"not completing his daily quota" (*défaut de tâche*)—routinely punished by "complete withholding of food." Within the next week, his *registre* was twice again marked for the same offense and now he was hauled up formally before the Disciplinary Commission, consisting of the

Hauling Timber, by Francis Lagrange

camp's commander and several guards assisted by a clerk, that meted out internal sentences. Presumably to teach him a severe lesson (no records of the deliberations were kept), the Commission sentenced Médard to eight days of solitary confinement for the first offense and to an additional thirty days of solitary for the second. (The maximum sentence that the Disciplinary Commission was permitted to pronounce was thirty days per offense.) Because the *relégation* had a certain independence from the rest of the penal colony, and because few *relégués* left memoirs, we have only a couple of written descriptions of the punishment cells used during Médard's time, but they seem to have been very small, with a ceiling designed so a man could not fully stand up. The heat was said to have been unbearable. Prison doctor Rousseau described:

> A tiny grilled opening let in a bit of light and air. The prisoner slept on a plank. The furnishings consisted of two wooden buckets, identical in form but differing in purpose [one contained drinking water, the other waste]. No chair, no shelf, just the two buckets which, in the dark, the prisoner might well mix up and knock over. . . . Solitary confinement is limited to thirty days at a time. In case of consecutive sentences, the total number of days is served in doses of twenty days at a time, followed by twenty days of normal penal colony life.

George Seaton, the only *relégué* contemporary of Médard who left detailed records,[28] claims that the thirty-day limitation was not always respected.

> I have known of men who did three years in the [solitary] cells without ever seeing the light of day. They were the men whom the guards took a dislike to; crimes were invented just to keep them there. Most of them were driven mad by the sheer loneliness and boredom. . . . For a month I endured the loneliness of the dumb, growing weaker and weaker on my pitiful diet. . . . For two days out of every three we were on a diet of bread and water.

Médard emerged from his first twenty-day "dose" of solitary on 8 June 1934. But just before reentering for his remaining eighteen days, he was again brought before the Commission, this time for a new offense: "missing articles" (*défaut d'effets*), as he had been unable, at morning roll call, to produce one or another of the prison-issued pieces of clothing or bedding for which each inmate was responsible. And once again, the Commission pronounced the maximum sentence, apparently trying to break his will—thirty days in a cell. So, by the time Médard again went into solitary on 28 June, after his twenty-day stretch as a normal hard-labor *relégué*, he had accumulated forty-eight days of additional punishment, two and a half "doses" in solitary that were slated to last into late October.

During this period, every time he was not in cellular confinement Médard seems to have committed one or another infraction that added yet more time to his punishments. Only three days after leaving his cell for a twenty-day "respite" in mid-July, he was brought before the Commission for "urinating from the veranda of his barracks" and was sentenced to an additional fifteen days of solitary, theoretically stretching his doses in the cell well into November. However, on September 14, the day he was to enter solitary for his next twenty-day stint, the Clerk of the Commission recorded in Médard's dossier, "Pardon [*remise*] of all remaining sentences, by order of the Camp Commander." Médard, who by that time had served forty of the total of eighty-three days in solitary he'd accumulated during his first four months at Saint-Jean, was probably in sufficiently poor physical shape that the Commander thought he was at last gaining the upper hand.

Subsequent events, however, show that Médard remained incorrigible throughout his stay in the penal colony. Indeed, the pattern of offenses and punishments changed but little as the years stretched on. During the eight years and two months covered by Médard's *registre matricule* (some 2,980 days), he accumulated additional sentences of 1,729 days—58 percent of his total time in the *bagne*—in solitary or other cellular confinement.

12.5.34   Défaut de tâche.
19.5.34. I.   -do-
          II.   -do-
23 juin 1934 Défaut d'effets
21 juillet 1934 *surpris urinant de la Véranda de sa case,*
18 - 7 - 34   *Remise du rest à sa peine et du Cam.*
13 oct. 34   *manquant - l'appel*
22.12.34   *Scandale, rixe ⁊ coups réciproques avec son*
          Co. relegué 1738 ~~cidot~~ Hector
1.1.35   *Remise du reste Ct. du Directeur*
1.6.35   *Défaut de toile ou hamac - vol ⁊ patates*
8.6.35   *Vol ⁊ patates - Défaut de toile ⁊ pliant*
14.7.35   *Remise du reste % du Directeur*
10.8.35   *a quitté son chantier à 7 heures*
28.9.35   *a quitté son chantier à 9ᵉ sans autorisation*
9. . .   *Transformation d'une vareuse ⁊ laine.*
30.6.36   ᴵ *Vol ⁊ maïs, surpris par le veilleur ⁊ nuit à 4 heure*
          ᴵᴵ *manquait à l'appel du matin le 28/6/36*

Médard's *registre matricule* (detail)

Offenses, Punishments, and Reprieves Handwritten into Médard's

registre matricule.

[Indications in italics concern major offenses, adjudicated by the Colonial Courts.]

12 May 1934	Not completing daily work quota	
19 May 1934	I—ditto	8 days solitary confinement
	II- ditto	30 days solitary confinement
23 June 1934	Missing articles	30 days solitary confinement
21 July 1934	Discovered urinating from the veranda of his barracks	15 days solitary confinement
14 Sept. 1934	Pardon of remaining sentences, by order of the Camp Commander	
13 Oct. 1934	Absent at roll call	4 days solitary confinement
22 Dec. 1934	"Scandal," brawl, and exchange of blows with co-*relégué* 14733 Hector	15 nights in prison
1 Jan. 1935	[Holiday] Pardon of remaining sentences, by order of Director [of Penal Colony]	
4 Feb. 1935	*Prisoner Missing—Escaped*	
5 Feb. 1935	*Prisoner Found*	[@*12 Feb:*] *1 month prison* [*Saint-Laurent*]
31 May 1935	*Prisoner Missing—Escaped*	
1 June 1935	Hammock missing—theft of sweet potatoes [prisoner missing]	
5 June 1935	*Prisoner Found*	[@*18 June:*] *2 months prison* [*Saint-Laurent*]
8 June 1935	Theft of sweet potatoes— Missing canvas cover [for cot?]	30 days solitary confinement plus 2 months Saint-Jean prison
14 July 1935	[Holiday] Pardon of remaining sentences, by order of Director	
10 Aug. 1935	Left work site at 7 a.m.	15 nights in prison
28 Sept. 1935	Left work site at 9 a.m. w/out authorization	15 nights in prison
9 June 1936	Disfiguring a woolen jacket	15 days solitary confinement
30 June 1936	I. Theft of corn discovered by night watchman at 4 AM	30 days solitary confinement
	II. Absent at morning roll call on June 28	8 nights in prison
14 July 1936	[Holiday] Pardon of remaining sentences, by order of Director	
4[?]Aug.1936	Prowling about workplaces at 3 a.m.	15 days solitary confinement
13 Oct. 1936	Left work site at 7 a.m.	15 days solitary confinement
4 Dec. 1937	Attempted escape, caught in the act	30 days solitary confinement

19 Feb. 1938	1 woolen jacket	30 days solitary confinement
2 July 1938	Ripping up a blanket	30 days solitary confinement
26 July 1938	*Prisoner Missing—Escaped*	
13 Aug. 1938	*Prisoner Found*	[*@16 Aug:*] *3 months prison* [*Saint-Laurent*]
3 Sept. 1938	Engaging in immoral acts, carrying a sharp implement. Missing woolen jacket and shirt. No cloth, shirt, boots, cup, spoon.	90 days solitary confinement plus 2 months Saint-Jean prison
17 Sept. 1938	Destruction of prison property	Warning
1 Oct. 1938	Attempted to engage in acts of active pederasty upon [illegible], which led to a brawl	30 days solitary confinement
1 Jan. 1939	[Holiday] Pardon of remaining sentences, by order of Director	
9 Jan. 1939	*Prisoner Missing—Escaped*	
11 Jan. 1939	*Prisoner Found*	[*@31 Jan:*] *1 month prison* [*Saint-Laurent*] [*then @ 21 July:*] *6 months prison* [*Saint-Laurent*]
8 Mar. 1939	Attempted escape	30 days solitary confinement
24 Mar. 1939	Missing articles	30 days solitary confinement
1 May 1939	Defacing wall of his cell	8 days solitary confinement
	Found at 2 a.m. behind the rear courtyard where sweet potatoes are stored	30 days solitary confinement
29 May 1939	Infraction of the rules	4 days solitary confinement
3 June 1939	Pardon of 2 months by order of Comm.ˢᵗ· Supʳ.	
13 Sept. 1939	Missing articles	4 days solitary confinement
10 Jan. 1940	Possession of 2 knives and an awl	15 days solitary confinement
20 Jan. 1940	Pardon given for 2 months	
24 Feb. 1940	Missing from kit: woolen jacket, 1 hammock, 1 pair of boots, 1 washbrush	30 days solitary confinement (pardon of 2 months [word illegible])
5 Oct. 1940	Pilfering sweet potatoes	30 days solitary confinement plus 3 months Saint-Jean prison
11 Dec. 1940	Pilfering sweet cassava	30 days solitary confinement plus 3 months Saint-Jean prison
1 Jan. 1941	[Holiday] Pardon of 1 month prison, by orders of [Director ???]	
19 Feb. 1941	Possession of a knife	30 days solitary confinement
3 June 1941	*Prisoner Missing—Escaped*	

3 June 1941	*Prisoner Found*	*[@10 June:] 8 months prison [Saint-Laurent]*
28 June 1941	Destruction of property	30 days solitary confinement
10 Aug. 1941	Pardon of remaining sentences, by decision of the Chief in Saint-Laurent	
13 Sept. 1941	Urinates in a can which he empties in the middle of the barracks	15 days solitary confinement
15 Nov. 1941	Bad work attitude	15 days solitary confinement
16 July 1942	1. Theft of bananas	15 days solitary confinement
	2. Destruction of cloth trousers	8 nights in prison

By any account, Médard was an unusual prisoner, breaking the rules often and receiving more severe punishment than most. Many of his offenses seem a continuation of his favored subsistence activities prior to exile—theft of sweet potatoes, theft of corn, stealing bananas, pilfering sweet cassava. Others suggest rebellion and resistance—not completing his daily work quota, having a bad work attitude, urinating in a can that he empties in the middle of the barracks, defacing the wall of his cell, "losing" various articles, being absent at roll call, "losing" a woolen jacket and shirt, ripping up a blanket, destroying trousers, and disfiguring a jacket. Others merely seem to reflect his pre-*bagne* personality and habits—wandering off from work early, prowling around outside at night, and neglecting to keep his prison-issued gear in order.

As for Médard's several citations for "immoral acts," to the extent that they reflect actual events, they probably attest to available modes of aggression and rebellion more than to his sexual proclivities. According to his friends in Martinique, Médard showed little interest in sex, either before or after the *bagne*. On the other hand, although homosexuality in the *bagne* has been heavily sensationalized (with some writers estimating that 60–80 percent of prisoners, including *relégués*, engaged in homosexual practices), it was, by all accounts, part of everyday life. Médard's *registre matricule* records that eight months after his arrival, he was involved in an unspecified "scandal" that ended in blows with a co-*relégué* named Hector, for which he was sentenced to fifteen nights in prison; two years later, that he was marked up for unspecified "immoral acts" while holding a "sharp implement" and sentenced to ninety days of solitary confinement plus two months in Saint-Jean prison; and that in 1938, he tried "to engage in acts of active pederasty upon [illegible] which led to a brawl," for which he received thirty days of solitary. Since only acts of aggression involving excessive force (and leading to public mayhem) seem to have been marked up or punished, there is no way of knowing for certain whether Médard, like many other physically strong prisoners, had regular or occasional more-or-less consenting partners. But what we know about his apparent disinterest in sexual activities outside prison, and his apparent belligerence while on the inside, suggest that the incidents marked in his *registre* may well represent simply acts of occasional and sudden rebellion, lashings out against confinement.

In terms of escapes, Médard was in championship company—not as regards success but in terms of the number of serious attempts: seven (or nine, depending on how one counts) during the eight years covered by his *registre matricule*, punished by prison terms that ranged up to an unusually long eight months. Years later, after his return to Martinique, Médard would occasionally speak to friends of these adventures. It seems that rather than participating in the more usual kind of escapes—organized by several men together and involving the payment of cash to Indians or others ready to furnish canoes, sails, and other necessary materials—he simply took whatever opportunities presented themselves to head off into the forest. We know that escape was never far from the thoughts of *relégués*—over the course of the institution's existence, 22,750 escapes were recorded for a total of 15,995 men, one and a half per person. In 1940, 472 (of 2,312 *relégués*) escaped, of whom 420 were recaptured. Michelot cites the extreme case of one *relégué* who escaped nine times in five years during the late 1930s. The last time, he was brought in by a Saramaka named "Voisin" and sentenced to nine months of cellular punishment. Pierre writes of another escapee who was punished with four years of cellular reclusion and who "aged ten years" in the process.

Recaptured *relégués* generally received time in punishment cells—but not, normally, on the offshore Iles du Salut, where recaptured *transportés* were incarcerated. Nevertheless, Médard recounted horrific stories about the tiny chambers he was shut away in for long periods. "There were snakes all over the cell," he would tell Ti Louis during the late sixties. "If I took off my shoes, when I went to put them on in the morning, they'd be full of little green snakes." Julien Privat also told me that Médard had several times described to him the snakes that crawled around in his cell. And everyone who knew Médard after the *bagne* agreed that the reason he walked all bent over, neck fused to spine, is that the punishment cells in which he was kept were only a meter and half high, so that he could never fully stand up.

Whenever a prisoner escaped, "thirty or so Arab turnkeys armed with cutlasses would back up the guards, who were armed with carbines and revolvers." Sometimes, large-scale chases were organized, with Senegalese riflemen, guards, gendarmes, and Indian- and Maroon-manhunters, but apparently it was the professional, solitary manhunters who were most successful. Something of the excitement of this period was expressed to us when we lived in Suriname, where old Saramaka men used to tell us about their tremendous fear of escapees from the *bagne*. Well into the 1970s, Saramaka mothers still frightened their children by repeating the adage, "Little children cooked up with dasheen, that's the convict's favorite dish!"[29] Escapees in the forest were often starving, and Saramakas preserve numerous stories of their attempts, sometimes successful, to ambush, rob, or kill Saramakas who happened to cross their path. Books on the *bagne* recount how four particularly fierce North Africans, who had been sowing mayhem throughout the colony in the several months since their escape in early 1934, fell upon a Saramaka garden camp along the Oyapok and killed a woman. Before they could cross the border to Brazil, they were captured by Saramakas and, in return for a reward, turned over to the authorities. (Another account suggests that the Saramakas lynched them, with machetes and clubs.) Saramakas still say that "*alábi poité*" [Arab prisoners] were "the worst of the lot."

The war years were undoubtedly Médard's toughest in the *bagne*. On the eve of the war in July 1939, under circumstances that I am unable to squeeze out of the archival records, Médard was officially transferred from the *relégation collective* to the *relégation individuelle*, meaning he was free to live on his own anywhere within the colony, responsible only for reporting to the authorities twice a year. It appears that he chose to live on the edge of the *relégation* territory, along the river at Saint Louis, doing a bit of provision-ground agriculture by day and by night making artworks for sale in the Saint-Laurent market. However, his *registre matricule* continued to be marked up—and he continued to serve punishments, both in the old solitary confinement cells and in the prison of the Colony—throughout the next three years, very much as if nothing had really changed in his status. This may well have been due to certain unusual practices brought on by the war.

France's plan to close down the whole penal colony had been interrupted by the German invasion of the metropole. The rupture of shipping traffic caused the value of imports from France to Guyane to drop from forty-nine million francs in 1939, to four million in 1941 and to zero in 1942 and 1943. Like the rest of Guyane, the penal colony suffered mightily and new work and punishment regimens were introduced. Even the official French embassy publication admitted, "In 1940 the appointment of a new director trained in the penal camps of the Far East . . . caused regulations to be tightened and harsh disciplinary methods, long discontinued, were revived."[30] One of Médard's *relégué* companions, V. Garcia, reminisced about these years, when Lieutenant Colonel Camus was director of the *bagne*.

> He was sent out from the metropole with explicit instructions to destroy both *déportés* and *relégués*. And he took all necessary measures. . . . Regarding the *relégués*, he reduced rations to one-third of what they had been. . . . They gave you a quarter liter of broth a day—from 18 beans on, you'd be all right but they gave you on the average nine beans. So, there was hunger, anemia. . . . When Camus began his term, there were 1300 or 1400 *relégués*. Six months later, there were scarcely 600 left. . . . The gravediggers didn't have the strength to make the holes, so instead of digging a meter deep, they made it half a meter, and then after a while no hole at all. . . . [At the end of the war] When they weighed me at the hospital: 35 kilos . . . Fully clothed, 35 kilos. If I sat down, I couldn't stand up.

Mortality, which had been running at 5 percent annually before the war, rose to 48 percent for *relégués* in 1942, until conditions improved in 1944; between 1940 and 1943, more than half the general prisoner population died. With Camus's arrival, forced labor was reintroduced for the *relégués collectifs* and each had to produce his meter-cubed of hardwood or be deprived of all food. Médard, though technically free to live on his own, seems to have been "reinducted" into the *relégué* workforce during this time, under the Vichyist "Work, Family, Fatherland" decrees of 1942. Indeed, I would speculate that the otherwise mysterious notation on Médard's *registre matricule* "Apte—13 Juin 1942 [signed] Dr. Houdayer," was part of the desperate administrative attempt to harness additional labor to wartime tasks; between 1940 and 1943, men throughout the *bagne* were summarily reclassified (for example, from "unfit for medical reasons" to "fit for hard labor") in order to provide extra bodies for wartime needs. The "missing jacket, hammock, and boots" for which Médard was punished during this period suggest he participated in the widespread underground market to obtain food. And his trial for *évasion*, before the Saint-Laurent Justice of the Peace in 1941, which led to an eight-month prison sentence, specified that he had "left without authorization the territory of the *relégation* where he is required to reside," suggesting that during the war years there were indeed new legal impositions on the freedoms even of *relégués individuels* like Médard, rendering his 1939 shift in status from the "collective" to "individual" *relégation* relatively meaningless.[31]

By war's end, Médard would have found himself among only several hundred *relégués* still alive.[32] These remaining men were cleared out of Saint-Jean, to make room in the camp for European war refugees, and were then sent first to the Camp de la Transportation in Saint-Laurent and later to the Iles du Salut, before final release. Those *relégués* still alive at this point had the right to ask to be repatriated when and if they wished, with the first leaving in 1946 and the final ones—apparently including Médard—leaving Guyane in 1952–1953. It would seem that, for something like seven years after war's end, Médard lived on the outskirts of Saint-Laurent—at Saint Louis on the edge of the old relegation territory, next to the Amerindian village of Balaté—as a free man.

In 1983, at my behest, Ken Bilby interviewed a former convict, M. Brunoi, in Saint-Laurent. Brunoi was a Martiniquan who had been recommended to Ken by a *vieux blanc* because, he said, blacks normally stuck together in the *bagne*. "When I asked Brunoi about Médard," wrote Ken,

> he launched into a fifteen-minute monologue, a rapid recounting of what he remembered about the man, so that I could hardly get in a word edgewise. "He was a strange sort and liked to be alone . . . He was strange, always preferred to live alone, not quite right in the head; a husky, stocky man, very strong but he walked hunched over.

And he'd never shake anybody's hand. . . . He built a small *baraque*—
it didn't deserve to be called a house—decorated on the outside with
all sorts of little things. It looked a lot like a *chapelle* but it was very
small and it had a spire or tower on top. This was his only house in
Saint-Laurent. It was far out of town, right on the river's edge, in a
place near where Amerindians lived. . . . Médard was a *bricoleur*,
always making things—toys for children, miniature model houses,
and especially ships. He also made little wooden boxes with land-
scapes inside—you could look through a hole and see streets and little moving parts. He also made wooden cars with parts that really
worked. He was fond of small mechanical contraptions. He also constructed little cages, and sometimes statues. Once, he made a statue
of De Gaulle—all this while he was living in Saint-Laurent. His only
tool was a pocketknife. The people of Saint-Laurent never appreci-
ated what Médard made and never bought any of it. But occasionally
a tourist passing through, a foreigner, would buy something from
him."

Brunoi, Ken went on, constantly apologized for the "poor [*naif*] quality" of
Médard's work, repeatedly using words like *pas fin, brut,* and *pas raffiné*. Médard,
he said, was a *paysan* who could neither read nor write and therefore someone
whom Brunoi didn't particularly frequent—he wasn't Médard's buddy, they
never drank together or went places together. But as a fellow Martiniquan, he
knew a lot about him. He said that Médard left Guyane—by ship—around the
time his own son was born, which would place it about 1953.

In his later years, Médard told one of his Anse Caffard neighbors, Sisi
(Maturin) Larcher, that after being liberated in Saint-Laurent, he'd made a little
house "exactly like the one" he'd later built in Anse Caffard and that he'd lived
in it for several years on the outskirts of town. During some of this time, he told
Sisi, his eyes were totally white because of what he'd suffered in prison—he
couldn't see.[33] It was after some neighboring Indians stole from him that he
asked to be repatriated and, sometime during the early fifties, finally returned to
his native land.

MOST OF OUR FRIENDS in Martinique first remember seeing Médard only after his return from the *bagne*, in the early 1950s. They describe a white-haired, partly crippled figure, still very strong, largely silent—and an artist of mysterious genius. He now walked either bent over nearly double, leaning on a staff (his preferred mode indoors), or with chest out-thrust and neck and head leaning backwards, when he moved about outdoors. "They worked him too hard, they tortured him over there. He was chained in a cell *this* high [one meter], so he couldn't stand up straight," goes the received wisdom. Nevertheless, Médard seems to have picked up with little change the way of life he'd fashioned for himself before leaving for the *bagne*.

His first house—a tiny, decorated, wooden structure—was built near his mother's people in Corps de Garde (Sainte-Luce).[34] In 1983, we visited near there with Céleste Senzamba, then ninety-two years old, blind, and cutting the ends off greenbeans for dinner—she told us she'd been married to Médard's brother and that once Médard settled in after Guyane, he quickly began making artworks at night, always by candlelight. Médard seems to have spent the next decade and a half between this Corps de Garde residence and his old haunts at Diamant, gradually spending more and more time in the Diamant cave, which he slowly refurbished to its pre-Guyane splendor.

During these years, Médard would take *marchandise* both for himself and on orders—lumber and roofing tiles from the sugar factory at Lareinty, molasses from the distillery at Trois-Rivières—always on foot and always at night, covering distances of up to fifty kilometers at a time. As Ernest Larcher put it, "He was one hell of a thief, a thief's thief. He'd steal to eat and he'd steal for others—if you saw something you wanted, you'd tell him and he'd go get it for you. He'd steal molasses and then sell those molasses. . . . The man was a born thief." And, as before his banishment, Médard occasionally ran afoul of the law.[35] Tante Na remembers the gendarmes coming to get him when he was living in his Anse Caffard cave, near her house. But he wasn't gone for long.

Mayor Armand Ribier described Médard's miraculous prison break, also mentioned by others who knew him in the 1950s.

> In those days, the jail was made of masonry, not bricks—the walls
> were a mixture of masonry and earth and rocks and shells. Méda

managed to work a piece of conch shell out of a wall. He dug a tunnel underneath and came out the other side! I don't know how he did it. When they called me to look—when one considered his size compared to the hole—you couldn't understand it. No way. For us, someone of Méda's size couldn't have possibly passed through that hole. And there were no cracks in that building.

It appears that, after this particular escape, the gendarmes left Médard alone for some time.

Meanwhile, at night in his Diamant cave or in his house at Corps de Garde, Médard was making things—many things, at a frenetic pace. Sometimes, when local people went into Fort-de-France for the day, they'd see Médard, sack over his bare shoulder, unkempt and barefoot, going from shop to shop and bar to bar trying to sell one of his pieces. One old man remembers Médard carrying an elaborate ship on his shoulder during a 1950s Fort-de-France carnival, as people dropped coins in his hand. And Médard was a faithful visitor to local fêtes—at Sainte-Luce, at Diamant, at Anses d'Arlet. Each year he would attend the September fête at Petite Anse, staying at the home of his friend Ador Cuty and exhibiting his latest piece at the house of Paul Jean-Alphonse near the beach. He'd stand in front and beat an old snare-drum, and when people came, he'd ask a few pennies for a peek. A number of Petite Anse people recall the battleship, festooned with cannons, that he displayed one year at the fête. Pierrot Larcher, a successful seine-captain at the time, was especially impressed by a sort of puppet game—two men in a wooden box that Medard manipulated by horizontal dowels at a 1950s fête. Médard was also going house to house with his art, in both Petite Anse and Diamant. Génor Naud had a Médard-made weathervane in the shape of a cock atop his house during the 1960s, until a hurricane ripped it away. "It was so very pretty!" he told me, his wife adding, "It was made like a clock— a cock standing inside a clock—and it was yellow all over!" Tina Larcher remembers Médard's showing up at her mother's around 1960 and pulling from his sack a fantastical bust of a king—he expected "a few *sous*" for their having viewed it. Sometimes, Tina said, he'd come by to sell bottles of molasses out of his sack. And her brother, Emilien, told me that when he and his fisherman brother passed near Médard's cave, he'd motion them over to shore and give

"... pulling from his sack a fantastical bust of a king"

them *kwi* (calabash bailers he'd fashioned) or else piles of mangos he'd gathered at Anse Caffard, in return for a few fish. (Given the number of times I accompanied Emilien to drop nets of an evening, just offshore from Médard's place during the summers of 1962 and 1963, it is only chance that I never happened to meet him.) Sometimes during this period, Médard would sell mangos out of his sack in Petite Anse, as well. And when he wasn't selling molasses or mangos, he would have bottles of honey in his bag.

Médard's physical appearance, his nighttime wanderings far and wide, his inexplicable ability to create artworks, and his legend as a *bagnard* caused many people to be afraid of him. As Ernest Larcher put it, "Méda wasn't like other people, he was a really strong fellow, a man without fear, but he was ugly—even in the city, he'd walk around all dirty, and barefoot. All the little kids would point and call out, '*Ga Méda! Ga Méda! Ga Méda!*'" (Look at Méda!)

Around this time, according to a Petite Anse fisherman named Emile Jean-Alphonse, an older woman in Anse Caffard decided, as a present, to give Médard a woman for the first time in his life. So she told Madame Jeanne in Petite Anse, who was accustomed to sharing her favors for a modest fee, that a certain man would come visit her the next night, and Madame Jeanne agreed. Médard prepared himself, bathing and loading up a large basket with fresh garden produce. When he arrived, he shyly told Madame Jeanne he'd brought her a basket in return for a *ti bo* ("little kiss"). But, as Emile tells it, once she saw who it was, she said gruffly, "Out! No market basket and no '*ti bo*.'"

During the mid-1960s, Médard had some trouble with neighbors in Corps de Garde (or Trois-Rivières), apparently over some cash that had been stolen from his house. So he decided to move his residence to Diamant. Mayor Ribier described how, around 1967, Médard had come to him to request a bit of land so he could build a house. "I agreed and he chose that place at Anse Caffard near his cave. He carried the lumber from his other house at Sainte-Luce and made this one out of the same boards."

Médard's new house, which people say was in the same style as the one it replaced, seems to draw—as he himself claimed—on his experience in Guyane. Before leaving for the *bagne*, he'd never built anything like it. Yet on many of the "English" islands from which gold prospectors in Guyane originated, small, heavily gingerbreaded houses, raised on stone stilts, were the norm. It seems likely that Médard saw such houses in Saint-Laurent and drew his inspiration, at least in part, from them. A rare photo taken during the time Médard actually lived in the house reveals a French tri-color waving in the wind.

It was not long after Médard moved into his Anse Caffard house that neighbors began trying to get rid of him—apparently because they wanted to build on land nearby. Mayor Ribier fully enjoyed the irony of his story, as he told me what happened next:

> I don't know what sort of trouble he had with the gendarmes, but people had been filing complaints and one day I received a letter from the prefect, Monsieur Deliau, telling me I had one of the most beautiful communes in Martinique from a touristic perspective and here I was letting it be ruined by permitting people to do things like that house. And that he was ordering the "eyesore" to be destroyed. So, I responded, "Médard has no heirs, he's a man who lives alone, he has no means of subsistence, he has no place to live. If you make the mistake of razing Médard's house, I'll take my car, put Médard inside, and bring him to the prefecture, right to the Résidence Préfecturale. And his fate will be up to you. You'll have to decide what to do with him. Because he's a man without anything, a man who harms no one, a man who simply asks a place to live. Moreover, I see no problem with the house he made, I do not see that it 'ruins

Diamant touristically.' On the contrary, I see tourists passing by with their cameras and taking pictures of it." The prefect never responded.

One of Médard's neighbors during the time he lived in this little house, Tante Na, told me, "It's not that he didn't like people. He was just shy. All he'd ever say was '*Bonjour*' or ask my husband for a fishhook. He fished with a handline, off the rocks, and always grilled his fish on an open fire." He also spent a lot of time searching for *brigauds* [shellfish], and walking everywhere—but always off the roads, *sous les bois*." Her son, Ti Louis, added that he remembered Médard

Médard's lived-in house at Anse Caffard, ca. 1970

scavenging Camembert boxes, to make things from. Médard would invite him into his house when he passed by, offering him soft drinks. "He was always kind to me but if he laughed twice in a whole year it was a lot." Ti Louis stressed that most people were afraid of Médard, associating him with various supernatural powers, and that Médard spent many of his nights making artworks, alone by candlelight. Ernest Larcher, who also visited Médard in his Anse Caffard house, said, "He'd play the piano for us there, it'd go *tingtingtingting!*[36] He'd tootle his flute. He'd also made a kind of horn, out of zinc, and he'd play it for us. He even made a saxophone, not from wood but from some sort of aluminum. He'd blow it and it would play!"

Dinette Louisy, who owned a bar and sometime dancehall in Taupinière, had a large steamship she'd bought from Médard and strung with electric lights—*le Duc d'Aumale* she called it.[37] "When you asked Méda how he worked, where he got his gift," she told me, "he'd say, 'Don't even bother to ask. It's the secret of love—my own secret.'" Or, as Philibert Larcher once said of him, "In this life, there are some things that are beyond understanding."

"He'd play the piano for us there, it'd go *tingtingtingting!*"

By the early seventies, there were neighbors in Anse Caffard—including the *békés* who owned the land—who clearly didn't want Médard and his house to stay. Besides the police, who they got to bother him periodically, people began stealing from his garden and letting their animals eat from his garden at will. "People were really giving him a hard time," said one of his neighbors, Clairville Naud, "so Méda decided to head up to his old haunts at Bompí, near his father's folks." He joined his elderly friend (or relative?) Justin Zumbalá on Morne Pavillon (Morne l'Afrique), where he built himself his very last house, the one we visited with Julien and Tina. It wasn't long before Médard found himself quite alone, and increasingly ill, though he continued his creative productions.

". . . he built himself his very last house"

On one of his rare trips down from the mountain in 1973, he sold to a jazz musician a pair of colorfully painted plaster-of-paris, bas-relief plates that appear to be inspired by some sort of German or Alsatian beer advertisement in a magazine. They may well be his final artworks.[38]

Later that year, Médard lay sick for several weeks in his house, with no one to look after him. And, as Clairville told me, "When he was really in a bad way, they carried him from that house at Bompí directly to the hospital at Trois Ilets where he died not long after. In the end, he was just all tuckered out."[39]

Plaster plates by Médard Aribot, 1973

Phos, Pointe-à-Pitre (Guadeloupe)

III. Remembering Médard, the Seine of History

Where are your monuments, your battles, martyrs?
Where is your tribal memory? Sirs,
in that grey vault. The sea. The sea
has locked them up. The sea is History.
                    —DEREK WALCOTT, "The Sea Is History"

Dusk. The *Flight* passing Blanchisseuse.
Gulls wheel like from a gun again,
and foam gone amber that was white,
lighthouse and star start making friends,
down every beach the long day ends,
and there, on that last stretch of sand,
on a beach bare of all but light,
dark hands start pulling in the seine
of the dark sea, deep, deep inland.
                    —DEREK WALCOTT, "The Schooner *Flight*"

Médard's House at Anse Caffard. Top: 1983. Bottom: 1986.

Reconstructed house (postcard, ca. 1988). A painter at work, 1995.

Cover to the latest *Guide Gallimard, Martinique*

I NEVER MET Médard face-to-face. Ten years before his death, I spent some seven months in Petite Anse, just over Morne Larcher from his hidden cave. But it was still three or four years before the road over the morne through Anse Caffard and Diamant would be built, and six before Médard would construct his little house by the sea. Though I cannot pretend to evoke the world he experienced, I would like at least to bear witness from my own perspective to that early 1960s world I shared with him. It was a world peopled by fisherfolk for whom Médard's life history mattered a great deal.

Such a return to what people in Petite Anse call *avant* ("before," "the way things used to be") involves risks—nostalgia runs deep in 1990s Martinique. But, as Saramaka hunters say, if you don't stir up a hole, you'll never know what's in it. And there will be ample time, later, to examine the specific transformations that memories of Médard have undergone in the course of modernization.

"Your story," wrote former Harvard Professor H. Stuart Hughes in 1989, "is a period piece." I had written him for confirmation of a memory—a sort of mythoheroic turning point in the version of my life that I told myself—whose truth I now felt obliged to plumb. Not yet twenty-one, within the span of two months in 1962, I had met Sally at Harvard and then gone off for the summer to do fieldwork in Martinique, in the process falling in love with both.[1]

Early one August morning I had accompanied my new friend Emilien on the spectacular trip by fishing canoe to Fort-de-France, skimming through turquoise waters, capped by the whitest of foam, passing deep green forests and mountains, with the Mont Pelée volcano reaching for the sky in the distance. After I watched him sell his fish, amidst considerable banter, to a market woman by the side of the canal, we went ashore for haircuts (Emilien's barber working on my head with only the greatest reluctance, saying he'd never before cut the hair of a white man), and I wandered into a bookstore while Emilien purchased some fishing gear nearby. I bought a dozen books about Martinique—Michel Leiris's *Contacts de civilisations*, Eugène Revert's *La magie antillaise* (my project was to study fishing magic), Élodie Jourdain's pioneering study of Martiniquan Creole, a couple of books of creole folktales, and a half dozen books of local poetry, among which Césaire's *Cahier d'un retour au pays natal* and *Cadastre*, as well as Lilyan Kesteloot's just-published study of Césaire's work. As best I remember, I had never heard of any of these authors except Leiris, whose book I'd read in Widener Library in preparation for the trip.

I read and reread Césaire's *Cahier* in Petite Anse that summer and, on my return to Harvard in September, proposed to my tutor, a specialist on Rimbaud, that I write my senior thesis on this poem and poet. The professor said he'd never heard of Césaire but—if I would lend him some sample works—would take it up with his colleagues in the Department of Romance Languages. I offered him copies of the *Cahier* and *Cadastre*, I think. A week later, the verdict was handed down: having looked over the poems, the Department had decided that Césaire's work "might be of anthropological interest but was not of sufficient significance *as literature* to merit a senior thesis." I was upset enough by this incident, which I interpreted as racist and ethnocentric, to make an arrangement for Stuart Hughes to serve as "paper" advisor while Professor Vogt, in anthropology, actually supervised my thesis—an essay that never mentioned Césaire but did treat some of the realities he wrote about and managed (at least from my perspective today) to somehow combine a heartfelt romanticism with the scientism of the day.[2]

In 1996, as I read through my 1962 fieldnotes, the first word that springs to mind is innocence. But also enthusiasm, curiosity, and ambition. And a kind of solid middle-class American concern about inequalities and suffering in the world, amply leavened by the optimism of youth.[3] My letters to Sally that summer are all this and more, as I was trying to seduce her, to win her over to a way of life that included the romance of fieldwork (among other romances). Because my fieldnotes tend to be in a "scientific" mode, as I had been taught they should be, the letters provide a telling narrative accompaniment, a humanized version of what I experienced that summer.[4] (My citations are verbatim, though of course selective.)

> [early July, 1962]. . . . Dear S. In the last five years there've been four enchanted nights that have had a quality unlike anything else I've known—one spent on the floor of Monument Valley, Utah with Navaho wind gods sweeping across and

among fantastical red rock formations, another at the bottom of the Grand Canyon, a third on a beach in the shadow of a Loire chateau, and one high, high up in an Andean canyon, camping with the Incas and watching the flocks of llamas move in the moonlight on the valley floor. Last night night made a fifth.

At four o'clock, I left the land behind with Emilien (25), his "matelot" Hector, and a young boy, Emilien's nephew. We dropped our nets in the sea off Diamant and tied ourselves to a float to wait until the fish came. Slowly, very slowly, the sun sank behind the mornes and the Western sky became flaming red, then rose and pink, and finally bluish-black. The sea washed against the fragile gommier as we ate mangos in the salt spray without a word, each man thinking his own thoughts. Venus appeared and then other stars until we were floating under a magnificent, star-specked dome, watching lights on shore twinkling through the clear air.

Em told me the nets would be ready when there was a great "fire" in them at the bottom of the sea. And soon there was. Looking over the side of the canoe, we saw the nets glowing

"Last night . . . made a fifth." Ballpoint on onionskin, 1962

phosphorescent through the crystalline water. Each dip of Hector's oar sent beautiful blue and white sparkles, larger than a firefly and more enchanting, spinning away in a whirlpool. The nets were hauled in and I traced a phosphorescent "S" on my foot in blue sparkles, like Candide carving Cunégonde's name on trees.

Slowly, we rode the waves back, and as we rounded the point and could see Petite Anse, flames leaping from yellow torches told us that other canots had already returned. We beached the canoe, lit our torch, uncoiled the nets, spent an hour removing our fish, and returned to bed.

[July 1962] Writing by candlelight is a joy—it flickers around almost like another person. . . . Wilfried, the gentle madman, just visited. He walked up, entered my room, blessed me with the sign of the cross, took my pen from my hand and drew some radiating lines on a piece of paper. He always carries a twig with him with which he makes similar markings in the

"At four o'clock, I left the land behind with Emilien . . ." 1962

dust. He talks gibberish about trenches, guns, and Germans, and seems to be trying to draw a military map.

[27 July 1962] Yesterday was the most miserable day I've spent in a long time. I went out fishing with 15-year-old Toto and an older fisherman. The outboard kept breaking down and there was the inevitable rocking in the hot sun, the smell of spilled gasoline and fish dizzying my head. In utter humiliation, and in front of two nearby boats of watching fishermen, I k[n]eeled over the side and baptized the clear green water by the Rocher du Diamant with vomit. Oh how sick I felt. One thing only saved me from utter degradation. Toto, at almost the exact same moment as I, sank into the bottom of the canot and got sick all over himself. The fishermen seemed hardly impressed by the incident. The sea was rough and apparently this sort of thing occasionally happens. But the women! When they heard they went wild. Mme Naud nearly collapsed with

"We dropped our nets in the sea," 1962

laughter. The girls hit each other and giggled spasmodically. I went to bed. I don't know what would have happened had Toto not gotten sick.

[28 July 1962] Yesterday I sat for a while in a wonderful, big, colorful cement house where a 69-year-old patriarch presides over his brood of 24 kids! One is getting married this afternoon and I've never seen so many relatives in one house. The groom, Ti Jo, had an especially good fishing season last year and was able to build a house, hence the wedding. . . . If it's still light, I'll try to take some wedding pictures.

[3 August 1962] Last night I went fishing again with Emilien. It was even more beautiful than the last time and much more pleasant because Em and I disembarked for one of the two hours of waiting between dropping and hauling in the nets, to search for mangos on shore. We found two heavily laden trees and carried, in our pockets, shoes, and hats, 57 mangos back to

Wedding picture, Ti Jo and Marcelle, 1962

the waiting <u>matelot</u>, Hector, who was rowing just offshore in the canoe. We spent the next hour watching the sun set and the stars appear, and eating 15 mangos apiece. It was a delicious evening. As we returned home through the phosphorescent water, we rounded the point and there, hanging just above the western horizon, was the new moon, orange and mysterious. Em and H traced large, deliberate crosses on their chests as they saw <u>la lune</u>.

[early August 1962] This morning I was alone for 3 hours at work with a paintbrush. Emilien asked me to paint the name on his canoe—Notre Dame—while he repaired his nets. I did the best I could, though it is pretty crude. He seemed pleased and also asked me to paint on four crosses, which I did. Perhaps I'm spending too much time fishing and not enough on magic. I've been going to sea for five hours each evening. Last night, our nets got fouled in some rocks and were ripped to shreds. Now, hours of repair work. . . .

Emilien with the newly painted *Notre Dame*, 1962

[4 August 1962] I almost don't have time to write you, I'm so busy asking questions, playing cards with the fellas (who have names like Homère, Hippolyte, Hector, and even Charlemagne . . .) and finding out about magical practices. This morning I saw a man named Guilos putting a new <u>nasse</u> (fishpot) to sea. It has little crosses of <u>bois moudongue</u> and <u>acacia</u> tied on near each entrance. First he blessed it with <u>eau bénite</u> taken from the church, then he beat it with an acacia branch to drive out evil spirits. When the moon is right, it will be moved to its permanent location near Diamond Rock, provided it has not been stolen, bewitched, or carried away by strong currents—all real risks.

I also found out that the phosphorescent algae in the sea is the same stuff that makes the inside of tombs in the cemetery glow during the nights. . . . This afternoon talked with a man who is <u>marré</u> (bewitched) and hasn't caught a thing in a

Guilos (left) finishing a large bamboo *nasse*, 1962

month. If he had money, he'd go to a <u>quimboiseur</u> (he called him, for my benefit, a <u>docteur</u>) but he hasn't. I was also shown a large seine net that was bewitched. Pierrot, its owner, hasn't caught a thing in three weeks. Tomorrow morning I'm going on a new kind of fishing trip—for conchs, with large-meshed nets. Monday I'm going out with Pierrot and the big seine that's bewitched.

Last night, as usual, I went out fishing with Emilien, dropping our nets off a really wild coast, with sandstone

cliffs, and with goats and lambs roaming among the rocks. I
realized that what sailors in ancient times took to be "sirens"
calling out to them might have been goats, which bleat just like
women crying. I've never heard anything like it. Em and I
were both strongly attracted. Had Scylla and Charybdis been
near by, we would have fallen in gladly (or am I mixing my
myths?). Life continues very pleasant and stimulating—
except for seasickness.

[8 August 1962]. . . I went to sea à voile [by sail, not motor]
with Joacin, one of the few men who still power their canoes
exclusively with sails. Left in the dark at 5 am and didn't return
till 11. I spent the final couple of hours vomiting absurdly and
repeatedly into the exceptionally beautiful greenblue sea. . . .
Yet very glad I went, knowing that in several years this will be
gone forever.

Guilos (left) with his *nasse*

[August 1962] . . . .Emilien formally presented me with 1000 francs this afternoon which he forced me to accept as my share of our catches. He also gave me a man-to-man talk about how I should come live here permanently, since there is such fine fish, wonderful fruits, and luscious women, and people—he says—are happier than elsewhere.

[August 1962] . . . Last night we dropped our nets around a point to the west, just in sight of the lights of Fort-de-France. Gosh, it looked big! I remember so well how small FdF seemed the first time I saw it just a few weeks ago. Apparently, it has grown considerably. . . . There was hardly any talking in the canoe last night so I amused myself with many and varied thoughts. For more than an hour, I ran through the smallest details of Jackie Robinson's life, which I'd read about over and over—maybe even weekly—in Arthur Mann's biography, when I was eleven or twelve. Jackie was my greatest hero, my idol. But try as I might, I couldn't remember who the left fielder was for the '53 or '54 Dodgers, no matter how many times I ran through the batting order and replayed in my mind particular Giants'-Dodgers' night games I'd listened to on the radio, under the sheets, long after my bedtime. I felt very far from Martinique. . . . Just as I was reprimanding myself for not being more bold and asking more questions . . . I began aimlessly bailing the boat with a half-calabash and Em cried out for me not to turn over the bailer. By chance—the way I find out most things—the world of "things that bring bad luck" was opened up. Turning over a bailer, crossing ones arms in a canoe, and much else turns out to be forbidden—like walking near a pigeon-pea bush before going to sea. And a menstruating woman who steps over a net or touches a canoe is as dangerous as a dog who pisses on same. So, in spite of my shyness I learn things. As we sat rocking under the stars, I thought of how nice it is to have something you feel you can do well, and I slowly realized that I am beginning to think of myself as an anthropologist. It's a strange and pleasant feeling to realize for the first time that maybe you've got a métier that is already somewhat within your control.

[14 August 1962] I got a letter from old pal Renato yesterday.[5] It had been sitting three weeks in the American Consulate. Since I've heard from him, I've been homesick for my friends in Vicos. He writes, and it's true, "You lived in heaven last summer. Trees, streams, birds singing, and all around snow capped mountains, wonderful people, the strongest alcohol in the world—all a man could ever want." He also sent words of praise for last summer's trial marriage work from Cornell anthropologists. I'm convinced that this year's work will be better. . . .

I'm utterly fascinated by the variety of things I'm learning

Setting a net to dry, 1962

about magic. Jealousy and envy and suspicion are the basis of so much of interaction here! . . . Emilien has two uncles (his father's brothers) who are the most magically powerful men for miles around. Amédée, the great <u>quimboiseur</u>, has become my friend. His brother, Amélius, who is said only to do "evil," is terribly jealous of the famous sorcerer who cures people and canoes from the whole island. The evil uncle once told Emilien, in confidence, that if <u>he</u> had the books of magic his brother has, the sun would never rise again![6]

[23 August 1962] Early morning. Amédée has shown me many of his secret formulas though there are others about which he remains vague and private. He also showed me one of his <u>livres</u>—<u>Le Grand et Petit Albert</u>. His strongest magic, however, comes from notebooks handed down, supposedly, from the original Martiniquans, the Caribs. He has a little chapel in his house where he goes through all sorts of hocus-pocus. His new house, the largest and most modern in the village, is built

Amédée, Anno Henry, R.P., and Amédée's redoubtable brother Amélius, 1962

thanks to a grateful fisherman from faraway Bellefontaine who, using one of his "Carib" potions on a seine net, pulled in U.S. $9,000 in one day and gave $1000 to him. . . . My quimboiseur friend is not particularly impressive-looking or sounding. He has the air less of a physician than of a country veterinarian. Local fishermen all call him Papa . . . He says a lot of his trade is with lycée students from FdF who come before exams. I'll try to learn what to do so the two of us can get all A's next semester.

7 p.m. I've just chalked up my ninth hour of the day with Amédée. I'm feeling things out with him that I never would have dreamed possible a few weeks ago. Today I saw and taperecorded a séance. Papa gave me various formulas and promised to show me his really secret, ancient book next Tuesday. For the moment, I'm abandoning going to sea. Papa insists that the "Livre Caraibe" he'll show me Tuesday is his source for recipes to help students get good grades on exams!

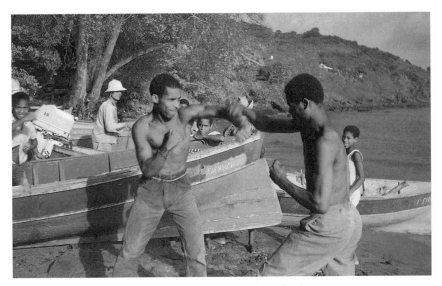

Two young fishermen—Hernoud and Hippolyte—clown for the camera, 1962

[26 August 1962] When not eating with the Nauds, or sleeping, my time lately is spent almost exclusively with Amédée. This morning he greeted me "Richard, the other day a rich hotel owner from the city came to see me. He said he felt that an enemy had set an <u>esprit</u> upon his hotel. He drove me in his car right to the front door. When we entered, I could see a toad on every single table in the dining room! It was the <u>esprit</u> who'd done that. This was a tough one, difficult, difficult, but I got rid of it that very evening. I banished it with a <u>parfumage</u> which I conducted while I recited . . ."

I watch clients come and go and listen as they obtain advice and remedies. His house is chock full of gifts from grateful clients. There's a $96 transistor radio given by a storekeeper who continues to send Papa 1500 francs a month; there's a large alarm clock; there are many small gifts from students who have passed their <u>bacs</u> thanks to the magical "rings" he makes for them to wear; and there are bottles and bottles of

Amédée and his sister Laurence, with the house built by seine-magic money

champagne on top of the sideboard. So far, most of his "livres" turn out to be 19th-century French mystical texts, though <u>Le Grand et Petit Albert</u> is supposed to go back to the thirteenth century. On Tuesday I will finally see his famous book of "Carib" formulas, which he insists were translated from Latin.

My 75-year-old, palm-reading friend Laurence, Amédée's sister, continues to kiss me frequently with her one-toothed grin. She gives me two eggs each day as I leave.

[27 August 1962] Amédée told me he won't be able to get his secret book until Thursday afternoon, so I'll have to wait till then to begin copying the magic formulas (if he really comes through with it—I hope so much he will!).

[30 August 1962] It is becoming increasingly difficult for me to see Papa. He has clients from FdF almost all day long, many of them bus or taxi drivers. In the waiting area outside the house, barefoot fishermen, hats in hand, mingle with smartly dressed FdF businessmen and parents of lycée students. . . . What a joy life would be if school were able to capture the excitement and fascination with learning that I sense here.

Looking backwards, I now realize that my growing concern with "magic" was far more than a boyhood obsession. That summer I was being drawn into a core region of Martiniquan lived experience, into what Glissant identified ten years later as a "spectacular" case of a local institution in the process of losing its socio-historical functions under the massive pressures of *francisation*. And one

Midday meal at the Nauds—Christiane, M. Christophe, Mme Naud, and Merlande

that Michael Taussig, writing of contemporary Colombia, understood more broadly as a fundamental "critique of the modern mode of production," a weapon of resistance against modernity itself.

As I sat on the grass with fishermen that summer,[7] methodically mending nets, most of the ongoing talk was about fishing—winds and currents, where the customs launch was currently patrolling, how one or another *quimboiseur* in a far-off village was performing one or another small miracle, and above all where the fish were. Men tentatively and obliquely searched for bits of potentially useful information, always reluctantly offered and always in veiled form—an ongoing game of feigning disinterest but keeping the talk flowing. "Sensitivity to envy," as Taussig found in Colombia, was "as necessary as the air we breathe," providing "a theater of possibilities" in which "implicit social knowledge roams and scavenges, sharpening its sensitivity, its capacity to illuminate, its capacity to wound." In the mornings, as often as I could, I visited with Amédée, who manned the front lines for his fishermen neighbors in the ongoing battle against evil.

In those days, Petite Anse was alive with spirits, devils, incubi, and flying witches.[8] On a daily basis, I was regaled with tales of remarkable encounters:
—In a fishermen's café in Anses d'Arlet, I overhear a man complain bitterly about an *esprit* that knocks loudly on his door each night, keeping him from sleeping. That same creature has put out his cooking fire a couple of times and last week stole his *zédui* (the wooden needle with which he repairs his nets). He has no choice, he complains, but to go to a *quimboiseur*.
—One night, Emilien tells me, his father surprised a mysterious woman combing her flowing hair in his canoe. Sensing danger, he ran back to his house to get a harpoon but when he returned she was gone. Following that, he had an unusual string of fine fishing.
—People remind me that nighttime brings dangerously alluring sights on the trail that runs through Petite Anse (fiery automobiles streaking by, unimaginably beautiful girls bathing in the sea, gnarled old women nursing babies on a rock, strange children wandering and crying out), as well as more obvious dangers. Rémy, known for his courage, has seen the devil more than once. In fact, when he went to wake up his crewman the other night, a giant horse-with-three-legs—Lucifer himself—fell out of the mango tree under which he was standing.

And coffins are often sighted at crossroads. When Gérard, another man known for bravery, came upon one in the middle of the path, he opened his knife, sat down on the box, and boldly asked, "Who's inside?" "Heat, heat," came the first answer. When he pressed, the woman's voice asked him if she sounded like thunder. No, he said. Like wind, then? No. Perhaps like running water? When he said yes, the coffin dissolved into a rivulet slanting off to the sea.

—I am instructed, repeatedly, that when walking at night, if I feel a tingling and my hair stands on end, there's a *bête infernale* in the vicinity, and I must quickly pull the pockets out of my pants, take off my shirt and put it back on inside-out, and open my pocketknife.

—Emilien tells me how, a few weeks before my arrival, a cousin of his went *à miquelon* (*lapèch-miklon*) with his father and was run through and killed by a leaping swordfish, as he hauled it over the side. The following week Emilien's brother Ernest, who hadn't been catching of late, went to a *quimboiseur* in a far-off commune. Before he even sat down and introduced himself, the *quimboiseur*

Ernest (Emilien's older brother), his wife Léonie, and Sico, Bernard, and Marie-Laure, 1962

said, "You are a very lucky man. The fish that killed your cousin was meant for you." And he was able to make him the protection that allowed him to continue.

—Fishermen who live closest to the shore talk of hearing loud rumbling and banging at night, as spirits knock around in the canoes, sometimes actually turning them over. But when men rush out to investigate, they find nothing.

—Josephe confides that Marie's mother was a well-known witch. She'd seen her several times, with her own eyes, flying through the night like a ball of fire.

—Soon after my arrival, a fisherman loses four fingers when his handline gets tangled. Divine punishment, say the men in the café. Everyone suspects him of being a *dowlis*, an incubus who—sometimes in the form of a rat—visits their houses at night to eat their food, steal their money, and take his pleasure with their wives and daughters. That man, they said, had even slept with his mother-in-law.

—French gendarmes in Anses d'Arlet regale me with tales of local black magic.[9] Recently, a pair of twins were kidnapped by a fisherman at Prêcheur or Bellefontaine. The man was caught at sea, with the tied-up children being readied to be put into a *nasse*. They assure me it's common for fishermen, particularly in the north, to be caught robbing graves for magical bait, used especially for dorados. Dr. Perronnette, inspector of public health, tells me that when two toddlers disappeared several years ago at Morne Vert, and it was thought that a *quimboiseur* had killed them to use their bodies, he was called in by the authorities to examine the bones at the *quimboiseur*'s house—they turned out to be chicken bones.

Homère Larcher mending a net, 1962

Amédée, whom I'd befriended partly with the help of printed recipes I'd copied from books in Widener Library and brought with me to Martinique, seemed to be spending an awful lot of his time worrying about people who were out to ruin him. In themselves, such concerns were not unusual—fishermen also devoted much of their time and energy to problems of envy. But Amédée's anxieties seemed particularly acute. Since he and his colleagues took full responsibility for making fishermen's lives liveable, perhaps it was inevitable that the personal costs would be considerable.

"Richard," he confided one afternoon in July,

> A fellow came to see me yesterday, a coolie-man. He walked in and shook my hand. That coolie-man squeezed my hand *hard*. Then I did my work for him. And he said, "I have no money." So I said, "No problem, don't worry," and he left. I was working for the next person. There were others sitting, waiting for me. And then I caught a glimpse of him, near the house, making all sorts of signs with his arms and fingers. During the night, I felt a sharp pain in my back and couldn't sleep. In the morning, I could feel something upon me. Yes! I could feel an *esprit* upon me. I could still feel that man's finger on me. Then I had a terrible headache. Terrible! Then I saw things, like crickets—but not crickets. Oh, but they stung, those fellas! So, I said a prayer against *esprits* and they left. I gave myself a bath, a protective bath. I said another prayer and I sent his things right back to him. And now I feel just fine and that fellow is caught! He'll be back in three weeks, sure as sure can be. But he'll be walking like this [mimes a hunchback]. He'll be coming to beg me to work for him. And I'll ask 75,000 francs to remove the thing.

And then Papa added, with a giggle, almost as an afterthought, "But the truth is I don't know *how* to remove the damn thing for him, since he's the one who started this in the first place!"

When the next year, newly married, I returned to Petite Anse with Sally for a four-month stay, Amédée was clearly in some sort of general decline. He seemed less mentally alert and increasingly—and, I thought, pathologically—preoccupied with a fear of others. There was now only one pharmacy left in Fort-de-France that he could enter without feeling an overwhelming sense of evil spirits all around him. Returning from town one day, he confided that he'd effectively parried a fierce spiritual attack by five rival *quimboiseurs* in another drugstore. Another time, he told me that a woman he'd never seen before came up to his house and set three *esprits* on him so that people from Petite Anse would no longer come consult him. (He was able to get rid of two of the spirits without difficulty but struggled valiantly with the third before besting it.) And the last time I saw him, near the end of our 1963 stay, he was putting up a high, rickety barbed-wire fence to encircle his house.

Nevertheless, that second summer, Amédée graciously let me record séances, copy down fishing magic recipes, and observe the psychology and economics of his trade. He also let me work with him in the dark room where he mixed and cooked his recipes—shelves upon shelves of carefully labeled bottles and jars and jugs containing hundreds of pharmaceutical products, bundles of herbs and barks and leaves, and his own famous *bains caraïbes*, which he prepared according to his Latin recipes.

I witnessed scores of séances. Most were routine and apparently efficacious. When Didier Larcher stopped by—as Papa's poor cousin, he was not expected to pay for the visit—he said his net had caught nothing in three days. Amédée quickly tore a blank page from a notebook and wrote out a prescription, as Didier beamed: "Tie together one branch of acacia, one branch of calabash, and one branch of *guimauve*. Beat the canoe all over, then throw the bundle behind you into the sea." Then he went into his back room and brought out a bottle of reddish liquid, whispering: "Take three drops and rub them on your hands [Papa demonstrated as Didier imitated], three drops on the door of your house, three drops where you keep your money, three in your canoe, and three on the net—do it three days running." Then some relaxed talk about how vexing it was that some people spend their time preventing others from catching fish—Didier admitted he suspected Sebastianiste (an elderly alcoholic woman who liked to sing) and Papa quickly said "Yes, beware of Baniss'!"—and Papa told a few stories about miraculous cures he'd effected for clients from here and there. After Didier left, Papa gave me the formula for the 3-drop bottle: four products he'd bought at the pharmacy—*lavande ambrée*, *essence de consoude*, *poudre obligatoire*, *essence d'acacia*—and a pinch of earth.[10]

For bigger players—seine captains during the current season, *miklon* fishermen during the winter months—he prescribed more complex preparations, such as this *bain caraïbe* for canoes, which he let me copy from a worn notebook:

> Boil together: river water, sea water, 9 leaves *bois canon*, 9 limes each
> cut in three, 9 leaves cacao, 3 shoots of *mahot*, 3 shoots of *chadron
> bénit*, 3 shoots *coudrel*, 9 leaves *bois caca*, 3 shoots *arada*, 9 leaves *gros
> thym*, 1 white pigeon pea, 1 root *bois moudongue*, and 1 root
> *simarouba*.[11] After it's well boiled, add: earth, holy water, alkali,
> *baume du commandeur*, tincture of benzoin, *essence de rose*.

In the small world where fishermen daily braved the seas in their fragile canoes,
jalousie (envy) was their greatest preoccupation and fear. Papa Amédée—pious,
intelligent, generous, living alone at the edge of society under constant fear of
attack—played a salutary role in all their lives. For he furnished them with what

Didier ("Bous-kaka") Larcher mending a net, 1962

Césaire has called "miraculous arms"—fierce weapons against envy. I must confess, somewhat sheepishly, that he never did show me his *Livre Caraïbe*.

THINKING BACK ON Petite Anse in 1962–1963—besides fishing and magic, which so filled my days and nights—my mind tends to wander over certain set-piece memories (similar, in at least a superficial way, to those growing-up-in-premodernization-Martinique memories captured with such literary verve by the novelists Joseph Zobel, Patrick Chamoiseau, Raphaël Confiant, and Ina Césaire). Though my fishermen friends and I were quite unaware, this was in fact the twilight of an era. The coming decade would bring them a paved road and cars, electricity, telephones, piped-in water, TV, newspapers, large-scale emigration of their younger sisters and brothers to the metropole, and intense pressures for *francisation*.

For me, these 1960s *lieux de mémoire* include the arrival and departure of Misyé Maxime's blue *bombe*, the aging bus that linked Petite Anse and Fort-de-France via Anses d'Arlet each morning and afternoon; the occasional wake I attended, with its animated all-night taletelling; the Anses d'Arlet fête, with its dice tables and the happiest merry-go-round music in the whole world; and

Misyé Maxime atop his *bombe*, 1962

dominos and cards in Mme Naud's café, where fishermen gathered of an evening whenever, because of bad weather or some other reason, they were not taking their dropnets to sea.

Zobel's *Diab'-la*, set in Diamant, describes the evening return of the bus:

> It was a vital organ of the village, like the sea or the "Seven Sins" café. In the morning, this one had sent off a basket of red snapper, that one a bucket of lobsters. This one has a brother or sister who is supposed to visit, or a friend who had collected the week's money from the fishmongers in the market and would meet him in the Seven Sins to give him his share. And, after all, one has friends here and there—in Lamentin, in Petit-Bourg, all along the route—who might have sent along a package or at least a greeting with the driver or one of the passengers. . . .
>
> "Missié Loulou, don't you have anything for me?"
>
> "Missié Loulou, did you see Nonotte? What did she tell you for me?"
>
> Phlegmatic behind the wheel, the driver takes care of each responsibility one by one—bottles, demijohns, crates, and packages, vials of medicine, sacks of bread, bags of candies, crumpled letters. Everything people had asked him to buy for them in the morning; everything that relatives and friends had sent along.

In a time without telephones, without a real road (or local cars)—and with only the rare transistor radio—Misyé Maxime's *bombe* was the daily link with the wider world. In each direction, he loaded up the roof and rear of the vehicle, as well as his pockets and the area around his seat, with trussed fowls, cartons of produce, bundles wrapped in brown paper and tied with cord, baskets of fish, and carefully written notes on folded sheets of paper. At various points along the route he would stop the bus and get out to knock on the door of a house and pick up or deliver a package or message, while the passengers patiently sat and waited. The trip—which today, if it's not rush hour, can be made in forty-five minutes—normally took three and a half hours.

Sally's presence during the summer of 1963 allowed me an entrée into the previously closed world of fishermen's wives and daughters. We found family units, even from a 1950s U.S. perspective, to be both strong and surprisingly hermetic. And the gendered separation of spheres—women controlling domestic space, men roaming the outside world—seemed striking. Our surveys found that well over 90 percent of Petite Anse's several hundred people lived in households comprised of a fisherman head, his wife, and assorted children.[12] If there was any of the fabled "matrifocality" of the Caribbean, it inhered in the preponderant role played by mothers within the domestic domain. Families were large—Emilien had eleven brothers and sisters, Merlande nine. And it was women who managed the domestic economy and saw to the moral as well as formal education of the children. This responsibility for moral education was paramount, and mothers were expected to be severe and disciplinary in instilling values of respectability. Women also participated indirectly in their husbands' fishing success or failure—by adhering to the various taboos surrounding their "polluting" potential, as women, and by taking care of the domestic portion of fishing magic prescriptions (washing the house with appropriate preparations, burning candles or magical lamps while their husbands were at sea). Sensitivity to envy strongly curtailed visiting, except between sisters or mothers and grown daughters. Yet any woman could tell you, at any time of the day, exactly which canoes were still at sea and which had already returned.

Sally performing an unspecified ethnographic act, 1963

That summer, Sally spent her days sewing, baking, and chatting with Emilien's mother and his unmarried sisters and cousins (half of whom would leave in the next few years for a life in metropolitan France), and visiting with fishermen's lonely wives while they worried about their husbands and awaited their return from the sea. Women's economic dependence on men seemed overwhelming, and, except for their children, women seemed far more isolated socially than their husbands. (Sunday mass, whether at the local chapel or the church in Anses d'Arlet, provided the only regular public occasion for women to gather; few fishermen ever attended.[13]) Children were constantly being sent on errands outside the house—little girls spent much of their time heading tin cans or small buckets of water from the spring or (depending on where in Petite Anse the family lived) the well or even standpipe, and they did most of the shopping (one or two items at a time) from the tiny local groceries.

Mme Naud's grocery-café is another privileged site for my personal nostalgia. In 1962 I lived in a room in a nearby house owned by the Nauds and ate my meals with them. When Sally and I returned the next summer, they had fixed up their tool shed for us, though we continued to eat with the family. The Naud house abutted the combination rumshop and grocery run by the matriarch. Over the counter, mainly during the day, she doled out saltfish, matches, onions, flour, sugar, rice, and dollops of margarine or tomato paste weighed out on brown paper, as well as cooking oil, rum, and kerosene for lamps (customers brought their own empty bottles). Mme Naud kept track of accounts in a thick notebook

Children fetching water, Petite Anse 1962

and patrons paid when they had cash.

Patrick Chamoiseau caught the spirit of this kind of grocery in his sensitive memoir of Martiniquan childhood:

> The hardest thing was having to return a purchase. "Go tell the lady that the bottle isn't full." Or, "Oh my, this isn't what I wanted, there's too much, there's not enough, it's not fresh, look there's rat shit in it . . ." The little kid would carry back the incriminating merchandise. His worried head would be trying to find a diplomatic way to explain it to the grocery-lady, especially since their entry in the credit ledger was always more or less bulging. He had devised the general form "Mama says there's a problem . . ." To which the grocery-lady would barely react. Leaning on her counter, she'd simply ask, "What sort of problem, then?" And he would enter into the details of his mother's complaint. Which might be:
>
> "She says that there's something in the lentils."
>
> "What sort of thing?"
>
> "I didn't understand exactly."
>
> "What do you mean, you didn't understand? In my lentils there's nothing but lentils, right?"
>
> "Yes. That's what so strange."
>
> "What do you mean, strange?"
>
> "There's nothing but lentils—except for one lentil that isn't a lentil."
>
> "Are you trying to say that there's something in my lentils?"
>
> "I didn't say that, no."
>
> "Well then, what *did* you say?"
>
> "What mama said was . . ."
>
> "Let me see for myself."
>
> And she would discover, for herself, the rat shit, the dead roach, the little stones in too great quantities, and she would utter a curse, cross herself twice, and silently exchange the pitiable goods.

In the evenings, at Mme Naud's tiny square tables with homemade stools, fishermen gathered for dominos, rum, and talk of the sea. On holiday evenings, an accordion, shack-shack, and drumsticks-on-a-crate provided music, and the Naud girls, who ranged from eight to twenty-five, provided dance partners. The regulars included Frazius Canton, the boatcarpenter who repaired fishermen's *gonmyé* in his openair workshop by the sea (and who had served in the army with the Guadeloupean who pulled the trigger at the Diamant massacre); Pierrot Larcher, seine-master and Mme Naud's brother-in-law; the generous and gentle Exentus Lebel, teased for looking so "Congo"; and various younger fishermen, including would-be suitors of the Naud teenagers.

It was in that café in 1962, before an interested crowd of ten or fifteen drinkers, that I deployed some of the tricks taught me for the purpose by my uncle Nat (an accomplished cardsharp). And surely this helped enormously in gaining me entrée to Amédée and all that. (By having learned how to "force" a card, I could, in those days, permit a man to "pick a card, any card," show it around, replace it in the deck and reshuffle while I went to the hearth, took some ashes, and rubbed them on my naked chest where, mysteriously but boldly, would appear, say, "2D"—the two of diamonds, or whatever card I had decided to force and whose image I had marked, invisibly, with a bar of soap on my body.)

Frazius at work, 1962

Exentus in Mme Naud's store, 1962

BUT IT IS ANOTHER rumshop-grocery—Emilien and Merlande's "Le Rayon"—
that affords the most privileged, and temporally continuous, window on Petite
Anse then and now. It is also a site where a great deal of talk and play about
Médard has taken place over the years. It all began in horror.

One clear day in 1970, far from the sight of land, Emilien—who was hauling
a fighting swordfish over the gunwale of *Notre Dame*—slipped and fell backwards, cracking his spine on one of the hardwood ribs of the canoe. Merlande—
who never sent letters—had painstakingly written us in New Haven, telling us
that Emilien would probably suffer permanent paralysis.

Soon after Emilien's accident, unbeknownst to us, Merlande and others in
Petite Anse heard a radio report saying that a "Monsieur Richard"—whom they
took to be me—had been captured and killed in Vietnam. They apparently
mourned my death as Sally and I, in our own more quiescent way, lamented
Emilien's fate. For several years, preoccupied with other matters (young children, changing jobs), and somehow afraid to face Emilien, we avoided contact.
And then in 1975, unannounced, we drove a rental car up to The Sunbeam.

Who was more shocked and more happy? Emilien, who looked as good as ever, and Merlande, sitting outside their new little café, both of whom thought I was dead—or Sally and me? (After two years and several operations in Brittany, Emilien had returned to Petite Anse with a lifetime disability pension and an interdiction ever again to go to sea.)

In those days The Sunbeam was a tiny rumshop, with cement floor and bamboo walls, topped by a couple of sheets of "galvanized." When Mme Naud passed on and her little store shut down, The Sunbeam expanded accordingly, picking up that clientele and adding its own, largely Emilien's old fishing friends. One summer, ten years after Emilien and Merlande began their new storekeeping lives, I tried to describe The Sunbeam as emporium, poised significantly, as it then seemed to me (in the words of Clifford Geertz), "on some sort of fault line between the large and the little."

> One of the half-dozen such rumshop/stores in the *quartier*, The Sunbeam is less cramped physically than most (measuring three by four meters). The rambling, galvanized tin structure has a counter at one end for rum drinking, candy buying, and weighing and paying

Emilien and Merlande in front of The Sunbeam, 1986

for groceries; there are sacks of animal feed, rice, and sugar ranged along the walls; boxes of salt cod, canned goods, and cosmetics are stacked against shelves; wire racks as well as miscellaneous wooden and glass cabinets are filled with everything from tomato paste, onions, and sardines to antimosquito coils, toothpaste, and tennis sneakers; and Hawaiian-style shirts hang from the ceilings alongside buckets and sausages. Since the coming of electricity, cold drinks and popsicles have been big sellers, and the store now has two freezers and a large refrigerator. Attached to the store is the proprietors' bedroom and kitchen, as well as an opensided terrace with tables and chairs where patrons can drink, or sometimes eat, overlooking the sea. Trucks make deliveries to the store as part of a series of regular rounds—beer and ice cream arrive on Fridays, dried goods on Tuesdays. On a typical day, the store grosses about $120 (U.S.)—two-thirds groceries, one-third drinks and ice cream—as a result of some 185 individual sales. (In other words, the average sale comes to less than a dollar—a handful of gumballs, a loaf of bread, or a pound of

R.P. behind the counter of The Sunbeam, 1986

dried peas.). . . . During July 1983, the store stocked some 213 different items or brands. And of these 84 percent were imported from outside Martinique—from 31 countries and from every continent except Australia. . . . Quite generally, there appears to be a rigorous separation of production from consumption, with many products undergoing a remarkably roundabout itinerary on their way to Emilien's and Merlande's. Take, for example, a certain brand of orange juice, sold in the store with a label vaunting *"le soleil de Californie toute l'année."* It specifies further that the contents were made from California concentrate, canned in the Netherlands, imported to Paris, and then shipped to Martinique, where (for a price) one could drink a can just outside the store in the shade of a lovely citrus tree.

But it was in the evenings that The Sunbeam really sprang to life, with its front porch, lit by a kerosene lamp and adjoining the road, being the favored spot for lounging, drinking, arguing, and watching the world go by. Derek Walcott, writing of Saint Lucia (our next-door island, which you can see on the horizon from The Sunbeam[14]) in "What the Twilight Says," caught the flavor of this special kind of evening spectacle, before rampant modernization, including television (first *Dallas* and *Santa Barbara*, now Brazilian telenovelas), swept it all away. "The theatre," he wrote, "was about us, in the streets, at lampfall in the kitchen doorway, but nothing was solemnized into cultural experience." The theatre of the poor,

> where everything was possible, sex, obscenity, absolution, freedom, and not only freedom to wander barefoot, but the freedom made from necessity, the freedom to hack down forests, to hollow canoes, to hunt snakes, to fish, and to develop bodies made of tarred rope that flung off beads of sweat like tightened fish-lines. There were other theatres too. There was the theatre of degeneracy. Not clouds of heroes, but of flies. The derelicts who mimed their tragedies, the lunatics who every day improvised absurd monodramas, blasphemous, scabrous monologues, satirists, cripples, alcoholics, one transvestite, one reprieved murderer, several hunched, ant-crazy old women.

All of these types, and more, frequented The Sunbeam. And when Médard—shirtless, crippled, sack-of-miracles over his shoulder—would come by near the end of his life to show off his latest creation, he fit right into this wonderful if fragile world. After his death, Médard's memory, as embodied in that wooden "*photo*" high up behind the counter, held him a special place in the clouds of words that filled this firmament. Through that special hunk of wood, memories of the *guerre du Diamant*, the *bagne*, and colonial oppression continued to swirl through The Sunbeam. Which is where we first encountered them in 1978.

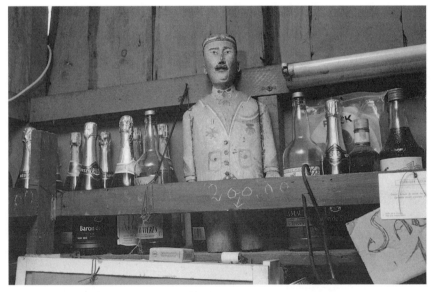

That wooden "*photo*" high up behind the counter

11 DECEMBER 1995, our first day back home in Anses d'Arlet after a semester of teaching in Williamsburg. We are awakened, as on most mornings, by the distant, wavering sound of a conch shell, blown to summon the seine crew for the first haul of the day.[15] When I drive down to town to buy bread, the catch of wriggling jackfish is already being distributed on the beach across from the grocery. As I cross the street, the owner of the new Madinakay Studio-Hotel rushes up and asks, "Excuse me, Monsieur—Can you tell me the name of the man who built that little house in Anse Caffard, the convict?" "Médard," say I. "But Médard *who?*" I answer, "Aribot." With a smile of triumph, he says people had told him "le Canadien" would surely know. When I ask, he explains that it's for a contest in *France-Antilles*—Martinique's only newspaper. They'd printed a photo of the house and required people to know the full name of the *constructeur* to qualify for a prize.

My aim here is to explore how one generation's powerful historical metaphors could so quickly become the next generation's trivial pursuit. By taking the literary equivalents of the circuitous paths through the forest favored by Médard, I will try to shed light on how a people's central mnemonic for colonial repression could find itself transformed, in less than two decades, into the anodyne and picturesque icon on the cover of France's best-selling tourist guide to Martinique.

WHEN PEOPLE BEGAN telling me about Médard twenty years ago, with affection and sympathy, they stressed his singularity—as a loner, a simpleton, a man of supernatural strength, an artistic genius, a gentle eccentric, and possibly a madman. I want now to attend to two aspects of this notion of difference—both quintessentially Caribbean and closely bound up with Médard's life and memory. The first involves the relationship between madness and colonialism. The second concerns the theater of marginality.

Let us begin by asking, in broader terms, why madness (eccentricity, deviance, highly dramatized individuality) is such a marked and salient category in the (post)colonial Caribbean. The answer, I believe, is that the construction of madness in the twentieth-century French and British West Indies is built quite directly on the ruins of colonialism. "Proper" language, schoolbooks, European history, uniforms, and other trappings of the colonizer make up the building blocks of this particular imaginary. The importance madmen and other marginal people hold in the daily life of ordinary folk stems from the ways that they crystallize, in dramatic (often parodic) form, central aspects of colonial relations. The Caribbean theater of madness and marginality, familiar to every resident, holds up a bright mirror to colonialism, standing that rigid order on its head, and in so doing provides powerfully charged popular entertainment. Three literary examples, chosen from a much larger corpus, may help introduce the theme.

There's a passage from *A Brief Conversion*, in which Earl Lovelace signifies lovingly on Walcott's "alphabet of the emaciated" from *Another Life*. Describing small-town life in Trinidad, he tells us:

> There at the roundabout is Corporal, barebacked, wearing his own homemade baton at his waist, standing in the middle of the road, directing traffic. On his head is a chamber pot, his helmet; his leggings are a tangle of dried banana leaves wrapped around his feet, from ankles to his knees. He is barefooted.
>
> Earlier, I had passed Mussolini on a bench. He is an old stickfighter who keeps vigil at that corner. . . .
>
> When I get to Federation Cafe, I will see Science Man, who my father says, 'book send mad', who, during the war, they say, was sentenced to a term in prison for making a radio. . . . Britain, in her unchanged dress of red, white and blue; Graham, with his hernia; Pretty Foot, our transvestite; Fowl, who still crows like the cock he stole from Mother Alice, the Shango priestess. These are our celebrities. Their escapades, their fights, their moments of madness, their sayings, these are the subjects of our conversations. . . . Until that Thursday evening, I had not put them all together in that way. It was then that I felt the weight of their apology and defeat for the first time; and, for the first time, I looked at our town.

Or again, the extended gallery of characters that V.S. Naipaul offers in *Miguel Street* includes another prototype.

> Everybody in Miguel Street said that Man-man was mad, and so they left him alone. But I am not so sure now that he was mad, and I can think of many people much madder than Man-man ever was. . . .

One day I met Man-man at the corner of Miguel Street.

"Boy, where you going?" Man-man asked.

"I going to school," I said.

And Man-man, looking at me solemnly, said in a mocking way, "So you goes to school, eh?"

I said automatically, "Yes, I goes to school." And I found that without intending it I had imitated Man-man's correct and very English accent.

That again was another mystery about Man-man. His accent. If you shut your eyes while he spoke, you would believe an Englishman—a good-class Englishman who wasn't particular about grammar—was talking to you.

Man-man said, as though speaking to himself, "So, the little man is going to school."

Then he forgot me, and took a long stick of chalk from his pocket and began writing on the pavement. He drew a very big S in outline and then filled it in, and then the C and the H and the O. But then he started making several O's, each smaller than the last, until he was writing in cursive, O after flowing O.

When I came home for lunch, he had got to French Street, and he was still writing Os, rubbing off mistakes with a rag. . . .

I went home, changed from my school-clothes into my home-clothes and went out to the street.

He was now half way up Miguel Street.

He said, "So the little man gone to school today?"

I said "Yes."

He stood up and straightened his back.

Then he squatted again and drew the outline of a massive L and filled it in slowly and lovingly.

When it was finished, he stood up and said, "You finish your work. I finish mine."

And Raphaël Confiant provides a recent Martiniquan illustration in the tragicomic figure of Cicéron Nestorin, who went to Bordeaux to study medicine and returned, four years later, not only mad but with an unbounded enthusiasm for the poetry of Aimé Césaire (a writer for whom author Confiant nurtures a vitriolic disdain). Cicéron writes slogans on walls and carries around cardboard signs, generally stating truths or asking questions that others dare not utter: WHY HAVE THE BÉKÉS ABOLISHED THE SUGAR FACTORIES? And he is never seen without his sack filled with dictionaries. Late in the novel, there is an exuberant scene in which, stuck up against the windowpane, Cicéron makes love to one of the Syrian storekeeper's white mannequins, finally ejaculating (shades of Fanon) to the cry of "*Vive Schoelcher!*" Later, he rejects these dark-haired beauties, each of whom he has named for an Italian movie star, in favor of a newly arrived blond object of desire, whom he calls Ingrid. Because Cicéron knows everything about the *quartier*, having been born and bred there, and has complete freedom to move about, he is able to stand on the streetcorner making speeches about exactly who's sleeping with whom and making obscure, hyperliterary placards about it all as well. Cicéron, "who dreams of a lost Africa and recites at every opportunity the verses of Aimé Césaire . . . has been positively 'unbrained' [*décérébré*] by reading too many books of medicine." Or, as ordinary Martiniquans say of madmen—and workers of black magic as well—they're generally "people who read too much."

Like the region's novelists, for whom colonial madness has been such an important trope,[16] anthropologists have often found themselves sucked into this vortex. In the late 1950s, British anthropologist Peter Wilson went to the tiny island of Providencia for dissertation research. Immediately, he ran up against a man named Oscar, who later confided, "They call me a madman, but I am proud of this, for there is method in madness. . . . You see, Professor Oscar Bryan Newball is of the eighth variety, a man of keen insight and wide vision." Wilson writes, "I began taking notes from him and about him almost as soon as I arrived on the island. It was unavoidable, really, because he latched onto me from the beginning, and I was immediately fascinated. I soon became deeply involved, for in a frightening but illuminating sense, he became a part of me. I could see in him part of myself, as I suspect everyone on the island could see something of themselves in him."

Twenty years later, British psychiatrist and anthropologist Roland Littlewood arrived in rural Trinidad, intending "to study local knowledge of health and sickness" in a fishing village. But before long, he too found himself deeply involved with a "mad" person, in nearby Hell Valley. He stayed off and on for a year, as a semi-follower of Mother Earth, a woman who (in part because she required the members of her community to go naked) was regarded locally as insane. Littlewood's book presents a phantasmagoric picture of the postcolonial Caribbean, partly through the eyes of Mother Earth, that better captures structures and experience than many a traditional monograph.

Years ago, in his pioneering study of colonial madness in Barbados, anthropologist Lawrence Fisher argued that it is "only in literature" that Caribbean madmen "clearly comprehend the nature of their society." But Littlewood's multifaceted portrait of Mother Earth, like Wilson's sketch of Oscar, may now lay that assertion to rest. The dozens of memorable "madmen" of Caribbean fiction are not just literary tropes. In many cases, their real-life models see through what Albert Memmi called the colonialist hoax as no "normal" person can afford to. They are among us in every rumshop and at every crossroads. Many of them have things to say that others dare not utter. And, as the novelists have long understood, if we are fully to comprehend Caribbean societies, we need to take them seriously.[17]

The background is relatively transparent. In a region now colonized for five centuries, whose countryside was almost from the first subjected to industrial time and discipline, where the social system was designed to reduce the bulk of the population to nameless and interchangeable ciphers, where notions of European respectability have long been dominant, there has always been a subversive appreciation from within of the small act of difference, of individual style, of eccentricity. With expressive resources reduced by overwhelming external controls, Caribbean people have always asserted their individuality, and resistance, as best they could through verbal play, pilferage, satirical song, deception, and small acts of defiance.

Caribbean people (particularly in the non-Hispanic, more-continuously-colonized territories), have long been stretched between imposed yet often-internalized colonial values (regarding light skin, establishment Christianity, office-work, and other forms of "respectability") and locally generated, bottom-up values (egalitarianism, crab antics, African-American magico-religious expression, man-of-words exploits, and other forms of "reputation"). This constant tension or dialectic renders what some commentators have called "schizoid" behavior almost normal. Individuals must work out their lives in a world where the circumstances of life are deeply contradictory, leading to what Herskovits, writing of Haiti, labeled "socialized ambivalence"—closely related to what Du Bois, writing of the United States, had called "double-consciousness." In such societies, many of "the mad" are not just finding a personal way out—they are carving out a solution, however unreasonable, for a society-wide, existentially absurd situation. Their retreat or riposte, whatever its iconoclastic form, often makes social sense. And it's plain for all to see.

In Petite Anse, Médard was one of the star players among that gallery of characters, at once marginal and therefore absolutely central, whom the village held in special regard. Others I knew, either in Mme Naud's café or in The Sunbeam, included[18]

—Sebastianiste, the wiry septuagenarian who at daybreak and sunset would mount a volcanic boulder, rum bottle in hand, and belt out "*Ce soir, nous allons danser, sans chemise, sans pantalon*" [Tonight, we're going to dance, without our shirts, without our pants] followed immediately by a stirring, patriotic rendition of "La Marseillaise";

—Wilfried, who left the better part of his mind in a Nazi prison camp and now went about blessing people with exaggerated signs of the cross and tracing mysterious writings with a stick in the dust;

—Pipo, once a bright youth, now always the first to approach tourists and con them (with considerable skill even when drunk) into buying him a drink, and who, on All Saint's Day, chased by the ghost of the man he once killed with a knife, races in absolute terror, looking repeatedly over his shoulder, along the darkening beach;

—Dédé, who everyone says was a very intelligent boy, sleeps wherever he finds rest, wears whatever clothes he can scavenge, cleans fish in return for some scraps, and, in a falsetto voice, speaks a highly overcorrected, greco-latinate, quasi-macaronic French;[19]

—Rigobert, increasingly blind, exaggeratedly courtly, gently kissing women's hands, can generate extraordinarily flowery French phrases but curses up a storm in Creole when kids teasingly steal his hat;

—Elvire, in her forties, who still has miraculous powers to attract men, especially married men, through the use of herbs and *quimbois*, as well as by letting herself be seen naked, and who reduces them to jelly until they become her slaves for a while;

—Thierry, rarely sober, highly intelligent, always on the road and on the move between Anses d'Arlet, Petite Anse, and Diamant, singing and dancing, talking nonstop, telling everyone's secrets and scandals, miming colonial relations (parodic self-abasement toward whites), lots of self-irony, terribly proud of the old green military jacket he sports, tied with bright orange sash.

The actual cast is, of course, much larger and includes some of the lame and the halt, the mentally handicapped, a flamboyant loose woman or two, a handful of people who've been (to borrow Aimé Césaire's memorable phrase) "dynamited by alcohol," and others recruited to play bit parts in the ongoing local theater of daily life, set on the stage of the rumshop porch, which is by sudden turns cruel and tender. And there are also those who are marked for life, and provide continuing entertainment and teasing, merely because of a single moment of weakness. Bel Komisyon ("Beautiful You-Know-What"), for example, is stuck with that nickname because in a moment of exuberance the morning after his marriage, he boasted in the rumshop of the unusual delights of his wife's *koukoun* and whenever he shows up, thirty years later, is still burdened—through gentle but pointed taunts—by that indiscretion. Or there's Bous-kaka ("Purse-of-shit"), who was entrapped by a group of women who knew his propensities for petty pilferage and dropped a sack-cloth purse filled with shit-wrapped-in-newspaper on the floor of a grocery, where he eagerly "stole" it and, as soon as he thought he was alone, greedily reached in to get his loot—and who bore that nickname for the next half-century.

Behind each character—each provider of endless entertainment and discussion—there's a story, told and retold. And (post)colonial realities are rarely far from the surface. Take Pipo, today the pathetic pointman of the Petite Anse welcoming committee whenever tourists pull up. A schoolteacher in the southcoast town of Sainte-Luce, a youthful companion of Pipo, recorded the relevant parts of the longer tale:

> Pipo, a born fisherman who came from Petite Anse, one of the
> *quartiers* of Anses d'Arlet, showed up one day to stay. Though a fine-
> looking man, he was illiterate and unable to put together two words

of French. At the parties and dances he would always attract the prettiest tourists, but he'd lose them as soon as he opened his mouth. For Pipo had an absolute mania of wishing to carry on a French conversation despite his handicap. So, I agreed to become his professor. In order to help him keep his dance partners, I devised a system: I counselled him to engage in conversation only after having danced four or five times in a row with the same girl, excusing himself for not being able to express himself in French because he was English-speaking. But as luck would have it, on his very first sortie, his partner turned out to be a teacher of English. He struggled to get out a few words, but the woman was gone. Another time when he was dancing with a local girl, he began in frustration to jump around like a goat in an anthill, but the girl was soon sitting down without him.

It was not long after that Pipo, having been told by another Petite Anse fisherman that he'd had too much to drink, went to his rented room, came back with two knives, and in frustration plunged both into the broad back of his unsuspecting friend. After seven years in prison for murder, now speaking passable French, he spends his time scouting the road for tourists—when he is not preoccupied with outrunning the pursuing ghost of his erstwhile victim.

As Walcott wrote (and he could have been speaking for the residents of Petite Anse in the 1960s and 1970s),

> These dead, these derelicts,
> that alphabet of the emaciated,
> they were the stars of my mythology.

Or as Lovelace replayed it, "These are our celebrities. Their escapades, their fights, their moments of madness, their sayings, these are the subjects of our conversations. And about each of them is a story: pride that has fallen; ambition that overleaped itself. Each story ends victoriously in defeat, penance, apology. This was our folklore." Memories of Médard, as colorful a star as any other in the Petite Anse firmament of the 1970s or early 80s, must be understood as part and parcel of this broader Caribbean theater of memory.

But Médard also embodied the carnivalesque spirit that was so central at once to Caribbean life and to local discourse about the colonial past. For denizens of The Sunbeam, Médard's memory preserved in heightened and dramatic form their own colonial struggles, all the intricacies and contradictions of Martiniquan identity in the days before rampant *francisation*—the 1925 *guerre du Diamant* and the role of his *"photo"* of the colonel, his arbitrary sentencing and the long years in the *bagne*—"not for having killed, not for having raped"—but for what people understood as determined resistance to colonial authority. But also recall that the best-known victims of his prodigious thefts were the Compagnie Générale Transatlantique, the *békés* and their factories, and the local gendarmerie. And that his artworks, made from the detritus of industrial society (cellophane from cigarette packages, silver paper from gum wrappers, bentwood from boxes of Camembert), constitute a commentary on Prospero-Caliban relations, an obbligato on the theme of colonial power and domination—vividly decorated colonels, generals, and kings; the French tri-color; warships and cannons; pianos, dancers, and fancy-dress balls; and whitefolks disporting themselves in German beerhalls, not to mention his solemn marking-of-the-hours on an overturned iron pot. Victim, in peoples' memories, of unspeakable colonial repression, Médard was nevertheless seen to have had the last laugh, through his exuberant, semi-parodic artworks. The carnavalesque and the uncanny permitted Médard to somehow (as Simon Gikandi wrote of novelist Sam Selvon) "defy the logical discourse of colonial modernism" by deploying "forces of chaos and madness amidst the official order of things." In *A Brighter Sun*, Selvon had reported, deadpan, that

> There was a change in the economic and social life and outlook of Trinidadians in 1941. United States personnel arrived, and the construction of bases provided work at high wages—higher than anyone had ever worked for before. Clerks quit their desks and papers and headed for the bases, farmers left the land untilled. . . . A man named Afoo Dayday was caught urinating behind a tree in a park and was jailed.

One imagines that Médard, with his peculiar genius, would have grasped both Selvon's characteristically Caribbean artistic technique—and Afoo Dayday's personal *geste*.

IN THE POST-COLUMBIAN Caribbean, trying to catch hold of history, coming to terms with the past, has always posed special difficulties—for both the elite and the unlettered. For the zero-moment is marked by irremeable rupture and pain. Not surprisingly, violence, torture, and blood course through the works of the region's great writers—from Carpentier, Césaire, and James to Lamming, Naipaul, Glissant, and Walcott. A character in one of Paule Marshall's novels explains to visiting anthropologists, "Ah, well, ah, history. . . . Any of you ever study it? . . . Well, don't if you haven't. I did for a time—West Indian history it was and I tell you, it nearly, as we say in Bournehills, set out my head. I had to leave it off. It is a nightmare, as that Irishman said, and we haven't awaked from it yet."[20] And Martiniquans, I would argue, experience the more general condition in an especially acute form.

Colonized for more than five centuries, quintessentially Western, Caribbean peoples face the challenge of somehow recasting the modernist paradigm of progress, unashamedly triumphalist and Eurocentric. How at the same time to appropriate and subvert the central ideas associated with modernity? How to write in the colonizer's language and assert one's own vision of the world? How at once to represent and resist the March of History set in motion by Columbus? How to play off one part of oneself against another?

Over the years, Caribbean intellectuals have rehearsed many of the difficulties, from the vitriolic queries of V. S. Naipaul:

> How can the history of this West Indian futility be written? What tone shall the historian adopt?

or the pointed asides of Édouard Glissant about

> the loss of collective memory, the careful erasure of the past . . . the obscurity of this impossible memory

or Aimé Césaire's allusions to

> this land without stela, these paths without memory

to the stark conclusions of Derek Walcott:

> In time, the slave surrendered to amnesia [and] that amnesia is the true history of the New World

or Orlando Patterson:

> The most critical feature of the West Indian consciousness is what Derek Walcott calls "an absence of ruins." The most important

legacy of slavery is the total break, not with the past so much as with a consciousness of the past. To be a West Indian is to live in a state of utter pastlessness.

George Lamming provided a particularly poignant literary expression of this existential situation in his first novel, *In the Castle of My Skin*, where he describes the thoughts and conversation of two Barbadian schoolboys in the 1930s:

> He asked the teacher what was the meaning of slave, and the teacher explained. But it didn't make sense. He didn't understand how anyone could be bought by another. He knew horses and dogs could be bought and worked. But he couldn't understand how one man could buy another man. . . . Slave. . . . Thank God, he wasn't ever a slave. He or his father or his father's father. Thank God nobody in Barbados was ever a slave. . . . They laughed quietly. Imagine any man in

Fishermen playing cards, 1962

any part of the world owning a man or woman from Barbados. They would forget all about it since it happened too long ago. . . . It was too far back. . . . And nobody knew where this slavery business took place. The teacher had simply said, not here, somewhere else. Probably it never happened at all.

More recently, Lamming has reflected on changes—and continuities—in Caribbean people's historical consciousness regarding resistance:

> We know, to a degree we did not know some decades ago, that Africans and Indians have a remarkable record of resistance. . . . But this knowledge is still largely archival. It is locked up in an enclave of scholars. . . . It is a knowledge which still awaits mass distribution, and which, therefore, has not yet become the shaping influence on the consciousness of those whose recent ancestors had made it possible. It is not inscribed in consciousness.[21]

But though, as schoolchildren, Lamming and these other Caribbean writers shared Walcott's experience of their pasts coming to them largely through the perspective of Westminster, Madrid, the Hague, or the Quai d'Orsay—

> I saw history through the sea-washed eyes
> of our choleric, ginger-haired headmaster,
> beak like an inflamed hawk's,
> a lonely Englishman who loved parades,
> sailing, and Conrad's prose[22]

—they have, against all odds, also begun pointing the way toward possible escapes.

Alejo Carpentier, in the famous formulation emerging from his confrontation with the Haitian Revolution, proposed that the history of the Americas, "*por los fecundos mestizajes que propició*," is nothing "*sino una crónica de lo real-maravilloso*" (that fertile mixings have turned the history of the Americas into a chronicle of magic realism). In this same register, Lamming reminds us of the redemptive potential of Caribbean folk wisdom: calypsonian Lord Kitchener, commenting on the Soviet triumph in space signaled by the launch of Sputnik, sang "Columbus didn't need no dog"—at once, Lamming hints, wryly acknowledging the hegemony of Western History (the definition of Columbus as a Great Man) and effectively subverting it (along with its triumphalist narrative of Western progress) through carnivalesque ridicule. Similarly, Wilson Harris has criticized the intellectual West Indian perspective that stresses an absence of ruins or a sense of pastlessness in the folk thought of the Caribbean, calling on historians to seek out "an inner time," to break out of the traditional "high-level psychological censorship of the creative imagination" that has hamstrung critical Caribbean scholarship. "I believe," he writes, that "a philosophy of history may well lie buried in the arts of the imagination." Glissant, who conjures up the need for "a prophetic vision of the past," asserts that "the struggle against a single History, and for a cross-fertilization of histories, means at once repossessing one's true sense of time and one's identity. It also means posing in an entirely new way the question of power." And Walcott's advice is complementary: "History remains for the Caribbean the territory of the imagination and memory, and that imagination is not innocent but experienced"; "The children of slaves must sear their memory with a torch"; and "The truly tough aesthetic of the New World neither explains nor forgives history."

It is these latter waves—the crests conjured up by Carpentier, Lamming, Harris, Glissant, and Walcott—that we shall try to catch for the shoreward ride.

MARTINIQUE, WHICH ONE RECENT student has dubbed the "Isle of Intellectuals" (and which is reported to have a higher concentration of diplomas per square kilometer than any country in the world except Israel), has already made a disproportionate contribution to these debates about the region's past. Politically and economically, today's Martinique, like its sister territories Guadeloupe and Guyane, stands out from its Caribbean neighbors by being part of Europe, lending its cultural politics a particular complexity. In the thirties, Césaire's explosive *Cahier d'un retour au pays natal* announced the birth of *négritude*, and a new poetics of resistance, written in what was at once extraordinarily powerful, masterful, and subversive French, began to spread its message wherever colonized peoples still suffered. One of Césaire's students in Fort-de-France's Lycée Schoelcher, although choosing prose rather than poetry, continued the literary assault in a yet more militant vein and was quickly heard round the world: Frantz Fanon.[23] (Walcott, in neighboring Saint Lucia, describes his own literary "discipleship" during this period to "the young Frantz Fanon and the already ripe and bitter Césaire [who] were manufacturing the homemade bombs of their prose poems, their drafts for revolution.") Glissant, a near contemporary of Fanon at the lycée, remains a major contributor to world literature and theory through his wide-ranging essays, poetry, and novels focused on neocolonial and postcolonial realities. And more recently, three younger Martiniquan intellectuals who call themselves *créolistes*—Jean Bernabé, Raphaël Confiant, and Patrick Chamoiseau—have published, amidst much hoopla, a literary manifesto (called *Éloge de la créolité*) in which they offer their own perspectives on recovering the island's past:

> Our History, or more precisely our histories, are shipwrecked within Colonial History. Collective memory must be our priority. What we once believed to be Caribbean history is no more than the History of Colonization of the Caribbean. Beneath the shock waves of French history, beneath the Great Dates marking the arrival and departure of colonial governors, beneath the uncertainties of colonial struggles, beneath the standard white pages of the official Chronicle (where the torches of our revolts appear only as tiny blotches), there was our own obstinate trudging-along. The opaque resistance of maroons united in their refusal. The new heroism of those who confronted the hell of slavery, using obscure codes of survival, indecipherable means of resistance, an impenetrable variety of compromises, unexpected syntheses for living. . . . Within this false consciousness we had but a bunch of obscurities for memory, a feeling of bodily discontinuity. Landscapes, Glissant reminds us, stand alone as inscriptions, in their non-anthropomorphic way, of at least some of our tragedy, of our will to exist. Which means that our history, or histories, are not totally accessible to historians. . . . It is no accident that, when it comes to Caribbean history, so many historians use literary citations to try to grasp principles that they can only graze with their usual methodology. . . . Only poetic knowledge, romantic knowledge, literary knowledge, in short, artistic knowledge can reveal us, perceive us, bring us back, evanescent, to a reborn consciousness.[24]

It was with motives not unlike those expressed by this modern Martiniquan literary troika, and fresh on the heels of my historical investigations with Saramaka Maroons, that I first began my engagement with memories of Médard. I was well aware of the ways in which the French congeners of Walcott's ginger-haired headmaster or Lamming's grade-school teacher had imposed Colonial History—remote and irrelevant to daily life—upon generations of Martiniquan schoolchildren. And it wasn't long before I had my first encounter with Médard's sister-in-law, Céleste Senzamba, then ninety-two and blind, who—when I mentioned my interest in *istoua* (history)—recounted, with great excitement, nonstop, the story of Joan of Arc, remembered from her primary school days before the turn of the century, calling out at the appropriate moment in the story, in one of the few French phrases she knew, "*Sauvez la France! Sauvez la France!*"[25] I nonetheless felt confident about uncovering, beneath this colonial veneer of History (from Joan of Arc to de Gaulle and after), hidden layers of history, called by other names and inscribed not in books (the people among whom we lived were barely literate) but in language, in proverbs, in metaphors, and in the land (and sea) itself. From my experience in Saramaka, I was ready to find traces of the past in unexpected places, playing ever-changing roles in ongoing social and political life, and being preserved, transformed, or obliterated according to the location of particular individuals and collectivities in relationship to particular events and actors, past and present. By the mid-1980s, in my ongoing explorations of memories of Médard, I felt I had found a set of traces, a series of remembered fragments about the past, that might be an ideal allegory for my more general contention that, *pace* some of the more pessimistic assessments cited above, Martiniquan peasants and fishermen did preserve a heroic, anticolonial vision of the past and that collective amnesia was more an invention of bourgeois intellectuals than a rural reality.

Indeed, in 1985, in the wake of that truck ride up Morne l'Afrique with Tina and Julien and the countless discussions with Philibert, Génor, Clairville, Dinette, Ernest, Mayor Ribier, and so many others, over a span of eight years, I was able to write with assurance that

> Today, in all the fishing villages along the southern coast of Martinique, almost anyone can tell you that Médard, that enigmatic,

silent sculptor who died a decade ago, was sent to the French Guiana prison camps for having made a perfect "*photo*" (a sculpture in wood) of Colonel de Coppens. And they will point to Médard's miniature gingerbread house on the cliffs by the sea outside Diamant as evidence of his artistic genius. *Tout moun* (absolutely everyone) knows that Médard once saw Coppens, that he fashioned his image in wood with every detail, from facial expression to military medals, exactly in place, and that he was condemned to the prison camps for this act of gross impertinence.

In the late 1970s, at the time I began to explore Médard's story, its power seemed tangible to rural Martiniquans. Although his penultimate house, once a brightly painted, gingerbreaded jewel of bricolage, with spinning weathervanes and tiny, awninged windows looking out toward Diamond Rock, now stood in ruins, whenever local fishermen, artisans, or peasants passed by, on the road or at sea, they remembered the man and his story. Their world was still hemmed in by sufficiently palpable (post)colonial structures and relations for them to recognize in Médard's struggle, though it occurred in the 1920s at the height of classic colonial domination, something very much their own. I felt I had found a story that revealed a meaningful (if relatively subterranean) aspect of the way these people situated themselves in the world. And I was able to conclude my 1985 article, on the strength of these beliefs, by claiming that "For Martiniquan fishermen all along the southern coast, the story of Médard and the 1925 shootings in Diamant—though nowhere written down—forms a central chapter of their modern history, of their meaningful past."[26]

Today, less than two decades later, I can no longer sustain that claim. Few people below the age of fifty remember anything at all about Médard and even fewer know that there was ever a "war" in Diamant. Leaving aside the survivors from the generation that first shared their memories and thoughts about Médard with me, most of their children and grandchildren today can tell me only that Médard might have been a convict (or was he a soldier? or an outcast? or a simple madman? or might he perhaps have been a slave?) who long ago lived in that strange little house at Anse Caffard. It is as if the massive steamroller of French (post)colonialism, with its destructive bending of consciousness and identity, has finally made a sweep through even the most rural, least modern areas of the island. What two decades ago my local friends understood as a story of heroic resistance to an almost incomprehensibly arrogant oppressor is today largely leeched of meaning—at least that kind of meaning. Médard's story, along with so much else about colonialism that was meaningful until recently in rural Martinique, is on the road to becoming official folklore for people who are increasingly (if still only partially and not necessarily irredeemably) learning to use French models of how to think and act.

What we are witnessing, I would argue, might be called "the folklorization of colonialism," or "the postcarding of the past." Indeed, during 1987, influenced by state efforts to recuperate the *patrimoine culturel* (the official heritage of this corner of France), as well as to promote tourism, a local youth group sponsored by the municipality of Diamant renovated Médard's house, cleaning up the graffiti slapped on by some Rasta visitors, repairing the carpentry, creating a picturesque rock-inlaid walk leading to the front door, repainting the wood in approximations of the original colors and, *voilà*, every tourist shop in the capital of Martinique began selling postcards labeled "Diamond Rock and its legendary 'House of the Convict.'"[27]

Nataly Jolibois's self-described "impressionist" painting of Médard's house, 1995

Southcoast fishermen's gradual "forgetting" (or silencing) of Médard as a symbol of struggle and anticolonial contestation parallels the current reshaping of Martinique's past by the island's most visible intellectuals. Though the precise linkages are difficult to tease out, it is clear that both rural fishermen and urbane writers are responding to the immensely changed circumstances of rapidly modernizing Martinique. Those writers who call themselves *créolistes*, from the generation of intellectuals now in their forties, provide a useful illustration of the ways the past is currently being reconceptualized.[28]

During the past ten years, the leaders of the *créoliste* movement, Patrick Chamoiseau and Raphaël Confiant, have, between them, written a literary manifesto, a history of Antillean literature, and a number of novels and memoirs that have won just about every major literary prize in France, including the Prix Goncourt. In the process, they have proposed a radical revisioning of Martinique's past.[29]

Writing against the *négritude* of Césaire, which they argue overprivileges the African side of their roots, they stress the multiplicity of Martinique's heritage—what they call *diversalité*. They proclaim themselves to be "Neither Europeans nor Africans nor Asians . . . but Creoles . . . at once Europe and Africa, enriched by contributions from Asia, the Levant, and India, and including also survivals from Pre-Columbian America." They insist that Martinique has always been an unusually diverse society—ethnically, racially, and linguistically—and that the Old World societies from which immigrants arrived were cultural monoliths. Moreover, the French Antillean plantation is seen as a relatively "gentle" institution in the broader Caribbean context: masters and slaves are said to have worked side by side, both having suffered the deprivations of emigration and transport and engaging in frequent cultural interchange; truly "harsh" slavery is displaced onto other colonial powers, like the Spanish, English, or Dutch.[30] As for maroons (the rebel slaves who had been so heavily romanticized during the heyday of the *négritude* movement), the *créolistes* tend to view them as having taken the easy way out by abandoning the plantation hot-bed of creolization and merely "americanizing," adapting to a new environment rather than fully "creolizing." For the *créolistes*, maroons remain uncultured isolationists, "on the margins of general [historical] processes . . . spiritually mired in times past, with their loincloths, spears, and bows . . . their bamboo bracelets, chickenhawk feathers, earrings, and designs traced in ashes on their faces."

The real heroes of this particular vision of Martiniquan history are the plantation slaves who, "secure in their secret dignity, often laid the groundwork for what we are today, and did so more effectively than many a maroon." More specifically, it is the *conteur* (the "man-of-words") who replaces the maroon as the heroic figure par excellence. "Among the most docile of slaves," the *conteur* has "almost the quality of an Uncle Tom, whom the master doesn't fear," which allows him to spread a subversive message of day-to-day resistance through all manner of verbal ruse. And the *créolistes* choose to portray their own literary activities as those of modern-day *conteurs* (or *marqueurs de paroles*) in much the same way that Césaire and his followers had viewed themselves as metaphorical maroons.

This particular revisioning of the past fits snugly into its historical moment. If today's Martinique, with its deep imbrication in France/Europe, can be conceptualized in an analogous mode to a slave community within an all-encompassing plantation system, then a self-proclaimed *marqueur de paroles*, the agent of a ruse-based subversiveness comparable to that of the slave-era *conteur*, becomes a much more appropriate contemporary figure of resistance than the fiery maroon rebel of yore. And an imagined *diversalité* or *métissage* can be packaged as a consumable cultural product (as Françoise Vergès has argued) along the lines of the United Colors of Benetton, effectively serving as "an 'artifact' in the Great French Museum of Human Diversity so long as the historical conditions that gave birth to this diversity—colonial wars, slavery, the construction of the French nation—are denied or swept under the rug."

It is partly for these reasons that the celebration of an "authentic" Martinique plays so well among readers in the metropole, as well as on the island, today. And I believe that the literary works of the *créolistes* are, on the whole, complicitous with the celebration of a museumified Martinique, a diorama'd Martinique, a picturesque and "pastified" Martinique that promotes a "feel-good" nostalgia for people who are otherwise busy adjusting to the complexities of a rapidly modernizing lifestyle. As literary critic Richard Burton has argued, "*Créolité* is in practice often retrospective, even regressive, in character, falling back, in a last desperate recourse against decreolization, into the real or imagined plenitude of *an tan lontan* (olden times)." In this regard, one might argue that the *créoliste* movement is ensnared in one of the traps of modernization, risking the kind of "patrimonialization" of which Walcott wrote: "Stamped on that image is the old colonial grimace of the laughing nigger, steelbandsman, carnival masker, calypsonian and limbo dancer . . . trapped in the State's concept of the folk form . . . the symbol of a carefree, accommodating culture, an adjunct to tourism."

The prize-winning *créoliste* film, *L'Exil de Béhanzin*, throws into relief many of the particularities of the *créolistes*' historical agenda. Indeed, this 1995 film might be seen as a comprehensive allegory of the *créolistes*' vision of the post-Emancipation history of Martinique: immigrants arriving from backward, monolingual, monocultural lands to discover a sophisticated creole world-in-the-making that is bubbling with ethnic and linguistic diversity. Chamoiseau's screenplay is hung on the scaffolding of historical event—the exile of King Béhanzin of Dahomey, whose empire was crushed by French armies in 1894 and who spent a dozen unhappy years in Martinique, living through the devastating eruption of the Mont Pelée volcano in 1902. Yet despite director Guy Deslauriers's claim that "we tried to stick as close as possible to historical reality," the main story line is invented from whole cloth and the depiction of central psychological and sociological realities is historically ungrounded. It is the particulars of the historical invention, combined with the authors' insistence that it is "historically accurate," that interests us here.[31]

The lyrics of the movie's theme song (written by Chamoiseau) express the heart of the plot, the redeeming power of *créolité*: *L'anmou rivé fè'y oubliyé péyi Dahomé . . . I fini pa enmen'y pasé tout péyi-a i té pèd la.* ("Love succeeded in making him forget the land of Dahomey . . . He came to love her even more than the country he lost.") The *belle créole* who, according to the film's fiction, instantly erases the African king's love of his country is the green-eyed Régina (played by France Zobda), first seen in a group of comely laundresses disporting themselves among the boulders of a tropical river. Their melodic chatter and rippling laughter could have served as the sound track for a nineteenth-century operetta, and their ruffly, off-the-shoulder blouses could have come straight off the racks of an upscale Parisian boutique—though a few capricious tumbles in the clear, rushing water quickly make their wearers look more like college coeds in a spring-break wet T-shirt contest, revealing that Ms. Zobda's physical charms consist of more than her sparkling eyes and radiant smile. Régina is *créolité* incarnate: *Toutes les terres, toutes les cultures, toutes les traditions* (a composite of "all lands, all cultures, all traditions"). And her house, a prototypical *case créole* ("traditional" creole cabin), is a little stage set with decor of the sort that can be found in modern Martiniquan museum displays, the lobbies of hotels that host *ballets folkloriques*, and pricey gift shops at the new airport—neat as a pin, with attractively arranged "traditional" basketry and pottery, but with none of the diacritics (for example, walls covered with pages torn from old newspapers) of a lived-in creole house.

As depicted in the film, Béhanzin (played by the Jamaica-born Delroy Lindo, with a francophone dubber providing his voice) embodies Africanity. Set next to photographs of the historical Béhanzin, the actor's features are rougher and "blacker"—in short, more what a present-day Martiniquan would call *nèg-kongo* ("African" or savage/primitive). And in virtually the only segment of the plot in which he takes the initiative, the otherwise passive Béhanzin has a premonition of trouble, leaps from his bed, and succeeds in saving Régina from a deadly snake bite through mystical African lore. Early in the film, Béhanzin confronts the dilemma of modernity—via the anguishing question of whether he should permit his son to be sent to lycée to learn Western ways. His decision to permit the boy to attend school, in order to equip him for the coming struggle, is made in the context of his shock upon discovering cultural diversity. "In contrast to his African homeland, the island of Martinique is inhabited by a diversity of people, who came from Africa, Europe, and Asia—a melting-pot startling enough to impress the African king, no matter how god-like." In Chamoiseau's own words (at the film's premiere, 28 March 1995), it was a "tremendous mixture of peoples, of languages, of colors, that Béhanzin discovered in America [Martinique]— epitomized by *la belle créole*." Or, as the film's director put it, "Béhanzin arrived in a land in full effervescence, boasting Arab, Chinese, East Indian, and White peoples.[32] . . . He is faced with the difficult question—difficult because he has no ready answer for it—of why this part of the world has such a fantastic mix of peoples. And what could it all lead to? A hundred years ahead of his time, he was pondering the *problématique* of intercultural encounters."

Suffice it to say that, in contrast to his movie version, the historical Béhanzin was a sophisticated, highly cultured god-king, who reigned over a large empire with numerous language and ethnic groups, a developed system of classes, and constant interactions with rival European—and African—powers. The acceptance of Western education for his son was hardly innovative; Béhanzin's own father, the redoubtable King Glélé (Gléglé), was formally educated in Marseille. And as for choice of women, the Dahomean monarch probably had as wide a range as any man on earth. Historically, then, Béhanzin (like most of the Africans who arrived in the New World as slaves) was in fact far more cosmopolitan, in terms of linguistic and cultural *diversalité*, than the Creoles whom he encountered in Martinique.

The film's take on marronage is enunciated early on, after the horse-drawn carriage in which Béhanzin is being transported is accosted by a frenzied, barefooted, spear-wielding black man. As my notes record the scene,

> "It's a half-crazy *nègre marron*!" exclaims Béhanzin's guard. And he warns the maroon, "Get outta here, leave us alone. This is Béhanzin Ahydjéré." Immediately, the maroon prostrates himself, waving his arms up and down in movie-swami fashion and chanting (in Creole) "*Béhanzin Ahydjéré rivé, rwa la, lafrik-la la,* (etc.)" [B.A. has come, the king is here, Africa is here]. B steps over to raise up his subject, who runs off, shouting (presumably to his fellows in the forest): "The king has come! We'll kill the whites! We'll be free!" As the two men return to the carriage, the guard explains to Béhanzin with marked disdain, "Those maroons! It was easier to just run away from it all than to stand firm and confront the white man in the cane field."

How wonderful to imagine, a half-century after the abolition of slavery, a wild Martiniquan maroon—and a youngish one at that—who is up-to-date on current events in Africa! In a second appearance, this time off-camera, the maroon is heard crying out under the captive king's window, "Béhanzin Ahydjéré, Béhanzin Ahydjéré. *Rwa nou rivé*! *Rwa nou*! Our king has come! Our king!" And the maroon returns once again at the very end of the film, in a deranged state, wildly tossing volcanic ashes in the air so that they fall all over his head.

It is hardly surprising that Africans, including some of Béhanzin's direct descendants, who saw previews of the film at a festival in Burkina Faso, reacted

negatively. In those excerpts from their comments shown on Martiniquan television, the Dahomeans complained that Béhanzin, a powerful leader and national
hero of resistance, was depicted in the film as a pitiable, broken man who lacked
cultural credibility. "They're presenting him as a king who can't even speak his
own language correctly," objected one. They also complained about his patent
passivity and undignified, instantaneous enthrallment to a creole woman. (Even
the Martiniquan audience sitting around us in the theater found this dimension
of Béhanzin's filmic character ludicrous; when one of the four African wives
who accompanied Béhanzin to Martinique sensuously unveils her spectacular
body beside the king's bed and he simply turns his back, dreaming of the *belle
créole* whom he has at that point laid eyes on only twice, and briefly, the audience
erupted in guffaws of incredulity.) As if to emphasize this perspective, the film's
official poster miniaturized the whole African continent to fit into a small part of
the map of Martinique. The *créoliste* image of the defeated African, whose
humanity was redeemed by his encounter with creoleness, provides stark contrast with the postcolonial African vision of the last great Dahomean resister to
European empire.

The Martiniquans who make up the local audience for this film (and for the
novels of Chamoiseau and Confiant), though they tend to be better educated
and more urbane than the habitués of The Sunbeam, share much with these latter folk—in particular, an acceptance, however grudging, of the inevitability of
the logic of political and economic integration into Europe. Such an acceptance,
even when accompanied by sporadic expressions of cultural resistance and par-
ticularism (sometimes even led by the *créolistes* themselves), ultimately requires
a muting of conflict between Martiniquans and the French. And it leads almost
inevitably to a nostalgia-based, vaseline-filtered view of the past and to a
broadly participatory, rather than contestational, political practice in the present.

Colonial nostalgia, 1990s Martinique-style, provides another entrée into this
tangle of interlinked phenomena—so central to understanding what has happened to memories of Médard during the past two decades. Consider, as an
opener, the following (as reported by *France-Antilles*): Just off the north-south
road that skirts the Atlantic coast, "a mini-village made up of rural cabins from
the 1950s . . . permits the new generation to discover the scenes their ancestors

knew, the way of life of their parents and grandparents. . . . Four years in the making, this open-air museum is a gem of tradition. On Sunday afternoons . . . members of the folkloric troupe Madinina install themselves there to recreate a living portrait of that bygone era." A few kilometers to the south, in the cove of Anse Figuier, another privately run museum, the island's first *écomusée*, also targets the 1950s —"the traditional society we have forgotten in our rush to modernity . . . *la Martinique profonde.*"

Alongside these idealized recreations of the good old days of not so long ago, generally depicted as a timeless and ahistorical moment, there is another mode of institutionalized nostalgia—restorations of elegant eighteenth-century plantation houses, filled with period furniture. It may be worth noting that there is very little information provided, in either the "1950s" or the eighteenth-century exhibits, about the social relations of production—the fact that most of the work in both periods was done by agricultural gang labor (whether by slaves or waged men and women). Nor is colonialism more than a silent backdrop in either context. The 1950s exhibits, ostensibly depicting the domestic economy, focus on such activities as household food processing and artisanal production. And the eighteenth-century restorations portray leisured life in the great house. Both of these pastorals exude contentment.

More generally, nostalgia for the "ancestral" way of life, for "the way we used to live," is omnipresent in 1990s Martinique. Celebration of the *patrimoine* permeates the press, radio, and TV, animated by artists, musicians, dancers, taletellers, writers, theater groups, and cultural associations—with considerable financial support from the state (for example, the Conseil Régional). Commercialized folklore is available at every village fête and large hotel, and it floods the airwaves. One might well ask, Why this surge of interest in the everyday life of only a few years ago? Might this not be a powerful case of what Fredric Jameson has called "nostalgia for the present," a desperate hanging on to a rapidly disappearing way of life?

I would argue that the early 1960s in fact marked a watershed in Martinique. It was at that time that France began its concerted, aggressive program of development and integration that transformed this island neocolony into a modern consumer society with the highest standard of living in the region. Infrastructure boomed: roads, electricity, telephones, and piped water arrived in the most remote communities, and the airport, hotels, and marinas were dramatically expanded. Social programs (a panoply of welfare benefits, pensions, and unemployment insurance) pumped cash into family budgets. The standard size of houses tripled even as family size began to plummet. Agriculture was encouraged to atrophy as service industries (including tourism) and the civil service burgeoned. The number of cars per family quickly came to rival that in the United States, increasing tenfold between 1960 and 1990. Supermarkets, as well as megastores for building products, appliances, and other consumer goods, sprang up across the landscape. In the context of both France and the wider world, Martinique (along with Guadeloupe) became the largest per capita consumer of champagne anywhere. The media were modernized—both the daily newspaper *France-Antilles* and the nightly news broadcasts on TV date from 1964—and contributed to making the French language an important part of everyone's daily life. Fort-de-France mushroomed to represent nearly half the island's population, as people abandoned the countryside in droves. As the economy "modernized," unemployment skyrocketed, leaving between 20 percent and 60 percent of the active population, depending on age, officially unemployed (though often financially comfortable). And large numbers of Martiniquans were lured to the metropole in the 1960s and 1970s by official French programs designed to fill particular employment niches, creating the present situation that finds nearly 40 percent of the population settled in the Hexagon.

This unusually rapid modernization, largely imposed from the metropole, is profoundly assimilationist in spirit. And it demands the concomitant rejection of much of Martiniquan culture as it had developed during the previous three centuries—at least as a viable way of life for today's forward-looking generation. One television ad ridicules the country bumpkin, visiting his bourgeois cousins, who grates fruit to make juice rather than buying it readymade in a carton at the supermarket, and another mocks the simpleton who hacks at trees with a machete when a gasoline-powered brushwacker could fell them at the touch of a button. Such promotional campaigns have successfully created a whole range of "needs," such as electronic front gates, home security systems, bottled mineral water, travel agents, and canned dog food, that were virtually unknown just two decades ago.[33] And, in terms of values and self-perception, Martiniquans have been encouraged to situate themselves as thoroughly modern, bourgeois members of the First World (and Europe) and to look with benevolent condescension upon, say, Haitians, Saint Lucians, or Brazilians as their disadvantaged, sometimes picturesque, but backward Third World neighbors.[34]

Yet despite all this, Martiniquans (most Martiniquans) do not feel fully French. Nor, of course, do most Frenchmen consider them to be. At best, they are Frenchmen-with-a-difference, in part because of the racial discrimination they confront at every turn. In Paris, Antilleans are routinely confounded with, for example, illegal Malian immigrants in police sweeps of the subway. And more subtle psychological pressures are common as well:

> French [jazz] fans . . . are often confused hearing Michel Sardaby [often described as a "world-class jazz improviser"] play piano. His fire, confidence and experience, combined with his dark skin, can lead them to believe he's American. Frenchmen come up to him and speak English. When they discover he's actually Antillais, he says, "their tone changes. They talk to me like a child, they rub my hair and tell me how much they love the biguine and rum. I hesitate to talk about it."

And back home, where white immigrants from metropolitan France now constitute more than 10 percent of the island's residents, the battle for who "owns" Martinique is played out through hundreds of minor confrontations each day: a retired metropolitan gendarme complains to the police about the loud music at a Martiniquan restaurant next door and a highly politicized court case centered on charges of racism ensues; a Martiniquan protests that a tourist has blocked the entrance to his house with his rented car and a fist fight breaks out; and disputes flair up with increasing regularity over the hiring of metropolitan workers for local construction projects or in civil service positions. For Martiniquans, these kinds of incidents are tremendously charged and leave unresolved the personal tension inherent in being simultaneously Martiniquan and French.[35]

Two decades ago Glissant argued that cultural symbols of Martiniquan identity—music and dance, the Creole language, local cuisine, carnival—take on remarkable power in such contexts by fostering in people the illusion that they are representing themselves, that they are choosing the terms of their "difference," while at the same time obscuring the rapidity and completeness of the assimilationist project. This focus on *le culturel* and *le folklore*, he wrote, serves both the assimilators and the assimilating, by lulling the latter into complacency and helping mask the crushing force of the *mission civilisatrice*. Richard Burton, writing in Glissant's wake, has more recently argued that the agricultural (and, in some communes, fishing) base "on which traditional creole culture was founded has been eroded beyond all possibility of restoration, leaving that culture—where it survives at all—increasingly bereft of any anchorage in the actual lived experience of contemporary French West Indians and, as such, subject to a fatal combination of folklorization, exoticization, and commodification." The modern Martiniquan, he claims, is "as much a spectator of his or her 'own' culture as the average tourist: 'culture,' like everything else in Martinique today, is, it seems, something to be consumed rather than actively produced in a living human context."

Having made our home in Martinique for the past decade, Sally and I certainly understand what Burton, an occasional visitor to the island, is referring to—and understand his outrage.[36] Yet his requiem for Martinique's "traditional" culture requires additional commentary. The "*tristes tropiques*" narrative, which went with the territory of so much traditional anthropology, has been effectively

Rowing off the town of Anses d'Arlet, 1962

called into question during the past couple of decades—and in any case never sat very comfortably in the Afro-Caribbean. And this image of the erosion of "traditional creole culture . . . beyond all possibility of restoration," though widely touted by Martiniquan intellectuals,[37] is ultimately dependent on reified and outdated notions of both "tradition" and "culture" that cannot do justice to ongoing developments on the ground.[38]

SOME VIGNETTES based on recent experience may help texture this master narrative of loss and add hints about current renegotiations of identity. I begin with several events, sponsored by agencies of the state but planned and carried out very much by Martiniquans, that collectively speak to these issues. In these contexts, one sees up close some of the ways that memories of oppression, inequality, and struggle are being replaced by nostalgia, complicity, and celebration. And one sees the active reinvention of history, identity, and consciousness in particularly Martiniquan ways.[39]

☞ December 1995. Pasted to the wall of the grocery where I buy the newspaper each morning, a poster publicizes Anses d'Arlet's annual Culture Week. Besides the usual displays of traditional dance and drumming, storytelling, and crafts by performers from other parts of the island, it announces an evening "Spectacle by the Sea" to be put on by the Theater of History, a professional troupe from the capital.

On the appointed evening, Sally and I headed down the hill and arrived just in time to greet the mayor and his entourage, gathered on the esplanade above the beach. We also shook hands with José Alpha, director of the Theater of History whom we'd met several years earlier, and St.-Oïde Marie-Angélique, a local fisherman who had been recruited to help with the sound-and-light spectacle. Soon, dramatic music (among other selections, "In the Hall of the Mountain King" from Grieg's *Peer Gynt*) swelled from banks of giant speakers, and tall columns of spotlights focused on the nighttime bay.

"*La pêche miraculeuse de 1944*," as Alpha called the play, was narrated before a microphone by an actress in impeccable, limpid French—in the literary past tense, punctuated by an occasional quotation in Creole ("Et Ti Passio courrut chez Raoul, '*Pè Raoul, vini wè sa, gadé sa*'").[40] The narrator began, "The story we are about to tell may be a legend for some, while for others it may seem like a dream, a mystery emerging from the imagination of a few elderly fishermen who lived that day in 1944, one of the enigmas of the sea." She then recounted how, one afternoon in 1944, while returning from Fort-de-France in his canoe, Albert Theneran surprised an enormous school of *bariolé* (skipjack tuna), larger than any ever before seen in the bay of Anses d'Arlet. At this point, the music surged and a fisherman from Petite Anse called out from his canoe, fifty yards offshore, to Ti Passio (Passionisse Jean-Alphonse) and St.-Oïde, standing on the esplanade, that there were boatloads and boatloads of fish all around him. St.-Oïde carefully read some lines before the microphone, describing the activities the announcement set in motion—including having the conch-shell blown to alert the town—as a few men began pulling on the lines of a seine that had been deployed before the start of the spectacle. After St.-Oïde's text described how the whole town had turned out to *fè ralé, fè ralé*—haul in the ropes—the narrator led both the cast and spectators in a rhythmic work chant, as the net was hauled in. And then, with the drums reaching a crescendo, in the middle of the diminishing oval formed by the incoming seine, the star of the show—a full-figured siren in a sequined bathing suit, who had been supine on a rubber raft in the dark—slipped into the sea and, under the glare of the spotlights, swam ashore to perform a "sexy" dance on the esplanade and writhe around suggestively on the sand, to the beat of a couple of female drummers with elaborately corn-rowed hairdos. She then distributed chunks of bread, representing abundance (and the distribution of the miraculous catch) to all within her reach. And once she had finally danced herself out, the creature was gingerly carried by St.-Oïde and Ti Passio back to the sea, where they let her swim free into the depths (onto her rubber raft).

Sponsored by various government agencies, the island's main vernacular theater group had developed the four-page script based, in part, on discussions with local fishermen. The walk-on, nonspeaking cast consisted of the mayor's men (his municipal councilors and employees) plus a few of his fishermen kinsmen, and Ti Passio and the gentlemanly St.-Oïde, both now septuagenarians. There weren't a lot of spectators—besides the mayor and his group, just the usual Saturday night crowd out on the esplanade, lining the rail one deep. Alpha directed with verve, himself controlling the sound system and lights, gesticulating like an orchestra conductor toward this or that actor or drummer. He clearly enjoyed having been granted the resources necessary to create and then realize this performance, "based," as he said to us proudly after the show had ended, "on a local legend."

A couple of days after the fact, *France-Antilles* published an enthusiastic account:

> ALL DAY LONG THE TOWN OF ANSES D'ARLET WAS ABUZZ WITH TALK
> OF THE SPECTACULAR SHOW—"THE MIRACULOUS CATCH OF 1944,"
> featuring the dancer Sonia Marc—which local fishermen presented
> the previous evening on the water. . . . This creation of José Alpha's
> Theater of History will later be reenacted for TV under the sponsorship of the municipality of Anses d'Arlet.

Yet when I asked Angéline, who runs the grocery, what she'd thought of the show, she shrugged. "When I saw that what they were doing was pulling in a seine," she said, "I decided to go home to bed." Indeed, despite the newspaper hype, in Anses d'Arlet nobody at all seemed to be talking about the previous night's spectacle, the climactic event of Culture Week. I made a point of listening in the rumshop: not a word. I brought it up with loungers on the waterfront: utter indifference.

In this case, I would argue, such indifference might best be read as a quiet form of resistance. What, after all, could Arlesiens be *expected* to say of such an event, in which their everyday lives are turned into folklore before their very eyes and, in some sense, with their own passive complicity? When the sounds and sights of seining (which, during the season, still wake up the town each morning) become officially celebrated and textualized by city intellectuals in the name of the cultural patrimony, how else can local people resist the pressure to see themselves through the eyes of others?

The idea for the evening spectacle had sprung from the Municipal Office of Culture's hope that local people—in particular fishermen—might this year be "integrated" into Culture Week. They contacted Alpha, who liked the idea and, in preparation for his commission, chatted several times with local fishermen—at the *mairie*, where hardly any showed up, then at a bar and a fisherman's house, where it went a bit better—about "big catches" they remembered, pressing for "the earliest," which they eventually decided was sometime "during Vichy" (*an tan Robè*). Although the fishermen were generally reticent, Alpha managed, as he later told me, "to summarize the story, and do a bit of fictionalizing as well." He also chose a plausible date for the event—to lend it historical authority.

In their discussions, the fishermen also had taught Alpha that schools of tuna and other pelagic fish almost always follow a "pilot"—a single fish of another species (often a shark or a ray) that leads them for hours and, if

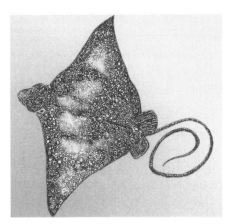

A *lanj* or *wakawa*

pulled from the sea, causes the whole school to dive into the depths and disappear.[41] And in answer to Alpha's questions, the fishermen told him that in that 1940s catch, the pilot had been a *lanj* (an eagle ray, *Aetobatus narinari*). Alpha's artistic imagination equated *lanj* (which can also mean angel) with a mermaid—though local fishermen, who know a lot about mermaids [*sirèn, mama dlo*] do not associate the two—and *The Miraculous Catch* was born.[42] When Alpha pressed the fishermen about the fate of the *lanj* that day, they finally admitted they'd simply killed and eaten it. Finding this poetically infelicitous, and even believing he might—through his script and their participation in the spectacle—relieve what he perceived to be the fishermen's pent-up guilt about this long-ago act, he decided that in the play St.-Oïde and Ti Passio should free the *lanj* from the seine and lay her back in the open waters to return, perhaps, another day, with another bounteous catch in tow. Indeed, Alpha considered adding another invented detail—having the *lanj* cry out from the seine (in Creole), "Set me free, Set me free," with the youngest child of that day's master-of-the-seine being the only one who could hear the plea—but the logistics became too complex, as the actress didn't have the strength to swim around in the nighttime waters sufficiently long for all this to take place, and it was written out of the final script.[43]

When I discussed the performance a few weeks after the fact with St.-Oïde, his characteristic politesse gave way to disapproval. Though proud of the role he had played, he complained that he'd been unable to persuade Alpha about the proper portrayal of the *lanj*. The actress, he insisted, should have worn a long, full skirt that covered her from waist to toes and spread out, to mime a ray, on the surface of the water. Once she swam ashore according to Alpha's scenario, they should have carried her back, quickly and gently, into the sea. Her dancing and, especially, all that writhing around on the sand, he said, was *malpropre* (in bad taste, obscene), and in any case, the real *lanj* has a form that tapers into a fishtail, not spread-open legs! He had suggested to Alpha that he get local children to swim around en masse within the seine, simulating the agitation of the circling *bariolés*, but Alpha hadn't taken up the idea.[44]

St.-Oïde seemed eager to tell me his version of what happened the day of that catch—how the fish were first sighted by Romuld Jean-Alphonse on the heights near our present house and how Romuld yelled down the hill and the cry was relayed, until St.-Oïde and others down in town rushed for the seine canoes. And how by then the school had veered toward open water to the north, but, luckily, a fisherman on his way back from the city, meeting the churning *bariolés* head on, was able to make enough of a commotion beating an oar on the surface to turn them back into the bay, where the seines could encircle them. He also said that the decision to eat the *lanj* rather than returning it to the sea was a whim, entirely without further consequence.

For present purposes, I would stress that Alpha represents *The Miraculous Catch of 1944* as true vernacular history (people's history, the fruit of oral testimony), part of his larger project "to depict the places, the events, and the people of Martinique and to valorize the memories of the old folks." For I would class it, instead, as another example of the tendency for the modernizing Martiniquan state (and its agencies) to turn selected aspects of the everyday into Historic Event, to transform those features of the quotidian that interfere with "development" into Official Folklore. However innocently (and I certainly do not mean to question their motives) José Alpha, his Theater of History, and the Municipal Office of Culture are contributing, I would argue, to a mystification that risks lulling themselves as well as those they portray into a false consciousness about the past, about identity, and about relations of power.

But no one is fooling St.-Oïde. He told me pointedly, toward the end of our conversation, "The mayor doesn't like to be reminded that there are still nearly one hundred working seines in Anses d'Arlet." After all, seining doesn't mix with the pleasure craft, the jet-skis, or the skin-divers that the modernizing commune is encouraging on its beachfronts. So there is a certain logic in the public celebration of "traditions" like seining as part of the cultural patrimony. For in the process, the serious work of professional fishermen such as St.-Oïde and his sons can be transformed into a fairy-tale, an evening's entertainment, and a showpiece of Culture Week.

As a further example of this kind of museumification or folklorization, with its relaxed attitude toward historical accuracy—always effected in the name of nationalism, island specificity, and identity—I would call attention to the latest *Guide Gallimard* for Martinique, written in part by local university professors and covering with apparent expertise everything from plate tectonics and marine life to history and literature. In a review of that work, Sally and I noted:

> It views ongoing cultural practices with a downward gaze, combining folklorization and museumification (with scarcely a word to let the reader know that Martinique's largest industry is tourism, which is wreaking great transformations throughout the isle). We are told, for example, in a handsomely illustrated two-page spread on the *gonmyé* (the fishing boat dating back to the Caribs) that this craft *"n'est plus utilisé actuellement que pour les courses traditionelles"* ["is no longer in use except for 'traditional' canoe races"]—and yet as we sit at the laptop and look out at Anse Chaudière through a papaya tree, we can see one *gonmyé* whose occupant is pulling fishpots, two others engaged in laying out a *balaou* seine, and a fourth making its way from the *bourg* of Anses d'Arlet toward Petite Anse. And the blatant appropriation of illustrations from foreign historical sources renders poor service to the text's arguments for Martinique's specificity. The authors give no indication, for example, that the *Indien Caraïbe* on page 76 is a Kaliña from Suriname. Nor that the most important depictions of slave life are also lifted wholesale (and without credit) from Benoit's lithographs of that Dutch colony, embellished with a newly constructed commentary implying that they show the particularities of Martinique—the text accompanying *Slaves Returning*

from the Fields (which Benoit titled *Slaves on Their Way to the Fields*) points to the unusual elegance of their clothing; Benoit's *Wigmaker with his Young Slave* is described here as wearing "the clothing of a freedman, proud that he need not carry anything himself"; the depiction of a slave fête, accompanied by a quote from Frantz Fanon, fails to mention that the image in fact shows the distinctive Surinamese *doe*; the entry on *le costume* ("In rags or nearly naked while working, the slaves liked to dress up, whenever they could, in fine clothing and jewelry") in fact shows typical nineteenth-century *"missie"* dress from Suriname; and even the vision of the heroic Maroon (here embedded in quotes from Césaire, Chamoiseau, Confiant, and Glissant) is illustrated by two uncredited images from Suriname—one a runaway slave and the other a slave(!) that Benoit drew carrying a basket for his master (who is here simply cropped out of the picture).

Culture Week's *Case Créole*

☞ After spending the evening watching *The Miraculous Catch*, we crossed the street to the Place de l'Eglise, where the *case créole*—a creole cabin erected by the municipality as the centerpiece of Culture Week 1994—was still standing. "The *case créole* is the most characteristic form of folk housing in Martinique," the head of the Municipal Office of Culture had begun his speech the year before. "Originally the dwelling of the Arawaks and then the Caribs, it was taken over by the early French settlers before becoming home to the slaves and, after abolition, to the peasantry. The *case créole* constitutes one of the greatest riches of our cultural patrimony." A number of dignitaries—the mayors of Anses d'Arlet, Diamant, and Trois Ilets, several members of the Conseil Régional and Conseil Général, a visiting Frenchman representing the National Bureau of Historic Buildings—and some seventy-five others had attended the inauguration of the *case créole*. A brochure explained that the purpose of the exhibit was "to permit younger people to better understand the history of their land by viewing the material culture of yesteryear."[45] Except that it had been sanitized—the cow-dung cement that normally chinks the walls of a *case créole* had been omitted—this exhibition house was pretty much indistinguishable from the home of Monsieur Ador, where Médard's colonel had been harbored until fifteen years ago.

At the inauguration, no one made mention of the fact that many of those present (or at least their parents) had once lived in such a house. Or that there were still a scattering of such houses at the edge of town, in Petite Anse, and, especially, on the beach of Grande Anse, where the municipality was in the process of razing them and moving the residents into public housing apartments, officially for purposes of public hygiene—but according to widespread rumors to make room for a large hotel. Indeed, from the eighteenth century till the 1980s, a row of similar *cases créoles* had lined the beach of Anses d'Arlet where we had just seen José Alpha's spectacle. Fishermen, their nets drying on poles above the waterline, had whiled away the afternoons in rumshops whose back doors gave directly onto the sand. There was little space for tourists and few visited. Then a decade ago, by orders of the modernizing municipality, the creole houses were razed, the inhabitants relocated to suburban-type homes on an inland savannah, and a white-sand beach, lined by a concrete esplanade modeled on the one in Nice, was put in place. Tourists came. Hotels opened. Drugs and burglaries arrived. Anses d'Arlet discovered it was postcard-picturesque.[46]

☞ In 1993, the theme of Anses d'Arlet's Culture Week, announced on posters pasted up throughout the commune, was the mysterious word *"Bityé."* At the inaugural celebrations—which, like all events at the *mairie*, were conducted in French—Michel Delbois, director of the Municipal Office of Culture, apologized that they had not used the local Creole word *bituwé* (provision ground, highland garden, swidden) on the poster and brochure, explaining that the only written version they could find was in a dictionary of Guadeloupean Creole. After reading a brief Creole poem he had composed about *bituwé* (and remarking that the language "must have sounded like Chinese to many of you"), he reminded the audience that *bituwé* had been part and parcel of the life of the older people present in the room (and he nodded, with a smile, toward his mother, amidst applause). And then Emile Capgras, president of the Conseil Régional, read a brief *éloge* to Martiniquan agriculture.[47]

Vice-Mayor Eugène Larcher thanked various state agencies for support of this year's Culture Week and introduced the evening's guest of honor, Monsieur Clairicia, the final manager/overseer of La Sucrerie—the distillery, owned by

The manager's house, La Sucrerie, 1996

the Hayot family, that dominated the economy of Anses d'Arlet (and still owns a predominant proportion of the commune's land) until the machinery was allowed to break down once and for all in the early 1950s. Clairicia read a hand-written memoir about his days as plantation manager, after which various digni-taries complimented him by stressing his fidelity and service to Monsieur Hayot. Finally, Mayor Olga Delbois presented a short reminiscence of how, as a teenager, he and his friends would snitch canes to eat but managed never to get caught by the redoubtable M. Clairicia. He also told how his own father, a Petite Anse fisherman, would seek permission in the off-season to make a *bituwé* on the high grounds of La Sucrerie, giving one-third of the charcoal he produced to M. Clairicia as the plantation's share. M. Clairicia, he stressed, had always been "correct" with his father and treated him fairly.[48] Delbois, like several other speakers, called Clairicia "a living library" of the history of Anses d'Arlet. And the mayor's *éloge* of the *bituwé* of long ago, like those of the other speakers, was Georgic in its sonorities. No one mentioned that, throughout the commune today, and even within sight of the ultramodern *mairie* in which we sat, there were scores of *bituwé* in which local families continue to grow ground provisions and make charcoal. And in the question period, when I pointed out that many of our neighbors still made and sold large quantities of charcoal—that *bituwé* were not simply part of the olden days—the speakers insisted that I was mistaken and (rather testily) that my misinformation was making Anses d'Arlet sound like Haiti.

Somewhat shaken by this exchange—and perhaps still under the influence of the champagne served with petit-fours following the Cultural Event—I went home and wrote a note about what I'd witnessed after leaving the *mairie*, at the other end of the street. (Sometimes even an anthropologist who spends much of his professional life questioning the notion of authenticity[49] has his moments of conceptual backsliding):

> Around Rosine's rumshop, we came upon a boisterous, picturesque *chanté noël*, five or so men playing accordion, drums, and shakers and scrapers inside under bright light, and outside—on plastic chairs spread around—thirty or so women belting out the songs. Marie [our closest neighbor] walked by and stood up in front to lead a song,

old Mme Jérome was sitting in the rear singing along, etc. Large groups of men lined the walls across the street, watching and kibitz-ing. The atmosphere was of a people's fête, happy, animated, sweet and rude at the same time, culture that has muscle.[50]

The official Culture Week festivities continued the next night with a lecture by historian Léo Elisabeth on "The History of Sugar in Anses d'Arlet." He spoke authoritatively about which planters owned what lands during which peri-ods, what they produced and how much they got for it, the rise and decline of various properties, and how the different branches of planter families intermar-ried. When, in the question period, I asked whether we hadn't heard the history of *békés* but not the rest, he reiterated that in the early years there were as many or more whites as slaves and that it was the original clearing of the forested land that was really tough—when the masters worked right alongside their servants. The history of sugar, he insisted, was the history of whites (though he did say, in response to a question, that at the height of Anses d'Arlet population growth, there were some three hundred whites but more than fourteen hundred slaves). It was a discourse we were familiar with from other recent histories: poor French settlers and their faithful African servants laboring side by side to create a brave new world in the tropics.[51] (Rather like the advertisements reported from 1995 Barbados for hotel floor shows, where visitors are invited to "see the cultures of the Caribbean as influenced by the Spanish, French and African *settlers*.")

☞ In 1989, we witnessed the local centerpiece of the Eighth Annual "Days of Tradition," sponsored by the Parc Régional de la Martinique and the Conseil Régional. The year's theme: The Sea and Fishing. The venue: the "local club" of Petite Anse, just across the road from the sand where several dozen fishermen beach their canoes and lay out their seine nets each morning. An outsider's view—from the latest *Guide Hachette*—helps set the scene:

> You drive through the village of Anses d'Arlet. The cliff-hugging coastal road gets even narrower, climbing incredibly steep slopes. The exceptionally dry climate in this part of the island lends the sea a surprising clarity, the ochre and beige cliffs plunge into a glimmer-ing, pure turquoise sea. The little road climbs bravely on, giving the courageous traveler the most beautiful panoramas one could wish

for. From certain spots on the road one can see the bottom of the sea, the quivering branches of coral. . . . Tiny, rudimentary huts, of cement blocks or bricks, the hamlet of Petite Anse wears its poverty like a badge. The earth, strewn with great dark boulders, is so arid that only brambles and small bushes manage to survive. Luckily, there is the sea. The fishermen of Petite Anse are well-known and, despite their isolation, people come from afar to buy their fish. It is true that these fishermen are not afraid of venturing great distances from the land.

Mayor Olga Delbois, who spent much of his childhood on this beach, opened the meeting, attended almost exclusively by fishermen and their wives, with the announcement that he had arranged with the Yacht Club of Schoelcher to orga-nize a regatta (for pleasure-craft) the coming weekend just off the coast. After the races, "typical seafood dishes" would be offered in Anses d'Arlet to the participants. Then two outside experts gave brief lectures about fishing: the first discoursed on "the image of the Martiniquan fisherman." He projected a slide of a *gonmyé*, another of an out-board motor, and then said that this type of craft, descended from the Caribs, is no longer used, having been replaced some years ago by yoles, first wooden, then fiberglass. Looking out the open door, we could see more than twenty working *gonmyé* pulled up on the beach.[52] The second expert, representing a

The beach at Petite Anse, with its Carib-style *gonmyé* (mid-1990s)

French state agency concerned with the sea, described how artisanal fishing was no longer economically viable because of depleted fish stocks, and that the state should therefore not lower fuel costs as fishermen demand because that way younger men will be discouraged from taking up the trade, which—he assured the audience—is already moribund. The fishermen and their wives politely applauded the experts and then adjourned to the refreshment table.[53]

EACH OF THESE state-sponsored public events (and one could adduce many many more) takes some aspect of daily life—fishing, housing, gardening, wage-labor, language—and transforms it into official folklore through a combination of distancing/exoticizing and sanitizing/laundering, in the process erasing or obscuring central relations of power. But such public events are barely the tip of the iceberg. For the major pressures on people to see themselves and their "traditional" lifeways as others (the French) see them normally come in far more everyday guise.

Not long ago, during what the French call "*les grandes vacances*" (summer vacation), a woman, her husband, and their several children returned from metropolitan France, where they live and work, to their native Martinique, for a visit to her mother. (At the height of "summer," some four thousand Martiniquans fly in from Paris each day.) Like many others of that generation (born around 1950), they had left the island with material encouragement from the government soon after high school to take up employment in the metropole. On this particular visit—the French government pays such trips for the whole family every three years—they brought with them the family cat, a five-kilo, impressively pedigreed "*chat de race*," which they had had specially vaccinated (three office visits) and otherwise prepared for the experience. On just the second day of their Martiniquan stay, the cat disappeared. Rural neighbors, out of earshot, joked that it had "marooned." A month later, when we visited the woman's mother (an old friend), her daughter's family was still in mourning. "The cat," explained the son-in-law, had "meant so much to the children!" and had itself been a replacement for their previous cat, which had fallen from their sixth-floor public-housing flat in France, precipitating costly consultations with a pediatric therapist who specialized in loss and grieving.

Martiniquan neighbors, however, found the whole business droll. For rural

Martiniquans, cats are utilitarian, rat-chasing animals (who also possess certain malevolent supernatural properties and, sometimes, particularly in the past, provided the stuff of a tasty repast). Kicking them out of the way is a much more common mode of interaction than caressing them. "Perhaps," people said, "the pampered 'Metropolitan Cat' [as it had become known] had marooned because it disdained '*la cuisine créole*'!" Two days before the family's return to Europe, the truly skeletal cat, which had no experience as a hunter, showed up but despite intravenous interventions from a Fort-de-France veterinarian (which provoked the mirth of rural neighbors), it did not recuperate sufficiently to board Air France with the rest of the family for the trip back home.[54]

The man of the house, in the home where the visitors stayed, is a mechanic/handyman in one of the island's large hotels and has often told us how bright young French specialists "up to their ears in diplomas" are sent out to fix major machinery—air conditioners or refrigeration systems—but end up calling on him, a semiliterate who still earns the minimum wage after twenty years on the job, to fix the damn thing once they give up. He openly enjoyed the episode with the cat—to him, the arrogant, inept Frenchman incarnate. Yet his feelings, and those of other Martiniquans who have stayed on the island, are less simple toward the cat's owners—who are, after all, their own children who through emigration have become not *métropolitains* (for white Frenchmen remain in a class of their own) but *négropolitains*, Martiniquans who to some extent have gone native in reverse, adopting (sometimes exaggerated) French values and behavior. During their visit, the owners of the cat enjoyed holding forth, for anyone who would listen, on the scandalous narrowness of local roads, the absence of sidewalks, the laziness of the workforce, and other lagging indicators of local modernity. At the same time, they frequently engaged in a very different but equally distancing and patronizing discourse of folklorization and nostalgia.[55]

The visiting *négropolitain*, eating at a fisherman's table (where we are also present), exclaims, "Isn't it *remarkable* how you fishermen can go out beyond the sight of land, without a compass, and find your way back! How ever do you do it?" As the fisherman patiently explains about winds and waves and mentions that shallower seas (as in the Saint Lucia channel) tend to be rougher, the visitor is moved to exclaim, "How amazing! Rougher where shallower! Who would have thought it?" At the same time, the visitor's wife, born and brought up in the fishing village, obstinately discusses the place and its inhabitants only as scenes from her childhood, creating a quaint, frozen-in-time relic. And, before leaving, they buy a small fishtrap, to hang on their wall back home in the Paris suburbs. (This particularly ostentatious brand of alienation has spawned its own jokes among Martiniquans: Have you heard the one about the local guy who returned from Paris saying he didn't know how to speak Creole any more?[56] He was poking around the yard, asking at every turn, "And what do call *that* plant? And *this* one?" He saw a crab and asked, "And what do you call *that*?" When the crab bit his toe, he immediately cried out, "*Sa ka modé! Sa ka modé!*" ["It bites! It bites!" in perfect Creole].)[57]

For Martiniquans who have stayed on the island (some two-thirds of the population), the pressures from such summer returnees are reinforcements (made especially poignant because the purveyors of French *mentalités* are in this case their own children, brothers, and sisters) of the alienating pressures they experience every day of the year—from the media (radio and television for all, newspapers for those who read), the workplace, the banking system, the social security bureaucracy, the postal system, the hospitals, the schools, the *mairie*, the *préfecture*, the state-run gambling outlets,[58] and the supermarkets. Recently, we were chatting with a woman from the agricultural north who was selling tied-up bundles of *onyon payi* (Martinique onions, a kind of chives) plus parsley in Anses d'Arlet, on the occasion of a large market day. A local woman came up and said she wanted only parsley—she wasn't "used to" Martinique onions and only cooked with *French* onions—so could she have a packet without the *onyon payi*? A third woman, overhearing, began cursing under her breath, saying, "Who does she think she is? Doesn't she remember what onions she cooked with when there weren't any *onyon fwance*? If she doesn't like local onions, fine. But does she have to *denigrate* them? Some people!" (or, in Zora Neale Hurston's North American terms, "My people! My people!"). Meanwhile, *France-Antilles*, reporting on that exact market day, wrote

Direct from producers to consumers, the market fulfilled its promise as clients gathered as early as 4:30 a.m. This periodic initiative is fast becoming a tradition in this little southern fishing commune, where vegetables are otherwise bought from passing trucks originating in the north. Arlesiens seem to welcome the market with enthusiasm, *as the organizers help them relive the whole folklore of the country, all the traditions of the island*, by means of showcase-sales of the fruits of the earth, the sale of local juice (sugar-cane juice) and honey, well-known for its medicinal effects. [My italics]

By its special gaze, the newspaper manages to transform buying the week's vegetables into folkloric performance. Reading the account, a woman—whether buyer or seller—is encouraged to see herself as part of a colorful, traditional market scene, part of the patrimony of the island. Or else to distance herself as thoroughly modern, not the kind of person to use *onyon payi*.[59]

We may return to the world of *quimbois* for one last set of examples of the everyday assault upon local culture. Glissant, writing in the seventies, paved the way in an angry passage about the difference between what he viewed as "normal" modernization and the massive pressures to modernize that the French have imposed on Martinique, and he identified *marronnage* and *quimbois* as the two major symbols of resistance. The state, he argues, deliberately set out to transform both of these, trying to persuade Martiniquans that *nègres marrons* had been bandits and that *quimboiseurs* are charlatans. In the "modern" Petite Anse of today, there is no question that the frequency of consulting the *quimboiseur* (and the daily use of "magical" products—to assure success in fishing, and for self-protection, health, commerce, school exams, love, and other everyday concerns) has somewhat diminished. But even more, such consultations have become more or less "shameful" or "embarrassing" and have thus gone partly underground. The daily newspaper *France-Antilles* has played a signal role in this process, as have television exposés that periodically present similar perspectives—a combination of sensationalist fascination and downward-gazing ridicule.[60] Four recent newspaper clippings give the flavor.

A "VOYANT" TAKES ADVANTAGE OF HIS CLIENTS

Yvon Varasse, nicknamed Django, plied his trade near the church of Sainte-Thérèse in Fort-de-France. Until the day the gendarmes discovered that Varasse had swindled a family from the south of Martinique, receiving a considerable sum of cash plus seven gold

Napoleons against the promise of better fishing results. Not satisfied with having cheated these people, the so-called *"voyant"* also took advantage—twice—of the youngest daughter of the family, age 16.

The *"gadedzafè"* had threatened the adolescent that he would put "spirits" upon her if she spoke to her parents about these goings-on. According to the victim, she was told that the sexual relations forced on her by the *voyant* were necessary for the success of his "work."

This new affair demonstrates once again—as if it were still necessary—how very numerous are the charlatans who do not hesitate to extract the maximum profit from the credulity of people who are already in dire straits. The victims, who believe they are going to better their situation, end up, as always, with nothing but disappointment.

Abuse of Power. Setting Himself Up as *Voyant*, Olive Ivrisse Took Advantage of His Clients

It is one of the most lucrative professions. And of a disarming simplicity, as long as you are a fast talker with a fertile imagination, and you're graced with the gifts of a conman and enjoy taking advantage of people, without worrying about where the necessary means come from or where it all might lead. In order not to hurt anyone's feelings, let's just say we're writing about men and women who, one day, suddenly decide they have extraordinary powers and put them at the disposition of the public, in order to "fix up" their problems of all sorts—emotional, physical, or moral. It takes no diploma to get yourself set up as *quimboiseur, sorcier,* or *gadedzafè.* Any place will do, as long as you're ready to take advantage of the misery, distress, credulity, and naiveté of ordinary men and women.

Women—there's the achilles heel of these pseudo-sorcerers. By nature rogues, they cannot resist the temptations of the flesh. By simple means of medicinal interventions, which destroy reflexes and create a sense of lethargy in the victim, they go on to take full advantage of her body.

It was after reading in this newspaper, twice within the space of several weeks, about sexual abuses committed by two pseudo-sorcerers, that a young woman presented herself to the detective bureau of the Fort-de-France police. A man claiming to be a *quimboiseur* had taken advantage of her when she went to consult him. Following up this complaint, the gendarmes arrested Olive Ivrisse, who had set himself up as *gadedzafè* in Fort-de-France. The details of the rape, which occurred in 1988, included the administration of some sort of noxious vapors which rendered her helpless and allowed him to have his way with her. . . . Ivrisse . . . was arraigned on charges of illegal practice of medicine and indecent assault and imprisoned in Fort-de-France.

THE *QUIMBOISEUR* TOOK ADVANTAGE OF HIS FEMALE CLIENTS

He was leading the good life, this *quimboiseur*. Thanks to his little office, which was rarely empty, the money flowed in and the *voyant-guérisseur* had accumulated a nest egg of nearly one million francs. And even better, this *quimboiseur* practiced therapeutic methods that were just a bit unusual when his clients were female.

If, to take an example, the woman was young and good-looking, he would frighten her by saying she was possessed by a *dorliss* [incubus]. And to exorcise it, he would suggest a method both radical and efficacious—sexual intercourse! With him, of course, and for the measly sum of 1700 francs . . . This is how Sylvie R. was forced to submit three times to the assaults of the *quimboiseur*.

But in the case of Madame G., a woman of 65 who sold candies for a living, the treatment was different. He contented himself with offering her a miraculous lotion for 25,000 francs. . . .

The criminal court sentenced him to five years. . . .

THE PERVERTED HEALER

The police have just put an end to the practice of a 59-year-old man who profited from his "consultations" to take advantage of his young victims. Three girls aged ten and fourteen have confirmed that they were abused by this man. Their parents had brought them to this *guérisseur* believing they had been bewitched, and having full confidence in F. Unhappily, once the girls were alone with him, he allowed himself all sorts of liberties. . . . Following up on the complaint of one of the parents, the police were able to arrest the man and charge him with corrupting a minor.

It is worth underlining the uncomfortable ambivalence of such reports, which write so disdainfully of "pseudo-sorcerers" and "so-called *voyants*," but suggest, by the same token, the existence of authentic, honest *sorciers*, *voyants*, and *quimboiseurs*. It is worth noting also that on the same page of *France-Antilles* as, for example, "Abuse of Power," there are five large, boxed ads, two with pictures, for a "*voyant*," "*grand voyant*," "*grand médium africain*," "*méthode égyptienne*," and a "*parapsychologue*." Local *quimboiseurs*, in contrast, hardly need to advertise in *France-Antilles*.

Zédui—needle for mending nets, carved in *zamouret* ("purpleheart") wood by Philibert Larcher, 1986

IN 1990, WHILE Sally and I were teaching at Stanford for the semester, Médard's story took an unexpected turn. Quite out of the blue, Michèle Baj Strobel—who taught art history in Martinique and knew of my interest in Médard—sent us a clipping from *France-Antilles*:

> "The True and Accurate History of Médard Aribot": A Sound-and-Light Spectacle written by Vincent Placoly, directed by José Alpha, with music by Léon Sainte-Rose, to be presented by the "Association Bel Age" and the "Theater of History" on the beach at Sainte-Luce, 5 May, 7 p.m., and on the beach at Diamant, 19 May, 7 p.m.

On our return to the island in June, Baj invited us to dinner with Alpha and Placoly (though in the end the latter was unable to make it).

Alpha enthusiastically told us that the production had drawn two thousand spectators at Sainte-Luce and nearly as many in Diamant. He stressed the grandeur of the spectacle, which he said used fifty actors, two sound towers, multiple banks of lights, neck microphones plus standing ones for the actors, and even a smoke machine. He also recounted how he and Placoly (the talented playwright who was then in the final stages of alcohol poisoning) had first come upon my 1985 *Caribbean Review* article in the Departmental Archives, how they had photocopied and then read and hashed it over during the following weeks, how they had gone out and interviewed a few of the people it pointed them to, and how they had spent whole nights drinking together and conjuring up a vision of what Médard's life might have been like. The Association Bel Age of Sainte-Luce, a senior citizen's group from Médard's natal commune, played a key role, supplying additional memories of Médard and participating in the spectacle itself. Alpha, as well as the *France-Antilles* clippings he showed me, described the productions on the beach as "triumphs."[61]

Alpha told me that in developing the script—in addition to the information in my article and the suggestions of the senior citizen's group—he and Placoly had "made up" or "filled in" events and characters that seemed to them dramatically interesting and historically plausible. Their goal was very much to catch truth through art—the unpublished script that Alpha kindly shared with me (for use in this book) is titled *La Véritable Histoire de Médard Aribot*. But it is subtitled *Vision Poétique*.

The particular vision they came up with is unblinkingly centered on the colonial past—oppression by the state, class and race inequalities, poverty of the masses. It deliberately celebrates the unique culture developed in the colonial communes of the island by introducing various figures, and trades, from the past—artisanal mattress-makers, market women, butchers, laundresses, the many and various types of sugar-cane workers. . . . But this celebration, in contrast to so many in modern Martinique, is not a whitewash. Placoly's script includes, at the top of the market scene, this explicit stage direction: "Avoid the appearance of a diorama or a postcard, even though characteristic gestures and words are to be used."

Alpha told me that in working on the project, he and Placoly were repeatedly struck by the absence of official documents, especially that no known photo of Médard exists.[62] So, he said, they conceived the idea of having a ubiquitous old-fashioned photographer, with a box camera on a tripod and hand-held flash, attempting to record the ongoing story for posterity. In fact, however, Placoly drew on well-known historical details for this aspect of the script, transposing events that occurred that same election day in Ducos and describing them in words that come almost directly from the *Historial Antillais* (to which he penned a handwritten reference on his scenario).[63] This is how Placoly's script positions the photographer on that fatal election day in Diamant, in a face-off with the colonel:

> COPPENS (to the photographer): Who gave you authorization to take photos?
>
> PHOTOGRAPHER: I work for anyone who pays me. . . . You have no right to erase the memory of history—the memory of what happens in my country.
>
> COPPENS: I'm the one who represents the law here!
>
> PHOTOGRAPHER: You haven't been elected yet.
>
> COPPENS: Listen! I've got the support of Governor Richard, the representative of France in the Antilles. And since you're so bent on capturing history, why don't you just write down that in the colonies of France, force will always determine the law.
>
> PHOTOGRAPHER: Buying votes at 1000 francs apiece, with the ill-gotten gains of the ten families who run the country as if they believe we are still in slavery-times, makes your so-called law weigh less than a sack full of wind.
>
> COPPENS: Lieutenant, arrest this Communist for me. . . .
> (the photographer is expelled with great brutality)
>
> COPPENS (to the gendarmes): Go ahead, start the voting. Let's get this farce over with.

The election scene itself, with the massed crowd at one end of the stage holding up colorful anticolonial banners, and the governor's troops and machine-gun in front of the *mairie* at the other, is the stuff of high drama. Night falls and

Coppens calls out to the police to seize the ballot box and bring it into the gendarmerie:

> (At the other end of the stage, the crowd raises Médard's frightening bust of the colonel. Coppens sees it and lets out a tremendous scream of terror and pain.)

COPPENS: Arrest the bearers! Arrest the carriers!

> (He falls [shot]. The bust of Coppens wobbles, as if one of the carriers had been wounded. And then, the enormous effigy tips over amidst great confusion. The smoke clears. The scene looks like the end of a battle.)

The script, which has Médard sentenced to the *bagne* for having made the effigy,[64] stages a scene in which his mother, Marie-Thérèse, bids him adieu. (In 1990, Alpha explained to me that, in order to better emphasize the link with Africa that is a leitmotif of their play, he and Placoly had decided to depict Marie-Thérèse, who was born in Martinique, as an African who arrived in 1877—the last year, they were told by a historian whom they asked, that a ship carrying Congos landed on the island.[65])

> MARIE-THÉRÈSE [in French[66]]: My son, my son, my little one. What have you done to make that ancient sadness, which haunted my childhood and youth, return to my gut, weakened by so much childbearing, by so many vain hopes tossed out on the gaming table of life, so much unexpressed love, so much affection held onto through thick and thin? Have I ever abandoned you, even for a moment—even when I wasn't right there? Have you ever ceased hearing the invisible voice of my heartbeats, which endlessly repeat, and hammer out, this scream: "I love my children and, in giving them life, I've given life to the mortar, to the peat, to the clay from which are molded the past, the present, and the future. I've retied the thread that my Hausa ancestors wove, with the patience of dreaming artisans, the thread that joined one mountainpeak to the next." Don't turn your back on me. . . . You don't turn your back on your own mother! . . . I've sailed a ship on the high seas, a ship of

torments. . . . Don't you see, child, women like your mother are condemned to live from one tempest to the next. One day, chained and dazed and beaten in the bottom of the hold, I dreamed that no child born of my womb would ever bear chains. And now that I'm an old woman, I see you and you're draped with chains like a knight of darkness, waiting for the ship of my nightmares to come carry you away from me. . . . My child, I make this wish: Before the gods, if they exist . . . may these chains lead you back to the land where I was born, so you can see, once again, in my place, the lion of the reeds and the antelope of the plains.

Late in the play, Médard returns from the *bagne* and meditates about the relative silence he has adopted:

"No Talking Allowed.". . . During the interminable days when the ship that was carrying me back from the *bagne* wandered the seas, I heard the rattling of chains against the wooden beams of the deck. . . . But as I came closer to the shores of my country, fresh blood coursed through my veins, a green dizziness sent my old man's head spinning, with my eyes turned white because I had seen Death. . . . I have neither the right nor the power to bring to justice those who wrongly sentenced me . . . Where are my mother and father today? . . . The air stinks of trickery and despair, of lethargic sleeps and lies, of blindness and stifling alkali. It kills, suffocates, strangles, anesthetizes anyone who has anything real to say. . . . Since birth, my heart has been set to the hour of night, the sarcophagus night, the pyramidical night, the Hausa night. . . . I was not born to the music of this world. . . . If I expose the froth of my saliva to the light of day, they'll find another excuse to enchain me. . . . All I have left is the work of my hands.

The play ends with a message of universality, as the elderly Médard, innocently playing his tiny piano to entertain some schoolgirls, is chased from the stage by an angry, "respectable" mother who dashes the piano to the ground and chides her children for wasting their time with "trash." Médard lovingly picks up the piano and "plays some simple notes, the pure music of hope."[67] Enter the senior citizen's group as chorus:

> Honorable Spectators, The time has come to drop the curtain. . . .
> But before you leave, young and old, rich and poor, whoever you
> may be, remember this well: How many Médards have you run
> across in your life without seeing them? Is it that they didn't speak
> up? Or might it be that we were afraid to hear what they had to say,
> that we were blinded by an inability to see things as they really are?

Of the five or six plays that Alpha's Theater of History has produced,[68] *The True and Accurate History* seems closest to the organization's stated goals of "valorizing (or celebrating) the memories of the old folks." The Theater's first commission (from the Conseil Général, in 1987) celebrated the inauguration of the Musée de la Pagerie, girlhood home of future Empress Joséphine, and depicted two incidents from the life of this figure, whose role in the restoration of slavery by Napoleon remains a matter of lively controversy in Martinique. The second commission concerned the colonization of Martinique by the French filibuster Pierre Belain d'Esnambuc in 1635 and had as historical advisors Léo Elisabeth and the official historical society of Martinique. Then came a commemoration of

Scene from *The True and Accurate History of Médard Aribot*, 1990

the eruption of the Mont Pelée volcano in 1902. And so on—ending with *The Miraculous Catch*. Between events and people that the history books recognize as "historical"—from d'Esnambuc and Joséphine to the Mont Pelée eruption—and the staging of "local legends" like *The Miraculous Catch*, the play about Médard would seem to hold a middle ground. Based ultimately on oral testimony (even if filtered through a journal article), it was—when performed—*meaningful* history, a version of people's own past that they could recognize and identify with.

Indeed, the 1990 Placoly-Alpha collaboration (with cooperation from the Association Bel Age) rescued Médard's story—but for how long?—from the process of terminal postcarding. In the two or three performances, Médard's memory was once again imbued with the powerful symbolic valence it had held for the fisherfolk I spoke with in the 1970s and early eighties. Over and above its artistic embellishments, this version of Médard's story focused on colonial repression and on the ultimate triumph of the human spirit. But it was not long before this *True and Accurate History* was publicly contested.

While working on the play, Alpha and another colleague had published an article, "The Legend and the Truth about Médard Aribot," in the state-sponsored journal of Martinique's *patrimoine*. Summarizing the Alpha/Placoly version of Medard's life (including the "fact" that Médard was sentenced to the *bagne* for having sculpted the colonel), the piece also proselytized for Alpha's "people-centered" historical research:[69]

> The Association Bel Age is well aware of the historical importance
> of oral testimony, so dear to our ancestors, and aware that these par-
> ticular pages of history have never piqued the curiosity of tradi-
> tional historians. In this regard, the Association wishes . . . to val-
> orize anecdotal history and invest it with all of its cultural force.

The first response to this article came in the form of a professional historians' disclaimer, written by the editors of the *Cahiers du Patrimoine*. It speaks directly to the issues of authority and documentation so dear to traditional historians.

> The text you have just read, which represents only the opinions of
> its authors, would seem to us to consist largely of legend. Whatever
> one might think of the colonial era, and in particular of the procon-
> sulate of Governor Richard, it seems clear that no individual could

be legally charged for having made a statue of someone, whether or not that someone was a colonel. We should also note that José Alpha has consulted the Departmental Archives and the contemporary press—and that while there is much on the tragic events of the Diamant elections there is not the slightest trace of any trial involving Médard Aribot. Moreover, the Conservator of the Martiniquan Bureau du Patrimoine alerted her counterpart in Guyane who, after having consulted the Archives of the Bagne, found no mention of Médard Aribot. . . . His life, however close to us in time, still entirely escapes us historically.[70]

The second response did not come until several years later but has broader implications and reached a wider audience. The weekend magazine of *France-Antilles*, under its "History" rubric, presented a two-part, illustrated article, "Médard Aribot, Artist or Convict?" Calling into service one of its favored tropes in writing about the Martiniquan past—what we might call "History as Mystery"—the newspaper employs ridicule and innuendo to attack the credibility of the Alpha/Placoly vision (and the 1970s/early 1980s fishermen's vision) of colonial realities as symbolized by Médard's life. Instead, very much in line with the zeitgeist of modern Martinique, it celebrates the artistic (folkloric, picturesque) aspect of his legacy. Though the article uses no new sources, it seems worth quoting at length because, when considered in light of the written and oral documentation in the present book, it has so much to teach us about the ongoing (re)construction (and the silencing) of history.[71] And also because, for the moment at least, it seems to have won the day in the consciousness of Martiniquans.

> **Médard Aribot, Artist or Convict?** His life seems closest to a marvelous folktale, however sad. Was he a convict? There's nothing that proves it. But that he was an artist couldn't be clearer! Once upon a time, there was a poor Congo-woman named Marie-Thérèse, who arrived in one of the last convoys of indentured Africans after Abolition. The year was 1877, she was only sixteen—a marginal woman, excluded from creole society because she was a Congo. On 9 June 1901, in the ruins of the Céron plantation at

Sainte-Luce, in the most miserable of circumstances, Marie-Thérèse Congo gave birth to a bouncing boy named Médard Aribot. And it was under the name of Médard that the boy, soon a strapping youth, a *nèg noua*, would earn his special notoriety.

What was the origin of his patronym, Aribot? No one knows. And no one knows what happened to his mother Marie-Thérèse either. . . .

But is there a single tourist who has passed through Anse Caffard in Diamant and not conscientiously photographed that delicious little multicolored house, said to be "of the convict"? Facing the illustrious Rock, restored by the painter Thierry Coco, it is a miniature masterpiece, the work of an original, of an artist partly mad.

This was Médard Aribot—builder, architect, carpenter, mason, and roofer, who gave free rein to his creative spirit between 1950 and 1960. . . . Whether in Sainte-Luce or Diamant, he was described as a loner, quiet, an escapee from the strict norms of his time. He went from place to place collecting detritus—old bottles, pieces of wood, packaging materials—not for utilitarian ends but to create new objects, forms, and sculptures, for all of which he was regarded with deep suspicion. Original, marginal, suspect, perhaps abnormal, speaking little, living alone and never having had a woman in his life, he was dismissed from military service as mentally unfit, his unsociability being confused with madness.

In 1925, Médard was twenty-five. May 25th witnessed the municipal elections and passions were running high. . . . Médard, who did not participate in politics and lived in some other world, happened to sculpt—without ideology, without partisan politics, but simply as a subject like any other—the bust of Colonel Maurice Coppens, a sculpture so realistic it constituted a satire of the candidate. Coppens's opponents paraded the effigy, at once mocking and true-to-life, in their electoral marches.

[There follows a brief account of the Diamant massacre, noting that there were ten dead and twelve wounded]. . . .

As Médard's staunch defenders tell the tale, "They needed a

scapegoat." And who better than Médard, that misunderstood pariah? It is said that he was condemned to fifteen years' banishment in French Guiana, though no one seems to know the name of the judge or the tribunal that sentenced him. There is no record of the matter in the contemporary press. Even the leftist papers, so ready in those agitated times to make accusations at the drop of a hat, contain not a whisper. "Médard came back from Cayenne fifteen years later, after 1940," say his faithful defenders today, even specifying that he was "crippled and twisted because they'd kept him in a tiny underground cell." But such claims owe more to dreams and imagination than to reality.

The Archives of the Bagne at Aix-en-Provence have not found a single trace of this alleged convict. If Médard Aribot ever went to French Guiana, it would have been for a wholly different reason and at some wholly different time. And as for the idea that he might have been registered under some other name, that is equally ridiculous.

Thus, the martyrdom of Médard Aribot must be considered a legend growing from the fertile popular imagination. . . . Such a legend could, of course, derive from a particular vision of reality, as the *Cahiers du Patrimoine* has pointed out, in which to make a portrait of a person means to bring a curse, or even death, upon him.[72] After all, in those days there were still many Congos living in Diamant. And Médard Aribot is said to have made the bust of the colonel only days before the latter's dramatic demise. In any case, this statue greatly contributed to Médard's legend. Until just a few years ago, it graced a fishermen's bar in Petite Anse. Now it is gone, perhaps stolen or simply "borrowed" by an anonymous admirer.[73]

Médard turned up again only after 1940. Where did he pass those long years—in the *bagne* (and why?) or in Martinique? That long, fifteen-year parenthesis will forever remain unexplained. Nothing in effect proves that he ever set foot in the *bagne* of Guyane. Perhaps he stayed in Martinique, perhaps he went to Guyane but not as a convict. No one will ever know. But he did reappear in Diamant in the 1940s where he continued to work as an artist. . . .

In the early 1950s, at Anse Caffard, he constructed that tiny house which first brought him fame. . . . He preferred working in miniature, but always with a sense of balance, and though he constantly changed colors he retained a strong preference for our national colors of blue-white-red. Didn't he go so far as to put a French flag made from tin on the facade of his house? He made a bust of Pétain, then one of De Gaulle. Indeed, he even created what for some remains his masterpiece, or at least his best-known work,[74] the bust of *The King of the Indies*. . . .

He died, indigent, in 1973, to the almost universal indifference of the general public.

In a reflection on collective memory in Martinique, sociologist Marie-José Jolivet observes that "To denounce the 'erasure,' to denounce collective 'amnesia,' is little more than to deplore the fact that collective memory is not what one would like it to be" (for example, the kind of heroic, counter-hegemonic version of the past that fishermen told in the 1970s). But historical consciousness—collective memory— is never monolithic. Whether in Martinique or the rain forest of Suriname, it is always embedded in ongoing social process. For Martiniquans, the meanings of the past actively reflect (and contribute to) the multilayered, fragmented, deeply contradictory realities of their social existence. Just as a leading republican politician assured me recently that "within every Martiniquan there lurks a Marie-Jeanne" (that is, a dream of independence), just below the surface of modernization and assimilation there lurks the spirit of resistance.[75] For the present, the anticolonial message associated with Médard has receded, almost to the point of flickering out. But circumstances change, and it would be a rash ethnographer who could feel certain that Médard and the *guerre du Diamant* might not emerge from their present "folkloric" trappings and assume their place as part of the richer historical experience that makes Martinique and its people all they are, or might one day become.

IT IS TO the mysterious *King of the Indies* that we grant the final word. For his image serves to summon up the meandering subterranean streams of historical consciousness that continue to course through Martinique. In the *Cahiers du Patrimoine*, José Alpha had illustrated what he called—following my 1985 article—*Le Roi des Indes*, and he wrote that this sculpture by Médard represents "the bust of a legendary figure whose secret only the artist knew." But sometime in 1986, Georges Radinez, a Martinique-born customs official then completing his nineteenth year in the grey surroundings of Paris, indirectly reminded me that historical consciousness is deeply rooted and that understanding the current postcolonial moment demands as much subtlety, and art, as an ethnographer can muster.

While visiting the Ville Lumière, I had happened to recount to Georges's Martiniquan/Parisian girlfriend (Liliane Larcher, one of Emilien's sisters) the recent personal discovery, in a fisherman's home by the sea near Diamant, of the haunting wooden sculpture by Médard—evidently a king, with a golden (cigarette-paper) crown, epaulets, medals, brown skin, and sea-blue eyes—that Nora Angély, who owned the piece, said (or so I thought I heard him say) Médard had told him was *Le Roi des Ingues*. "*Des* <u>Ingues</u>?" I asked, uncomprehending. "*Oui,*" said Nora. Trying again, unsure, I asked "*des* <u>Indes</u>?" "*Oui, oui, le Roi des Indes,*" I heard. And so, on the cover of *Caribbean Review* appeared, in full color, with its evocative name, *The King of the Indies*.

CARIBBEAN
REVIEW
Vol. XIV, No. 3
Three Dollars

The King of the Indies, on the cover of *Caribbean Review*, summer 1985

It was that far-off customs official who, by suggesting to his girlfriend that I had perhaps found an image of *"le roi* Béhanzin" (which had been spoken by Nora as *"le roi* Bé-zingue"[76]), ushered me into a privileged corner of the Martiniquan collective consciousness, one that Glissant, had I been more attentive, had already prefigured when he alluded to: "Béhanzin, 'King of Africa', mirror of the exiled . . . ever roaming through our unconscious." And, in fact, back in his kitchen in Martinique, Nora told me that Médard (barefoot, illiterate, "mad")—whose whole *oeuvre* might be read as a discourse on colonialism—had

Nora, in front of two framed paintings, a tapestry depicting German shepherds, a small conch shell, and some wiring leading across Médard's King to an amplifier set on the refrigerator (1986)

sculpted not *Le Roi des Indes* but *Le Roi Béhanʒin* ("a true *rwa kongo*," Nora added), the final ruler of Dahomey, the heroic resister to the French penetration of Africa, in the words of Chamoiseau's filmic maroon, "Our King."[77]

Le roi Béhanzin Ahydjéré, in exile in Martinique (postcard, ca. 1900)

THE POET OBSERVES the outward signs of island modernity. And restlessly questions his conscience.

> . . . that other life going in its "change for the best,"
> its peace paralyzed on a postcard, a concrete
> future ahead of it all, in the cinder-blocks
> of hotel development. . . .

> I watched the afternoon sea. Didn't I want the poor
> to stay in the same light so that I could transfix
> them in amber, the afterglow of an empire,
> preferring a shed of palm-thatch with tilted sticks
> to that blue bus-stop? . . .

> Art is History's nostalgia, it prefers a thatched
> roof to a concrete factory. . . .

> Hadn't I made their poverty my paradise?

The honest anthropologist must wrestle with similar demons (though in Martinique poverty may be less to the point than in Walcott's Saint Lucia). Clifford Geertz, writing (somewhere between exhaustion and ennui) of being an anthropologist at the end of the twentieth century, recently argued that "To convey this, what it is to be an anthropologist not off somewhere beyond the reach of headlines but on some sort of fault line between the large and the little . . . what is needed, or anyway must serve, is tableaus, anecdotes, parables, tales: mininarratives with the narrator in them."

But for many of my generation, this kind of being an anthropologist is not quite enough. For what if, with Glissant, we also want to accept the challenge "to struggle against a single History and for the cross-fertilization of histories, to rediscover at once one's true time and identity, and to question in unexpected ways the nature of power"? How might one also write about that?

FIN

"Did you ever hear of Napoleon," asked Atipa, "who used to be a general over there in France? . . . He married a woman from Martinique and cancelled emancipation so that the blacks wouldn't stop working in the canefields of his father-in-law. And the day they raised a statue to his wife in Martinique, a black man covered it all over with shit. It was the only thing he could think of doing. They sentenced him to three months."

[N.B. Slavery was abolished under the Convention in 1794, and reestablished by Napoleon in 1802.]

—Alfred Parépou, *Atipa (roman guyanais)*, 1987 [1885], generally considered the first novel published in Creole.

Joséphine, in her glory days

Notes

PART I

1. The roll call is long. To cite but two examples: In 1870, a popular insurrection centered in Rivière-Pilote saw hundreds of agricultural laborers burn plantations, resulting in four deaths—and an official colonial response sentencing six of the leaders to death, eight others to death in absentia, twenty-eight others to forced labor for life, and thirty-three others to more limited prison terms (Abénon 1982:414). In 1900, there was a wave of strikes among sugar workers, forcing the *békés* to renounce their plan for lowering wages—during which the *forces de l'ordre*, including a detachment of naval infantry, killed eight (or nine?) workers and wounded more than a dozen others (de Lépine 1980:17, Abénon 1982:424, Adelaïde-Merlande 1994:255, Darsières 1996:75).

2. "A cette époque, on dit, le clergé toujours marchait avec la noblesse. Nous sommes parti tiers état (nous les ti malheureux), tous ceux qui n'a pas de l'argent ceux sont des types du tiers état." The complete interview, mainly in French with some Creole phrases, was recorded on tape at the home of Philibert Larcher in Diamant on 28 May 1986. Quotes from Philibert later in this chapter are from that same session. It may be worth noting that Philibert's greatest pride was reserved for his role in the Resistance during World War II, when he served as a *passeur de gens* who braved Vichy reprisals to clandestinely transport—by sailing canoe, through mines and battleships—Martiniquans wishing to flee the occupied island to join the Free French via Saint Lucia (and thence to the United States). In addition to telling countless stories of his adventures during these nighttime sorties, he loved to display the personal letter of appreciation he received after the war from an aide to General de Gaulle. Philibert died in 1992.

3. The photo shows the entrance to the *mairie* in the commune of Trinité. As the *béké* industrialist Fernand Clerc notes in his annotation on the photo, which he sent to the minister of the colonies in Paris, "Not a voter in sight" (Archives d'Outre-mer, Affaires Politiques, carton 317).

4. This is the man named in one contemporary newspaper article "Lessanges" and in another "Faustin Lésanges." He was on the Bloc Républicain list for the municipal elections (*La Riposte*, 13 May 1925).

5. Several years before, Philibert gave a much shorter version of the events of 3 May to a local historian, who quoted him as saying, in full, "Around ten in the morning we forced the door of the *mairie*. Inside, ten men armed with clubs were waiting for us: policemen, customs officials, and rural police. I'd scarcely gotten through the door when I was smashed on the head and lost consciousness. Two others were wounded but I was the only one taken to the hospital in Saint-Esprit" (Maran 1986:207).

    The late Armand Ribier, then mayor of Diamant, told me in 1986 that "the man who struck Philibert was a certain Dessanges, a customs-man by profession." Ribier also claimed that, when the crowd of socialists stormed into the *mairie* at 8 a.m., it was Brigade Chief Battistini himself who, with the butt of his rifle, smashed the top of the ballot box to expose the three hundred fraudulent ballots. This story, placing Battestini as an unofficial socialist sympathizer, fits the allegations made by Governor Richard (see pp. 35, 37), that he was a friend of Lagrosillière.

6. De Lépine described early twentieth-century Martinique as "a classic colony, in that fundamental power resided in the French state, where the system of *'l'Exclusif'* continued to control relations with the metropole— Martinique exported everything that she produced, sugar and rum, to France, and she imported from France everything that she consumed, all the rest. . . . But at the same time, Martinique had a special colonial status, in part because of her age as a colony . . . and her people, who as slaves resisted less than those in other places the pressures of the masters, now vigorously desired not independence but complete assimilation into the French nation" (1980:8–9). He adds that while the British West Indian colonies were turning increasingly toward national independence, the French ones were moving energetically toward assimilation (Ibid.:14). Parry and Sherlock give a similar assessment of Martinique during this period, within the broader Caribbean context: "Politically speaking . . . [its history] was singularly uneventful. In form, government was representative on a wide franchise; in fact, the French governor was necessarily still the dominant power. . . Such

things as primary education and social services hardly existed. Economically and socially the history of Martinique . . . was one of somnolent stagnation punctuated by occasional riots or natural disasters" (1971:250).

7. Aubéry was married to the daughter of the island's richest man, Gabriel Hayot. A decade later in 1934, in one of the ugliest incidents of all colonial Caribbean history, he arranged for the assassination of investigative journalist and communist leader André Aliker. Celma's "La vie politique . . ." has some excellent pages on the events leading to Aliker's death (1981:336-47). She describes dispassionately and in detail how the industrial oligarchy of *békés* used intermediaries—civil servants and politicians—to control the economic life of the island, how they corrupted the civil service and the judiciary, keeping them at their beck and call, and how they controlled the elected representatives of the island in Paris. And how Aliker's investigative journalism about Aubéry's business dealings simply became too much for the *békés* to tolerate.

8. Lagrosillière seems to be referring to a common practice of the time for the governor, aided by the *parti de l'usine* (party of the sugar factory owners), to select out those civil servants who would not play ball and have them dismissed or transferred from the island for pretended violations. By the 1920s, this practice had become widespread and was the source of numerous letters of complaint to the minister of colonies. In 1924, the minister circulated a letter to all the governors of the "*vieilles colonies*"—"I am constantly besieged by civil servants with formal complaints regarding measures taken against them, in particular, transfers they consider illegal. . . . I hardly need remind the governors of the oldest colonies that I am firmly resolved to require political neutrality and absolute impartiality" (6 December 1924, cited in Mauvois 1990:91).

9. Colonel de Coppens—the rightist candidate for mayor of Diamant in 1925—had commanded a regiment of the colonial artillery and, after retiring from the military in 1920, served as "the specialist on economic questions in the Conseil Général of Martinique and is considered one of the most remarkable men in the colony" (*Petit Parisien*, 26 May 1925). He was married with four children and "during the course of the war had obtained numerous and

brilliant *citations*" (*Le Matin*, 1 June 1925). Born in the Martiniquan commune of Robert in 1873, he served in Indochina as well as in Europe during
World War I and had been decorated with the rosette of the *Légion d'honneur*, "*une belle citation avec palmes*" (a pretty medal with bars) (*La Paix*, 30
May 1925).

10. Lémery, who practiced law and served as *sénateur* in Paris, is described at
    this period of his life as "urbane, an elegant and articulate mulatto, an
    habitué of gracious dinners where he rubbed shoulders with ministers,
    politicians, high functionaries, and the influential journalists of the capital.
    He himself boasted of having the special friendship of the President of the
    République" (Mauvois 1990:53). Although he began his political career in
    Paris as a socialist, in 1906, he moved rapidly and increasingly to the right.
    By 1938 he had been decorated by Mussolini with one of fascist Italy's high-
    est honors (for having supported the invasion of Ethiopia) and then, in
    1940, served under the Vichy regime as minister of the colonies (de Lépine
    1980:11). For further biographical details, see Darsières 1996:276.

11. Lémery made the alliance clear when, on the eve of the cantonal elections
    of 1923, he told the mayor of Gros-Morne, "You have nothing to fear. You
    have the governor and the armed forces on your side. Everything will take
    place peacefully and, by orders of the minister, we will have the majority,
    exactly as in Rivière-Pilote [where, with the complicity of the gendarmerie,
    there had been massive electoral fraud]." And on election day, forty gen-
    darmes and fifty soldiers did, in fact, surround the *mairie* and kept at a dis-
    tance those from the opposing political camp (see Mauvois 1990:80–81).

12. Roughly 10,000 "Congos" arrived in Martinique in the late 1850s and early
    1860s. More precisely, between 6 July 1857 and 6 August 1862, 10,521
    Africans—including 9,925 from Congo Brazzaville or Congo Kinshasa—
    arrived on twenty-four ships as contract laborers. Of these, 70 percent were
    between twelve and twenty years old. By 1862, only 7,742 were still alive;
    most of the others had succumbed to illness. By 1900, there were 5,345 left
    (David 1978).

13. See R. Price 1966a on the ways that fishing has provided a way out of the
    master–slave (patron–worker) system for Caribbean men from the seven-
    teenth century to the present.

14. Richard's telegram to Hesse begins "Extremely urgent, personal and confidential—electoral campaign promises to be particularly violent. Local agitators crisscrossing colony preaching murder and mayhem" (cited at greater length in Mauvois 1990:110). The minister of the colonies had already sent special reinforcements to Richard for the elections: twenty-five men and an officer on 6 February and the naval vessel *Antares*, which, it was specified, would lie off Fort-de-France [or stay in port] "until end May" (Mauvois 1990:107).

15. The archives include various letters from the governor's political allies warning him, a couple of months before the event, that this special ballot box was to be constructed, as well as various testimonies from local gendarmes that were relevant to the trial against those responsible. In a "confidential" letter dated 13 May, the governor described to the minister of the colonies in detail how the Carbet *urne*, specially constructed by the socialists, had one-millimeter slits so that the presiding mayor could, from behind, slip ballots in unseen (Archives d'Outre-mer, Affaires Politiques, carton 317).

    The rightist French press reveled in such stories, tending to trivialize Martiniquan affairs, adopting a paternalistic, downward-looking gaze, and viewing the socialists as silly, naughty children. The special correspondent to *Le Matin* sent back the following report, right after the municipal elections of 3 May: Headlines: "MARTINIQUE, THE PROMISED LAND, WHERE EVERYTHING, even voters, grows with miraculous ease. Various examples of spontaneous generation between the opening of the polls and the vote count." Three of the socialist-run communes are offered as "examples"—the article claims that in Schoelcher, where 927 voters were on the lists, 6,190 ballots were counted, including 6,156 for the "Communist" list (and the total population numbered only 3,602); that in Morne Rouge, where there were 591 registered voters, 1,185 ballots were counted; and that in Sainte-Marie, where 3,043 voters were registered, just 1,390 were logged in as having actually voted, but the official results showed 4,526 votes for the socialists and only 14 for the rightists (7 May 1925).

16. A list from the archives, entitled "*SERVICE D'ORDRE DU 3 MAI 1925 POUR LES ELECTIONS MUNICIPALES*" gives, commune by com-

mune, the disposition of "gendarmes, soldiers or customs men." Diamant, though a tiny commune, received seventeen, only one fewer than Fort-de-France (Archives d'Outre-mer, Affaires Politiques, carton 777).

17. This photo is among those from Trinité sent by Fernand Clerc to the *chef de cabinet*, minister of the colonies, to bear witness to the municipal elections of 1925 (Archives d'Outre-mer, Affaires Politiques, carton 317).

18. Philibert's testimony is closely paralleled by that of his contemporary and fellow-fisherman Axionas Sénart, though I do not quote from it here. A recording of this latter's account of the 1925 elections, made in the late 1980s by the parish priest, B. David, was kindly lent me by Marie-Claire Joseph-Julien.

19. It appears that Governor Richard sent Brigade Chief Battestini, whose political sympathies he suspected, to another post that day and replaced him with Nouvel, who had led the recent assault on the sugar-strikers at Bassignac. Mayor Ribier of Diamant, when telling me the story of 24 May 1925, noted: "Brigade Chief Battestini, who had broken the ballot box on May 3, had been removed from Diamant and they'd sent the other."

20. These men may well have been using the widely known *maman-cochon* ("mother-pig") technique, taking a piece of paper—the mother pig—the same color as the ballots and folding it in such a way that it held, say, a dozen ballots and when slipped into the box allowed them to separate (Constant 1988:61).

21. A later official report specifies that by this time the crowd had heard of the murder of socialist *conseillers généraux* Des Étages and Zizine by a gendarme in Ducos and had become super-excited. It quotes the crowd as calling out "threats to Colonel de Coppens, to the president of the voting bureau, to the gendarmes and to the soldiers: 'You'll see tonight. We'll take care of you all. First COPPENS, then his running dogs, then his gendarmes and soldiers. We'll get all of you!'" "The moment," continues the report, "was truly propitious. The libations that had been consumed since the morning, the *'ponchs'* without which no election in the Antilles would be conceivable, had propelled a number of the demonstrators to the necessary degree of audacity" (Report of Inspector General Le Conte, dated 19 August 1925, Affaires Politiques, carton 3201).

22. By 9 August the Attorney General, needing justification for detaining "agitators," specified that these clubs "had been hidden in certain houses in town, in particular that of Emmanuel Roc, [socialist] candidate in the elections" (Beaudu, "Report to the Minister of the Colonies on the Events of 24 May," dated 9 August 1925, Archives d'Outre-mer, Affaires Politiques, carton 317).

23. An article in *France-Antilles*, largely derived from R. Price 1985, specifies, however, that the name of the machine-gunner was Méled Anglebert (Rabussier 1993a:49). The late Euphrasius ("Frazius") Canton, who served in the army with the machine-gunner, called him "Milèd" and told me in a 1986 discussion that he was a "caporal" or "sergeant."

24. One of the later official reports, bent on pinning guilt on particular individuals, specified: "The signal for the attack was given by Emmanuel ROC: 'Don't let the ballot box leave! It belongs to us. Bust it up. Don't let them take it to the gendarmerie. Let's get the gendarmes. Beat the shit out of them. Nothing will happen to you. Hurry, hurry!' The crowd responded by shouting out death threats. On the doorstep of his house, Tax Collector MENIVER (who only a short time before had been happy to receive from Colonel de Coppens the sum of five hundred francs, for which I have been shown the receipt) excited the assailants by pointing to the gendarmes, 'Kill them! Kill them! There's nothing to fear'" (Report of Inspector General Le Conte, dated 19 August 1925, Affaires Politiques, carton 3201).

25. Once again, Inspector General Le Conte's account (see previous note) escalates the stakes: "The band of some 500 demonstrators threw rocks, heavy seashells, and bottles filled with sand at the gendarmes and the soldiers—as well as shooting at them with revolvers. Hit in the face, Chief of Police Nouvel fell unconscious."

26. In front of the *mairie* of Trinité, May 1925. Fernand Clerc's annotation reads, "Trinité. Machine-gun at the door of the *mairie*. The populace massed behind barbed wire" (Archives d'Outre-mer, Affaires Politiques, carton 317).

27. This dispatch was published in *Paris-Soir* 28 May 1925, with the note that the Paris-based author was from Martinique, where he was visiting at the time (Archives d'Outre-mer, Affaires Politiques, carton 317).

28. Inspector General Le Conte quotes an unnamed source who claimed that in an electoral meeting in Diamant on 24 April, Lagrosillière had said, "If things like this had happened in Corsica, the voters would have picked up their rifles and stifled the fraud. . . . The four hundred voters of the [socialist] majority need only enter the *mairie*, delicately grab by the neck the forty who are in the minority, and toss them out the window" (Report of Inspector General Le Conte, 19 August 1925, Affaires Politiques, carton 3201).

29. Henri Thorel was, in fact, sixth on the list of Sainte-Rose in the elections (*La Riposte: Organe de la Jeunesse républicaine Martiniquaise*, 13 May 1925).

30. In a conversation with Inspector General Le Conte, Governor Richard gave fuller details about his choice of Cadrot, calling him "an energetic, level-headed, courageous man who—I must confess—is of the proper shade to impress the people of Diamant, who hate whites and everything they have to do with, with a hatred that knows no bounds" (Report of Le Conte, sent to Paris 19 August 1925, Affaires Politiques, carton 3201).

31. In giving his version of the events of 24 May, Mayor Ribier told me: "It was around four or five o'clock in the afternoon. Colonel Coppens had dined with the priest. He had a chauffeur named Hubert. When the machine-gun was fired, it had wounded the chauffeur. So, a fellow from Anse Caffard named Edvige Frédéric went to tell the Colonel that his chauffeur had been wounded. And the Colonel walked down from the presbytery where he saw his chauffeur lying on the ground in the street. As he bent over to see how badly he was hurt, he was hit by a bullet from the same machine-gun. . . . I don't know exactly how he managed it, but this same fellow, Edvige Frédéric—a veteran of the Great War—worked his way over to the machine-gunner and told him to hold his fire, the Commander was dead" (1986).

32. A later inspector general's report specified that "the eleven gendarmes and fifteen soldiers fired, during a period of about ten seconds, a total of 54 cartridges. . . . The troops continued to fire on those who were fleeing, according to the autopsies and medical certificates. Of the 21 people who were hit, the entry wounds for 11 of them show that they were hit either while they were fleeing or at the instant when they were already turning to run away" (Report of Inspector General Le Conte, dated 19 August 1925, Affaires Politiques, carton 3201).

33. Philibert told me that this man's name was Cléka, not Claka.

34. Mayor Ribier recalled these events in 1986: "So, the governor dispatched a boat—in those days there weren't cars like now—he sent a ship filled with gendarmes. But the people here, the fishermen, refused to disembark the gendarmes! They were out beyond the breakers and couldn't come in. Finally, they forced the men to go out in their canoes and bring them in. And that night, Diamant was under strict curfew. People couldn't go out or even have a lamp lit in their house. The gendarmes went around yelling, 'Close the doors. Close all doors. And shutters too. And extinguish all lights!'"

35. By August, as charges against Saint-Aimé were being further trumped up, Inspector General Le Conte reported that on 24 May, "About noon, Colonel Coppens came in to vote. He was followed very closely by a certain SAINT-AIMÉ Eloi (the man who would later be accused of having killed the Colonel and was one of the most aggressive of the demonstrators), who, when searched by the gendarmes, was found to have a dagger carefully hidden under his shirt." Later in the same report, Saint-Aimé is said to have been seen that afternoon, during the "rioting," pointing a gun at Chief of Police Nouvel (Report sent 19 August, Affaires Politiques, carton 3201).

36. Dr. Magallon-Graineau, socialist member of the Conseil Général and apparently in charge of the hospital at Saint-Esprit, pronounced the eulogy at the graves of his two murdered comrades. He said, in part:

> When I arrived a quarter of an hour after the event, there was nothing more I could do in my role as physician. . . . I saw the frightening cadaver of Des Étages, frozen in a look of horror . . . nose smashed in by the hard floor . . . struck dead before he knew what was happening, and Zizine, felled with almost a smile on his lips, stretching out a hand to touch that of Des Étages in a final fraternal gesture. And for three hours, a crowd coming from Saint-Esprit, from François, from Lamentin, from Petit-Bourg, from Rivière-Salée solemnly filed by the corpses, eyes filled with pity and consternation. This is what they did to our two friends!
>
> And the carnage continued, this time in the frightening hecatomb of Diamant. . . . One corpse! Two corpses! Three corpses! 4! 5! 6! 7! 8! 9! corpses. Ten corpses! A butcher's stall. A vision of Hell, a most horrible task: for the whole day of the 25th, my hands dug about in these poor caved-in chests, these burst hearts, this tortured flesh, piously profaning them. I am sweating blood! I am sweating blood! Yes, I want to transfuse into your veins all this horror, so that the memory of

those who died on our behalf will remain forever graven in your minds.

What an irony! Who would have thought, seven years ago as I dressed the wounds of the sons who were dying for Right and Liberty, struck down by German bullets, that today I would be performing autopsies on the fathers who died for Right and Liberty, struck down by French ones. . . .

Adieu Zizine! Adieu Des Étages! . . . . [Cited in Mauvois 1990:132-133]

Note that Martinique had furnished some fifteen thousand men to France's armies during World War I and that not much more than one in three survived to return home (Abénon 1982:426; Adelaïde-Merlande 1994:257 suggests a higher survival rate).

37. Cane-cutters were paid by the "task," which had since 1905 consisted of twenty piles of twenty-five bundles of ten one-meter-long canes—five thousand pieces of cane (de Lépine 1980:48).

38. The attorney general's report dated 9 August further specifies that "The aggressiveness of the crowd was such that, although being fired upon, some of the invaders lobbed rocks over the tops of the houses facing the barracks while others tried to scale the fence behind the building and fell back only when gendarmes Thoumassine, Delfour, and Brilh turned their revolvers on them" (Beaudu, Report to Minister of the Colonies, Affaires Politiques, carton 317).

39. On 21 August, aboard the steamship *Pellerin de Latouche*, in the first-class salon, while sipping champagne and bidding adieu to well-wishers, Governor Richard was shot five times with a revolver by one of the sons of Des Étages. Taken to hospital in Fort-de-France, Richard was awarded the *Légion d'honneur* by orders of Minister Hesse and finally left for France on 3 October aboard the Porto Rico. He never fully recovered from his wounds and died several years later.

40. Fernand Clerc's annotation reads, "Some idea of the atmosphere . . . . with a machine-gunner in front of the door to the *mairie* and the troops omnipresent. The populace is massed behind the barbed wire" (Archives d'Outre-mer, Affaires Politiques, carton 317; also cited in Celma 1981:354).

41. Philibert Larcher explained that the trials, parts of which he attended, were a travesty. The presiding judge, a *métropolitain*, did not understand Creole and hardly any of the defendants or witnesses could speak much French.

Philibert always got excited when talking about the trumped-up nature of the charges—"How in the world could Saint-Aimé have gotten his gun and shot Coppens right in the midst of all those gendarmes?"

PAQUEBOT " PELLERIN DE LATOUCHE "

". . . aboard the steamship *Pellerin de Latouche*"

PART II

1. Emilien told us he had changed the left arm from a horizontal position, palm up, to its present position after the statue fell and the arm came off. The arms, made of separate pieces of wood, appear to have originally been affixed with tree sap, probably *campêche*. According to Emilien, Médard often visited Ador Cuty. "Ador's house was his pied-à-terre in Petite Anse, his favorite place to hang out. That's why M. Ador owned the piece—but whether he bought it or Médard gave it to him, I don't know." The working notes Emilien watched us writing up describe the statue as follows: "47.5 cms high. Pants are blue with red dots. Jacket is yellow with red/brown/blue trim at wrists and a red collar (which has white trim). Face is same yellow as jacket. Hair, eyebrows, and moustache are black, lips are red, eyes white with black pupils. On his oversized, uneven-sized hands, there are red fingernails. Top of hat was dark blue but has been painted over red-

dish-brown. There are medals, a brown cross, red/white/blue ribbon, blue buttons, complex red tie, and pockets with buttons." Later, Dinette Louisy of Taupinière told us that Médard mixed his own paints and that his favorite yellow—the color of the "general's" face and jacket—was made from egg yolks.

2. Marie-Thérèse is described in the certificate as a "40-year-old day-laborer." Her two witnesses at the signing of the certificate were another day-laborer and a shoemaker, with only the latter able to sign his name.

3. Madame André Larcher, born in 1911 and a monolingual Creole speaker, reminisced for an hour or two with Sally and me, with the encouragement of her niece Liliane Larcher, at her home in Anse Caffard in 1986.

4. See Part I, note 12, above. Dinette rattled off the list of Congo names far too fast for me to write them down. I had to ask her to repeat them more slowly, for posterity, a few minutes later.

5. This passage prompted Ken Bilby to reflect, in an October 1996 letter to me:

There's an interesting parallel between the Diamant "war" of 1925 and the Bogle rebellion in Jamaica in 1865. Like Diamant, Morant Bay and the whole surrounding area in St. Thomas parish received a heavy concentration of post-emancipation indentured Africans (especially "Kongos"). Some of these Africans participated in the rebellion. Today, St. Thomas continues to be seen as the most "African" part of the island; the people are said to be "blacker" (and shorter in stature) than elsewhere in Jamaica, and those who practice Kumina are still called "Africans"; it's where Kumina religion introduced by the indentured Africans is centered (as Schuler shows) [see Schuler 1980]; some Kumina people can rattle off names of the Central African "tribes" of their foreparents; it's the poorest parish; descendants of the indentured Africans are especially concentrated in the sugar areas of the parish, and some still work on the sugar estates; because of its perceived "Africanness," the parish is still seen (by those so inclined) as the most "primitive" and "backward" part of Jamaica. But, especially among participants in Kumina and others of the lower strata in St. Thomas, this "Africanness" invests the memory of the Morant Bay rebellion with a powerful anticolonialist charge—one that is largely independent, I believe, of "official" government representations of Paul Bogle and the rebellion—to this day. The poorer people of St. Thomas, in particular, maintain a strong consciousness of the fact that "Bongo" people—"Africans" (including some of their own indentured ancestors)—played an important role in Bogle's rebellion. It's also significant (and recognized as such by local people) that the early Rasta movement got started here in "African" St. Thomas, as did the labor disruptions of 1938 that led to increased autonomy and eventual independence for Jamaica.

6. For older people in Petite Anse and Diamant, this recalcitrant-slave-in-a-barrel story is far and away the most commonly told brutality tale of slave times. Indeed, in many parts of Martinique, older people will point to the highest local hill and say, "that's where the *békés* used to roll down the slaves for punishment." For a lightly fictionalized version, see Confiant 1994a:143-44, and for a Guadeloupean version, Bébel-Gisler 1994:1.

7. Toni Morrison (1987:190) draws on the same trope in describing an exchange between a slave, Sixo, and his master, Schoolteacher, who surprised him in the act of eating one of the master's pigs.

> "Did you steal that shoat? You stole that shoat." Schoolteacher was quiet but firm. . . . "You stole that shoat, didn't you?"
>
> "No. Sir." said Sixo, but he had the decency to keep his eyes on the meat.
>
> "You telling me you didn't steal it, and I'm looking right at you?"
>
> "No, sir. I didn't steal it."
>
> Schoolteacher smiled. "Did you kill it?"
>
> "Yes, sir. I killed it."
>
> "Did you butcher it?"
>
> "Yes, sir."
>
> "Did you cook it?"
>
> "Yes, sir."
>
> "Well, then. Did you eat it?"
>
> "Yes, sir. I sure did."
>
> "And you telling me that's not stealing?"
>
> "No, sir. It ain't."
>
> "What is it then?"
>
> "Improving your property, sir."

8. This complete interview, recorded in 1986, is in Creole. Génor would have been about nine years old when these events occurred.

9. In August 1996, with the help of Hubert Larcher, I finally located Médard's seaside cave, which looks out at Diamond Rock through the crashing foam.

A giant landslide, apparently in the early 1960s, had rained down volcanic boulders from the heights of Morne Larcher and destroyed much of its splendor. But inside the entrance—formerly hidden by the dwarf *poirier* trees that cover the rocky hillside—the dark opening stretched upwards out of sight, providing more than enough storage space for the "merchandise" that Génor and others described.

10. This ship, made in the early 1970s, was bought shortly before Médard's death by Hubert Andrieu, the proprietor of l'Hotel Diamant les Bains, for two hundred *ancien* francs. Ti Louis confirmed this price when he told me that Médard normally charged three hundred to four hundred francs for a ship or other such large object. (Toward the end of his life, Médard also made small sailboats for the hotel to sell to tourists, according to the proprietor.) When we took notes on the piece in 1986, it was already well-eaten by termites, the wood paper-thin in places. "Length is 81 cms. Olive green with decoration in aqua, red, yellow, white. Silver paper in portholes. Includes megaphones, lifeboats, 'bentpipes,' protrusions of some sort, anchor, rudder (now missing), propeller on each side (now missing), keel."

11. Nankeen cloth was originally made in Nankin, China, from an unusual variety of cotton that was light yellow. By the early twentieth century, "nankeen" was commonly produced, with dyes, in Europe, especially for making trousers (O.E.D., s.v. *nankeen*). It was all the rage in the 1920s Caribbean (see, for example, Kincaid 1996:6, 151, passim).

12. At this point in the story, Madame Génor broke in to add that it was "A____ L____" who denounced Médard to the gendarmes. Génor said, "Yes. It was Diamant folks alright!"

13. Only two works of recent years have, in my view, fully succeeded—Bilby 1990 and Redfield 1995. Two other recent works have deliberately harnessed stereotype and cliché ironically, in order to sketch in a picture of the place (R. and S. Price 1992, 1995a).

Most literature on the *bagne* barely mentions *la relégation*. Almost all of the great memoirs (and pieces of investigative journalism) concern *transportés* or *déportés*—murderers, counterfeiters, political prisoners. (Seaton 1951 is an instructive exception, recounting the life of one of Médard's contemporaries in the *relégation*.) Here, doing my bit for history, I try hard both to stick to accounts of and about *relégués* and to use only materials relevant to the period of Médard's detention.

14. In 1985, traveling a circuitous archival path kindly cleared for me by Diane Vernon, I was able, through the good offices of Mlle. Marie-Antoinette Menier, to locate and gain access to Médard's conviction record in Paris, where the Archives d'Outre-mer were then located. It was the discovery of this document that led, a decade later, to my being able to obtain a copy of Médard's prison record during his time in the *bagne* (see pp. 102–105).

15. The final Conviction Notice of the Court of Appeals, dated 3 April 1933, further specifies that Médard "resided in Saint-Pierre" but that the crimes for which he was sentenced were "committed during a time when he was not present in Saint-Pierre" and took place shortly before his arrest on 1 November 1932.

16. In any case, Michelot reminds us that "From the murderer to the petty-thief *relégué*, while the reasons for their being sent to Guyane contrasted sharply, their punishments were essentially the same" (1981:232).

17. A *pied de biche* is a short claw-tipped crowbar, commonly used for breaking-and-entering. The *relégués* are reported, in turn, to have called the *transportés* by the derogatory nickname of *fagots* (Le Clère 1979:40).

18. Published statistics on the *bagne* are scattered and sporadic. Epailly claims, without citing sources, that during the whole history of *la relégation* (including both *individuelle* and *collective*), between 1 percent and 2 percent of the total came from Martinique (1994:163). Pierre gives the provenances of prisoners arriving in the apparently random year of 1926: there were 2 *transportés* shipped from Martinique and 5 from Guadeloupe—but no *relégués* from either. In that year, a grand total of 1,039 *transportés* and 278 *relégués* arrived in the penal colony (1982:315).

19. Epailly, citing no source, gives different figures but still in the same ballpark (1994:163).

20. Constructed in England in 1911, called the *Douala* (*Duala*) by the Germans, and used by them on the Hamburg-Cameroon route, the ship was ceded to the French at the Treaty of Versailles and rebaptized the *La Martinière*, to replace the *Loire*, which the Germans had torpedoed in 1916 (Donet-Vincent 1992:24, Findlay 1970:7, Michelot 1981:38). The *La Martinière* was, in

turn, sunk by the Germans in 1940, by torpedoes according to Findlay (1970:9), in an aerial attack according to Le Clère (1979:293).

21. Francis Lagrange, who signed his paintings with his nickname "F.LAG," arrived in Guyane exactly three years before Médard, as a *relégué collectif* (though he was later transferred to the category of *transporté*, following an escape and subsequent conviction for counterfeiting). One of the most colorful of all *bagnards*, he left several sets of a series of some twenty-five similar paintings of penal colony life, most of which are in private hands but one of which remains in the Musée Franconie in Cayenne. (On his life and work, see Lagrange 1961, Epailly 1994.)

22. "The arrival by ship up the Maroni is pure enchantment. One sees graceful coconut palms, pink-walled villas, and cottages set in fabulous vegetation, where purple hibiscus throw out their flames" (Alexis Danan 1934, cited in Michelot 1981:59–60) .

From the quay stretched a broad street, bordered on the left by the home of the Chief of the Port and on the right by a monument to Victor Schoelcher, liberator of the slaves. . . . Further along were the offices of the Compagnie Générale Transatlantique and those of the Penal Administration. A side street led to the brick factory and the slaughterhouse. Another was bordered by the postoffice, the courts, the public treasury, and the governor's mansion. Past the Camp de la Transportation, surrounded by high walls, and on to the several customs houses. . . . A military barracks and then the fine colonial hospital, built in 1912. . . . And the Chinese *quartier*, where the shops are. In the center of town, there was a public "*salle de fêtes*," the telephone office, the bank, and the church, and, just beyond, the cemetery. (Pierre 1982:72–73)

23. At my behest, Ken, kindly taking time off from his own doctoral research in Guyane, was asking around Saint-Laurent to see if any of the *vieux blancs*—former convicts—remembered Médard. As Ken described it: While speaking with such a man, a certain M. Baron who worked in the public hospital of Saint-Laurent (the former prison hospital), "another hospital employee passed by and overheard part of the conversation. He came up to me and asked if this Aribot was an '*ancien forçat*' [former convict] from Martinique. When I confirmed this, he asked whether he used to make various kinds of

'*trucs*' [things] with his hands. I said yes, and he told me then that one of the ships that Aribot had made was in one of the offices of the hospital" (Letter of January 1984).

24. The final, total number of *relégués* seems to have been 15,995, which suggests that Médard was among the very last to be registered (Michelot 1981:84). Epailly gives a slighter higher figure that includes prisoners who were transferred from the *transportation* to the *relégation* (1994:163). A further indication of the unreliability of published statistics on the *bagne* is that in a single edited work published by the Archives d'Outre-mer, Pierre gives the total number of *relégués* as 18,000 (1990:42) and Krakovitch as 15,600 (1990:39).

25. Details from Médard's *registre matricule* are taken from Archives d'Outre-mer, coté Colonies H 5319 (Aix-en-Provence), a copy of which was kindly supplied me in 1995 by Silvie Clair. The *registre* covers the period 22 March 1934 to 13 June 1942.

26. This place was often described as a true chamber of horrors, where men with tuberculosis and other lingering illnesses were left, largely without care, to slowly expire. Visitors, including physicians, were unanimous about its scandalousness (Pierre 1982:74). Médard's *relégué* contemporary George Seaton, who visited once to deliver stores, said: "A Hogarth would be needed to convey the abomination of that jungle hell. . . . Men with cancer, men coughing their way to a tubercular death, distorted syphilitics, lumbering victims of elephantiasis, monsters with ankylostomiasis, men without arms, men without legs, men without minds. . . . Idiots, their tongues lolling and their heads hanging, slouched and slipped like grotesque children. Some muttered to themselves, others giggled hysterically, a few were glassy-eyed and silent. . . . Perhaps worst of all was the smell" (Seaton 1951:68–69).

27. Michelot dates the ballet to 1935 and says that men fought with knives for Coronella's favors (1981:134). Belbenoit, a former *bagnard*, claims that he managed to visit the *relégué* barracks where Coronella lived, one night in the 1930s: "It was hard to believe that this was a man. The soft face, white with a thick layer of scented powder, the heavily rouged lips, the corsage of bright red Japanese silk, with a silk shirt of the same color, the high-heeled

blue silk shoes, were all those of a real woman. Even the lack of hair was concealed by a piece of silk wound round the head. . . . There were five or six more *relégué* women-men in the barracks dressed in female garb. They were dancing with their *forts-à-bras* to the music of an accordion" (1941:254–55). Le Clère adds, "Undoubtedly, there was little guards could do in the barracks where prisoners where shut up for the night without any surveillance and where young men were brutally forced to submit to older convicts. . . . In any case, the turnkeys—almost all Arabs and all homosexuals—decided which prisoners would sleep in which barracks" (1979:202, drawing on Péan 1934).

28. As this book went to press, on a visit to Cayenne, I was shown a privately owned manuscript written by another *relégué* contemporary of Médard, Marcel Dunand, who served as bookkeeper for the *relégation*. This 169-page retrospective diary (Dunand n.d.) covers the period 1927 to 1935 and repeatedly confirms the picture of life in St. Jean depicted by Seaton and others, without adding significant new information.

29. For various cannibalism stories regarding escapees from the *bagne*, see Michelot 1982:154–59.

30. On the genesis of this apologetic publication, see Donet-Vincent 1992:136.

31. I am grateful to Anne-Marie Bruleaux for providing a photocopy of the relevant document: Archives Départementales de Guyane, *registre* 3U 2/67, Arrêt de la Justice de Paix de Saint-Laurent-du-Maroni, dated 10 June 1941.

32. Michelot claims that on 28 September 1945 there were some 462 *relégués individuels* and 380 *relégués collectifs* in the *bagne* (1981:326). Epailly gives figures of 380 and 152, respectively, for 1 October 1946 (1994:164). See also *Report* 1946:14.

33. In the *bagne*, eye disease was a common consequence of long-term cellular confinement. Doctor Rousseau described in detail one such condition, known by the prisoners as *coup de lune*, that resulted from the dietary deficiencies of those held in cellular punishment and whose symptom was total night blindness (1930:127–28).

34. Some people place this house closer to Anse Céron or Trois-Rivières. One elderly woman named Matil, who spoke to us in Taupinière in 1986, insisted that his house had been near there, at Anse Céron (where Médard was

born): "It was absolutely chock full with goods—drums of kerosene, drums of cooking oil."

35. I have not gone through penal records to try to document Médard's minor encounters with the law after his return from Guyane and rely here solely on oral accounts.

36. This piano, now in the home of Albert Andrieu in Diamant, was bought by him from Médard in 1972. Its height is ninety-one centimeters. Médard made a number of other pianos, some of which are reported to have been taken by their owners to France.

37. There was a French mail boat called *le Duc-d'Aumale* that operated in the 1930s between Guyane and the Caribbean (Michelot 1981:253). Dinette's version was destroyed by a hurricane in the 1970s.

38. Bernard De Amil, a musician born in British Guiana and married to a Martiniquan, told us he bought the plates in 1973, shortly before Médard's death, for eighty francs. Médard offered them to him in Diamant but he didn't have the cash, so he took Médard back to his house to get it. He claims it was Médard's very first ride in a car. At De Amil's house, Médard accepted a soda and received his money. Our notes say, "The plate with three figures is 13 inches in diameter, the other 14 inches. The figures are in one-inch relief. Backs are rough, painted red. Colors: gold, bright blue-green, purple, silver, etc."

39. My copy of Médard's death certificate, issued at Trois Ilets, lists him as having died in hospital on 17 October 1973. The official place of death is listed as "Avenue of the Empress Joséphine."

PART III

1. My formal anthropological "training" to date had consisted of a freshman seminar with Clyde Kluckhohn on the Navajo (1959–60), a field methods course with Evon Z. Vogt designed to prepare me for summer fieldwork in 1961 in highland Peru (see R. Price 1965), and a reading course on anthropological theory with Vogt (1961–62). At that time, Harvard had no Caribbean specialists and I had little preparation for the specificities of the region. It was not until 1964–65, when I began studying informally with Sidney W. Mintz, that I read *The People of Puerto Rico* and began to under-

Sidney Mintz and R.P. in Santiago de Cuba, 1989

stand the extent to which the Caribbean and its peoples had, from early on, been in the vanguard of modernity (see, for example, Mintz 1966, 1996).

2. It was eventually published in revised form by Lévi-Strauss in *L'Homme* (R. Price 1964).

3. The equally youthful field experience of dance anthropologist Katherine Dunham in the Martinique of the 1930s was considerably less upbeat. She wrote Melville Herskovits about her difficulties in September 1935, apparently while in the fishing community of Vauclin: "This is a very difficult country. It is small, and the people are much amalgamated. There is much more to be done here psychologically than artistically or anthropologically. The country is slowly decaying and the people with it. I have not been so well here physically, partly because my work has gone so poorly, I suppose. There is just nothing to see, but I hang on, hoping" (cited in Clark 1994:197).

4. Sally had saved those letters for sentimental reasons, stashed in my mother's attic. I recuperated them from a ratty manila envelope and read them through for the first time since writing them, for purposes of this book, in 1996.

5. Renato Rosaldo and I—classmates—had become fast friends and in June of 1961 had set out together for South America and the adventure of our first anthropological fieldwork, Renato staying on in highland Ecuador (after we'd spent several days in Quito), and I continuing on to highland Peru.

6. Amélius was also known as being among the best educated, most urbane, of his generation. Now in his nineties, he still enjoys telling how, seven decades ago, he helped put his younger friend the novelist Joseph Zobel through school, and how he served as scribe for much of Petite Anse in the days when few could read, much less write, a letter. His recent years have

been devoted to *Le Feu*, the racing canoe he owns and enters in island-wide competitions.

7. "Summer" (like "winter") correctly represents my own northern perspective at the time. Fishermen, like other Martiniquans, think in terms of *livè-naj* (the rainy season, June–November, when coastal fishing is practiced) and *karemn* (the dry season, December–May, when men voyage *à miquelon* *[lapèch-miklon]*, far from land seeking pelagic fish).

8. As late as 1979, the force of such realities continued to surprise me. I had suggested to Michel-Rolph Trouillot, then a doctoral student who was visiting Martinique for a conference and who wished to get to neighboring Dominica to begin fieldwork, that he go to Petite Anse, introduce himself to Emilien and Merlande, and ask Emilien to arrange passage across the northern channel by *gonmyé*. A creoleophone Haitian of impeccable bourgeois background (see Trouillot 1995), Rolph later told us he'd spent the night and that they'd helped him on his way. But when we next saw Emilien and Merlande, they severely scolded us for having sent "the Haitian." They hadn't shut their eyes the whole night, they said, out of fear for the "voodoo" the Haitian might do. How, they asked, could we have been so thoughtless as to have sent a Haitian to stay in their house?

9. I was always taken aback by the vitriol fishermen expressed against the gendarmes (white Frenchmen), who periodically hiked in to check their papers and canoes. Indeed, I was struck that fishermen's pride in their own independence went with a relatively fierce defiance of any attempt on the part of the state to control their lives. These men were staunch republicans, with a keen interest in elections and politics, but they asked little from the state and seemed primarily interested in maintaining maximum elbow-room for themselves. (Contemporary political upheavals—the 1959 riots in Fort-de-France and the often-violent independence struggle in Guadeloupe—seemed to have few local repercussions or to evoke much local interest.)

10. Research with local pharmacists and in the library of the Faculté de Pharmacie in Paris revealed that the bulk of pharmaceuticals prescribed by *quimboiseurs* can be found in seventeenth- to nineteenth-century pharmacopoeias but are no longer stocked or used in France—though in the 1960s they still formed a major (for some, *the* major) part of pharmacists' sales in

Martinique. For details, see R. Price 1966b.

11. "Carib" leaves and roots such as these are all available in the market of Fort-de-France. In 1962, there were at least six women who sold such products full-time.

12. A couple of years later, a Harvard student whose senior thesis focused on the poorest area of Petite Anse (l'Anse, population 332) reported that some 88 percent of households consisted of a couple (or a widow/widower) and assorted children and grandchildren (Simmons 1966:115–16).

13. Fishermen, though believers, tended to be strongly anticlerical. (Local priests were all white Frenchmen.) Guilos once put it succinctly: "The canoe," he explained to me, "is the church of the fisherman."

14. For decades, there have been special affinities between Petite Anse and Saint Lucia's northern fishing villages. Several Saint Lucians are long-established members of the community in Petite Anse, and a handful of local men maintain second families across the channel, traveling back and forth by canoe.

15. Joseph Zobel, writing of the 1930s, poetically evokes the moment as Médard might have heard it, from his cave near Anse Caffard. "Dehors le jour s'éveillait et bâillait à grands bruits. Ocarinas de coqs, grincements de portes et claquements de fenêtres. Tintamarres d'ustensiles, voix, chansons. Du fond de l'Anse Cafard, montaient les trompes floues de la senne" (1946:29–30). (Outdoors, the day was awakening with a loud yawn. The crowing of cocks, the creaking of doors, the banging of shutters. Pots clanging, voices, singing. From the depths of Anse Caffard rose the wavering sounds of the conch, announcing the seine.)

16. Perhaps the best-known literary conjuncture of colonialism and madness occurs in George Lamming's *Of Age and Innocence* (1981[1958]), where the prophetic madness of the nationalist leader Shephard is interwoven with people's old-time memories of the original Tribe Boys' courage, where the island's madhouse disappears in fire on the eve of general elections, where the frightening, magical moment of nation-formation is arrested somewhere between madness and history, and where (in Shephard's own words) "the sea is silver and the mountains climb to the moon" (58).

    Three further examples, perhaps less well-known than those of the major novelists, are provided by Michael Thelwell, whose Black Raphael, River

King, in *The Harder They Come*, talks little but is strong and visionary (much like people's memory of Médard); by John O. Stewart, whose Pharoh, a sometime madman, sees right through the fancy-talk development schemes proposed by Teacher in the village Trinidad of *Drinkers, Drummers, and Decent Folk*; and by Anthony C. Winkler, whose *The Lunatic* foregrounds a ragged village madman named Aloysius Hobson, who talks with bush and tree, who claims his full name is "Aloysius Gossamer Longshoreman Technocracy Predominate Involuted Enraptured Parliamentarian Patriarch Verdure Emulative Perihelion Dichotomy Intellectual Chaste Iron-Curtain Linkage Colonialistic Dilapidated Impracticable Loquacious Predilection Abomination Vichyssoise Pyrrhic Mountebank Unconscionable Altercation Lookalike Partition Bosky Pigeon-Toed Dentition," and whose adventures encompass a broad range of neocolonial encounters, from taking part as "a spin bowler with a sly delivery" in an inter-village cricket match to servicing a sex-starved German tourist who engages him to show her "the real Jamaica."

17. Ken Bilby, seconding this point, noted in an October 1996 letter to me that

In addition to the "high" literary tradition, there also exists a more vernacular literature that recognizes the role of "madman" as commentator on the existential absurdity of life under the contradictions of (neo)colonialism. One example that comes to mind is a Jamaican play by one Festus Amtac Campbell called *Confusion at the Market Place*, privately published in 1978 with a few other plays in a booklet called *Echoes of Mount Portland*. The play, written in basilectal Jamaican Creole using an "intuitive" orthography, includes among its cast of characters "Jonathan—a lunatic—blind, ragged, at times a D.J., a politician and a lover. He speaks from out of his belly. He is the very epitome of pity but sometimes his words can burn like fire"; "Castell—said to be mad. Dresses in khaki suit, an old felt hat on his head and a parcel and metal stick in his hands. When walking his left arm is bent with the papers under it. The stick is used to touch victims he has arrested. He thinks of himself as a detective working for the Queen of England." And there are others. (These characters, whose actual names are used, were real denizens of the Port Antonio market when I lived in the area in the late 1970s; I often saw them while visiting the town and was taken aback by their commentaries on the absurd political situation at a time when Manley's government and Jamaica seemed to be falling apart at the seams; Campbell's rendering of their dialogue is quite true to life.) Since then, a whole genre of such vernacular plays—farces performed in Jamaican Creole and sometimes called "Roots Plays"—has blossomed. They're performed both in Kingston and provincial towns by touring companies. And "madmen" and flamboyant characters are staples of the genre.

18. I include people who played these roles at various times, often overlapping, during the past three decades. Several names have been changed.

19. He drowned in 1987, when the canoe from which he and two others were fishing with dropnets capsized, just off Anse Caffard, a few hundred yards from Médard's cave.

20. Significantly, Lamming and Walcott each use the same Joycean phrase, "History is a nightmare from which I am trying to awake," as epigraph for major texts—respectively *The Pleasures of Exile* (1992[1960]) and "The Muse of History" (1974).

21. Lamming continues, "The antagonistic weight of the past is [still] felt as an inhibiting menace. And that is the most urgent task and the greatest intellectual challenge: how to control the burden of this history and incorporate it into our collective sense of the future" (1995:25). Guadeloupean Dany Bébel-Gisler echoes Lamming's sentiments when she comments on the lack of popular (as opposed to intellectual) knowledge of resistance, by asking, "And what if we stopped seeing ourselves through the eyes of the other, the colonizer? If we tried to rediscover our own history? If the term *nèg mawon* no longer struck terror into the hearts of children and threatened the virginity of young girls, but referred to a heroic resistance fighter, more alive than Joan of Arc, Schoelcher, or de Gaulle?" (1994:234).

22. Naipaul, recalling his own schooldays, provides an additional example: "Trinidad was too unimportant and we could never be convinced of the value of reading the history of a place which was, as everyone said, only a dot on the map of the world. . . . This gave us a strange time-sense. The England of 1914 was the England of yesterday: the Trinidad of 1914 belonged to the dark ages" (1969[1962]:45).

23. Although Fanon often wrote and spoke of Césaire's influence on the students at the Lycée Schoelcher, and although the standard biographical works claim that he was Césaire's student, it now appears that he may never

have actually taken a class with Césaire. Lucien Taylor, who has made a point of looking into the matter (checking records in the Bibliothèque Schoelcher, interviewing Fanon's brother and Fanon's closest Martiniquan friend) reports that, to date, all evidence is negative (personal communication, 28 and 30 May 1997).

24. At the time that the Martiniquan *créoliste* movement emerged in the mid-1980s, related international crosscurrents, many centered in the anglophone Caribbean just next door, had already been swirling for at least two decades. As a metaphor or model for the development of Caribbean culture, "creolization" (a concept originally borrowed from historical linguistics) had long been debated and proclaimed by Caribbean writers and artists as well as Caribbeanist social scientists. For a sampling of this extensive literature, see the essays, dating from the fifties onward, collected in Brathwaite 1993 and, for other British Caribbean references, Walmsley 1992; for the Hispanic Caribbean, Fernández Retamar 1989 and González 1980; for diverse pan-Caribbean antecedents, including Martí and Toussaint, Gikandi 1992:16–17, and, of course, Ortiz 1940—as well as Mintz and Price 1992[1976], which includes relevant social science bibliography.

25. To better historicize this woman's enthusiasm, it may be worth pointing out the extent to which each generation of Frenchmen has reinvented Joan to suit their own needs, and how, after the French defeat of 1870, she became an ideal symbol of patriotic vengeance because she hailed from the recently lost province of Lorraine. It was during the 1890s that statues were raised in her honor in Nancy and Paris, the process of canonization was strongly pressed, and her image on horseback was plastered all over France. And it was at this time that French priests, sent out to Martinique, began telling the schoolchildren they taught—including Céleste Senzamba, who was then a schoolgirl—the glorious history of the Maid of Orleans.

26. In interesting ways, the world of 1960s and 70s fishermen paralleled that of city intellectuals. "Most plays of the period (c. 1960-75)," writes Juris Silenieks, "feature a spirit of confrontational combativeness and a commitment to intervene in the burning sociopolitical issues of the day. There is a tone of stridency, an attitude of self-righteousness, born from the intolerable feeling of repression and unfairness. . . . Quite often these dramatic works are

meant to be something like acts of accusation to condemn particular instances of colonial repression" (1994:518).

27. Until the mid-1980s, the house was still sometimes referred to in print as "the so-called House of the Fisherman" (Maran 1986:211), but after the restoration, the "House of the Convict" became standard. Not long after the house was fixed up, the Hotel Diamant les Bains had the ship, pictured on p. 69, repainted and installed in a glass case next to the reception desk, with a brass plaque reading: "Work by Medar Aribot Who Spent 30 years of his life in the *Bagne* of Guyane. Restored by Hubert ANDRIEU and Repainted by DJELO." During 1995, one of Martinique's TV stations used an icon of Médard's Anse Caffard house, rather like the drawing on the cover of the *Guide Gallimard*, to introduce its evening weather forecasts—showing it in a sequence of schematized clouds, rain, lightning, and sunshine. For the 1996 Carnival, the Queen of Diamant, who represented the commune in island-wise competition, was "dressed" as Médard's house. And in 1996, I began noticing young couples, including some from Petite Anse, who drove to the house direct from church, posing in their formal attire, using the backdrop for their official wedding photo. As this book goes to press, Thierry Coco—*conseiller municipal* in Diamant, who led the 1987 restoration—continues to harbor plans to move Médard's final house at Bompí down from the hills, restore it, and set it up as an attraction next to the one at Anse Caffard.

28. Much of my argument about the *créoliste* revisioning of the past is borrowed from R. and S. Price 1997, where considerable elaboration is provided. My broader engagement with the historical ideas of the *créolistes* is enmeshed in a debate about the conceptualization of Martinique within the Caribbean and should not be read as what Raphael Samuel has called "heritage-baiting"—the tendency of some cultural studies scholars to use "heritage" (or patrimonialization) as a whipping-boy, to view it as "the mark of a sick society, one which, despairing of the future, had become 'besotted' or 'obsessed' with an idealized version of its past" (1994:261). I believe that Samuel makes considerable sense when he notes that

If the parable of the motes and beams were followed, as it should be, few of the historians' practices would emerge unscathed. Are we not guilty ourselves of turning knowledge into an object of desire? And is it not the effect, if not the intention, of our activity as historians to domesticate the past and rob it of its terrors by bringing it within the realm of the knowable? Historians are no less concerned than conservationists to make their subjects imaginatively appealing . . . We use vivid detail and thick description to offer images far clearer than any reality could be. Do we not require of our readers, when facing them with one of our period reconstructions, as willing a suspension of disbelief as the "living history" spectacle of the open-air museum or theme park? Is not the historical monograph, after its fashion, as much a packaging of the past as a costume drama? And do we not call on our own *trompe-l'oeil* devices to induce a hallucinatory sense of oneness with the past, using "evocative" detail as a gauge of authenticity? (1994:271)

29. The *créolistes'* revisioning of the Antillean past deserves detailed comparative analysis with other attempts, such as that of Gilberto Freyre in 1920s Brazil, to construct foundational mythologies (see Oliven 1996).

30. It may be worth pointing out (following Trouillot 1995:17) that "Martinique, a tiny territory less than one-fourth the size of Long Island, imported more slaves than all the U.S. states combined."

31. In a half-hour-long 1995 TV documentary called "The Making of Béhanzin," various participants insisted on the historical veracity of the feature film itself. Not only did Chamoiseau and Deslauriers stress their attempts at historical accuracy, but the woman in charge of costume emphasized the "authenticity" of the king's headgear and pipe, the kinds of cloth used to drape the women, and so forth.

32. This statement of Guy Deslauriers betrays an implicit, unacknowledged subject position common to the great bulk of *créoliste* expression. Blacks can go unmentioned in the enumeration of Martiniquan diversity precisely because the speakers/writers are of predominantly African ancestry. For people who, a generation ago, might have been celebrating their *négritude*, the celebration of (for example) *indianité*—East Indianness—is an add-on; the African heritage is so obvious that it can remain un(re)marked.

33. On the randomly chosen evening of March 27, 1995, I jotted down the list of local sports covered on the 7:30 p.m. news (RFO TV). Martiniquans were shown engaged in track and field, bicycle racing, tennis, karate, soccer,

handball, basketball, volleyball, go-carting, golf, fencing, and a "traditional" sailing-canoe race. On subsequent evenings, the broadcast covered, among other sports, local rugby, stockcar racing, horse-jumping, gymnastics, ping-pong, body-building, horseracing, wind-surfing, judo, and radio-commanded model-car racing. It should come as no great surprise that in July 1996, a young metropolitan couple leased from Emilien and Merlande a corner of The Sunbeam with a window on the road and opened a pizzeria.

34. For discussion both of changes (and, above all, continuities) in Martiniquan ideas about "race" during this period and the denial by people today that there ever was a time when Fanon's (1952) descriptions held true, see R. Price 1995. The importance of skin color—in marriage, friendships, identity—bowled me over during my first stay in Martinique in 1962. On my third day on the island, my notes record, "a fisherman, after a short speech about how 'white or black, a man is, after all, a man,' asked innocently, 'Can you tell me precisely, exactly, what is the skin color of Monsieur Ray Charles? Is he darker or lighter than me?—of course, it's of no real importance, you know. But exactly what is the skin color of, for example, Nat King Cole?' etc. etc." And at my first dinner with my host family in Petite Anse, each of the seven children present was classified, at length and for my benefit, according to his or her proper "racial" category. Later, my notes describe a visit to a construction-materials company owned by the *béké* Hayot family: "A young M. Hayot goes around signing papers, looking cool in his chinos, docksiders, and Yale-Coop-type shirt. A café-au-lait woman, in heels, sits with the cash register. The salesmen behind the computers, who discuss purchases with customers and take their orders, are *mulâtres* or *chabins*. And all the blue-coated/jumpsuited men who work the lumber yard itself are dark black." The widespread Martiniquan essentialization of racial categories is nowhere more strongly portrayed than in the dialogue about women's genitals in Confiant's *Eau de café* (1991:85—for discussion, see R. and S. Price 1997).

35. A deeper analysis, inappropriate to develop here, would demonstrate that there has been a significant shift from the days when colonial policy, mandated in Paris, held sway in the colonies such as Martinique, to the present-

day, when a continued "culture of colonialism" (and a mass of metropolitan officials in the island) regulates many areas of life, despite the absence of official (legislative, judicial) policy on the part of the French state. As Ernest Wan-Ajouhu, former mayor of the important commune of François, has patiently tried to explain to me, today it is "agencies" of the French state in Martinique, not the state itself, that (operating in their own interests) make things happen. The justice system, for example, which any Martiniquan (from the poorest to the richest) can tell you works on two tracks, one for Martiniquans and another for metropolitans, is answering not to official colonial policy in this regard (as it did, for example, in the days of the *guerre du Diamant*), but to a persistent culture of colonialism that is practiced by the judicial system (and the Department of Public Works, and many other agencies of the state). For Wan-Ajouhu and others on the inside, this difference seems critical. For our purposes, the effects remain largely the same.

In a similar vein, many educated Martiniquans would argue that the 1960s'/1970s'/1980s' definition of the situation—the whole dilemma of assimilation—has been effectively laid to rest. For example, André Lucrèce writes, "Today, the stakes have changed. . . . After a long struggle against the policy of assimilation, the Martiniquan of 1992 knows who he is. The era of '*nos ancêtres les Gaulois*' is a thing of the past. . . . He can justly claim to be born of four cultures—African, European, Indian, and Amerindian. . . . He clearly affirms himself to be Martiniquan despite his French *carte d'identité* and French passport (which also says 'European Community'), both of which he sees merely as a practical convenience. He also affirms himself to be Caribbean and not European" (1994:45). And Lucrèce claims that Martiniquan culture is taking the world by storm: "Malavoi [a musical group] in Japan; Euzhan Palcy's film, *La Rue Cases-Nègres*, receiving a prize at the Venice Film Festival; the flutist Max Cilla in Canada; *zouk* music setting crowds dancing in Europe, Africa, and America; our painters who move between New York, Paris, and South America; Césaire at the Comédie Française; Glissant receiving literary awards in the United States; the Prix Goncourt for Patrick Chamoiseau; our literature spreading around the world" (1994:165). I would simply note that this type of triumphalist discourse—this ideological boosterism, still more programmatic than realized—has not yet made much of a dent on the consciousness of people in Petite Anse.

36. The delicate question of "subject position"—who has the right to speak about what to whom—and the related question of "authentic" voices become particularly contested in the postcolonial Caribbean (see Dash 1994:451). Sally and I present some relevant reflections regarding our relationship to Martinique (and to Martiniquan intellectuals) in R. and S. Price 1997, and I discuss the complications of doing ethnography in a place that is not, for us, "the field" in R. Price 1990b:22–24. It may be worth noting here that our eventual settling down in the Martinique of "today"—following our 1960s fieldwork and the more sporadic visits of the seventies and early eighties—began with a surprise call from Emilien and his brother-in-law Julien, squeezed into the only phonebooth in Petite Anse, to Paris, where we were on sabbatical in 1986. A house, they told us excitedly, had suddenly become available in the community, and they had taken the liberty of placing a bid for us. Were we finally ready to make good on our long-term dream—our promise—to become their neighbors? (The somewhat complicated circumstances of our decision to accept their generous offer need not detain us here. Those interested may consult R. and S. Price 1993.) Our actual installation on the island was administratively lubricated by Aimé Césaire, with indirect help from, of all people, Médard. In Paris, Sally had been interviewing writer-anthropologist Michel Leiris, then in his eighties, for an article in *Current Anthropology* and *Gradhiva*, and—because of his long-term interest in Martinique—had told him something of my ongoing research about Médard. Excited by the story, and oblivious to the time-zone difference, he phoned his old friend Césaire in the middle of the Martiniquan night to share it. And that launched a friendship, now a decade old, with the grand old man of Martiniquan politics, and literature.

37. Even Césaire, who had once written that "anthropology is the gaze of the white upon the black . . . an appropriation effected by imposing the categories of European thought" (n.d.), told us when we first met, in 1987: "We need anthropologists like you because the Martinique of today is no longer the Martinique you knew in 1962—that's all changed or disappearing. We now need anthropologists to record what's 'going' forever. . . ." Anthropol-

ogy, however, is changing. For example, Daniel Miller—focusing on "mass consumption"—has depicted the ways the modernizing citizens of Trinidad and Tobago have taken over imported commodities and images in the ongoing process of building a vibrant local culture as part of globalization (Miller 1994).

38. In a recent article on the cultural politics of tradition and modernity in Papua New Guinea, Errington and Gewertz (1996) run through many of the theoretical complications of this sort of analysis and present a useful bibliography. Bruner 1996 includes a sensitive discussion of the ways tourism affects the issue.

39. Most of my examples here, as elsewhere in this book, are drawn from the Anses d'Arlet/Diamant region, not because it is somehow "typical" of Martinique—no single region is—but because it is where the bulk of my experience (and Médard's) has centered. A general study of Martinique would need to attend more specifically to urban (and suburban) realities and to the discourses of the highly educated elites who inhabit those spaces. Here, though I attempt to take fully into account this broader picture, I keep my lens more narrowly focused.

40. In June 1996, José Alpha kindly gave me the unpublished script for his play to use in this book.

41. When fishing for pelagics—*lapèch-miklon*, miles from shore—men take care to leave the pilot once they've filled their canoe, so other canoes can get their share. Or, if the pilot is especially attractive (say, a good-sized shark), the fisherman catches it but doesn't haul it in, attaching the line to a buoy until all the canoes have taken as much as they can. And only then will he haul it in.

42. The fishermen Alpha spoke with, including St.-Oïde—as well as Petite Anse fishermen he didn't speak with—insist to me unanimously and emphatically that there is no association at all between *lanj* and women (or mermaids). Yet somehow in that mysterious process of quasi- ethnographic interviewing, the enthusiastic Alpha heard St.-Oïde tell him (or agree that?) a *lanj* is somehow a woman. (At least this is what Alpha told me in June 1996.)

43. Details of the making of *The Miraculous Catch* were kindly provided by

Michel Delbois, director of Anses d'Arlet's Municipal Office of Culture, in an interview on 2 May 1996. José Alpha himself added his own version on 26 June 1996, during a conversation at our house, in which he told of his plans to expand the script and film the spectacle for RFO Television some time in 1997. In that expanded version, the *lanj*, he said, might well cry out.

44. The attitudes of the several men in their twenties with whom I spoke about the spectacle were more generous to the dancer. One, who had pulled on the seine ropes during Alpha's spectacle, said appreciatively, when I asked what he'd thought, "We hadn't expected anything like *that* here in Anses d'Arlet!"

45. The subject was very much in the air. The 1994 telephone directory for Martinique included a heavily illustrated five-page section on "traditional housing," featuring the *case créole*, and this, in turn, was quite similar to the illustrated depiction of traditional housing in the *Guide Gallimard: Martinique* published earlier that year.

46. Anses d'Arlet has recently become a preferred site for the filming of music videos and TV ads. In 1996, one of the few remaining "traditional" creole houses on the main street served as visual backdrop for the introduction to Martinique of Renault's latest (most modern) small car—aptly named the Clio. The upbeat video, which shows the new car driving by the traditional house and along the modern esplanade, includes the whispered words (in English) "Oh, my love."

47. Capgras echoed Michel Delbois's discomfort about using Creole in the official setting of a cultural evening at the *mairie* when, after he had spiced his speech with a single Creole phrase, immediately said (in French), "Pardon my Latin!"

48. It may be worth noting that the managers (*économes*) of local sugarmills were notorious for exercising their *droit de cuissage*—their right to a sexual encounter in exchange for hiring a woman (as canecutter or other seasonal employee) or, in the case of hiring a man, to a visit from his wife or daughter. (And worth noting too that acquiescence in the same rite is rumored to be a requirement for getting a job in the modern *mairie*.)

49. See, for example, R. and S. Price 1995a.

50. In contrast to such small-scale, local, "traditional," almost spontaneous ver-

sions, large-scale official *chanté noël* have recently become widespread, sometimes—as at the refurbished plantation house Habitation Clément in the town of François—for thousands of participants. Sponsored by rum companies and airlines, such events now symbolize Martiniqueness for those at the vanguard of modernization. Indeed, a poll reported in *France-Antilles Magazine* (23–29 déc, 1995, pp. 48–50) found that while attendance at midnight mass varied inversely with educational level, "attendance at organized *chanté noël* is much more common among those with a high level of education and a comfortable standard of living."

51. In the projected Regional Museum in Martinique's sister-colony, Guyane, one of the expository labels stresses that "the earliest colonists, often poor, lived under conditions that were scarcely better than those of their slaves." And the brutality of slavery is relegated wholesale to the neighboring colony of Suriname. Guyanese slavery is presented in distinctly gentler terms, with emphasis on the significant presence of free blacks and mulattos and of small-scale European cultivators. The physical objects highlighted in the plantation section of the museum are pottery and a Creole stringed instrument allegedly made by an eighteenth-century slave. There is no mention of chains, iron collars, or other instruments of discipline and control. (For fuller analysis of this museum, see R. and S. Price 1994, 1996.)

52. There is, in fact, much of interest one could say about "the image of the fisherman" among urban Martiniquans. To cite just two examples: The owner of a major Fort-de-France bookstore recently insisted to me that the reason fishermen are still attracted to magic is that none of them know how to swim. (Back in Petite Anse, I confirmed my suspicions by a rapid survey—there are only two men in all of Petite Anse, including one who never fishes, who cannot swim.) And it is "common knowledge," even among scholars, that Antillean fishermen are lazy and easygoing, live from hand to mouth, and "rest on land for several days whenever they've had a good catch" (see, for example, Lasserre 1961:944–45, which cites additional literature)—all completely counterfactual assertions.

53. Glissant makes some apt observations on the exaggerated authority granted to outside experts in Martinique (1981:122).

54. In an earlier essay, I reported erroneously that the cat had caught the flight

(R. Price 1990b). In fact, it stayed, learned to hunt, kept its slimmed-down figure, and successfully went native. For the full flavor of this story, it may be worth registering here that, according to the *New York Times* (2 February 1990:A3), there are twice as many cats and dogs in France as children and that they consume more meat than all Spaniards put together.

55. Ken Bilby, in a letter of October 1996, has pointed out to me that in certain Parisian circles, the term *négropolitain* has rather different, far more positive connotations. Indeed, "Cameroon's most famous son," the jazz musician Manu Dibango, claims credit for having coined the term in 1984 and uses it to mean hipness, black cosmopolitanism, and pan-African sophistication (1994:134). Dibango's amanuensis writes: "This new sound is being created here in Paris, drawing on an environment different from its African roots. It's a cosmic product, invented by the Paris Negropolitans. . . . It permits all sorts of madness, in which I move effortlessly; people have to have this kind of madness for me to get excited. . . . Alpha Blondy has managed to leap the hurdles and make his *Interplanetary Revolution*. He announces the arrival of a negropolitan generation braver than that of its elders. He is a man of satire. His madness suits me" (Dibango 1994:120, 128). And Bilby wonders whether younger, hipper *négropolitains* might not actually be introducing new forms of cultural resistance to Martinique.

56. This kind of alienation is nothing new in the French Caribbean. In *Atipa*, perhaps the first novel published in Creole, the narrator says, "I'm telling you, local folks who speak badly of Cayenne do it to seem more sophisticated, to sound like whitefolks. I know some who hardly stayed two days in France and when they returned pretended not to know a thing about our country. They even pretended to have forgotten our language!" (Parépou 1987[1885]:68). And in *Black Skin, White Masks*, Fanon writes: "As soon as the 'newcomer' steps ashore, he makes things clear; he answers only in French, and he often no longer understands Creole. Local folklore offers a relevant illustration. After several months in France, a country boy returns to his family. Noticing a farm implement, he asks his father, an old don't-pull-that-kind-of-thing-on-me peasant, 'Tell me, what does one call that apparatus?' His father's only reply is to drop the tool on the boy's feet and the amnesia vanishes. Remarkable therapy" (Fanon 1952:18).

57. If I caricature here—and in such a brief evocation of the complex relations between on-island and off-island residents, it is almost unavoidable—it is to make a heartfelt point. Family ties tend to remain strong and there is a good deal of visiting, in both directions, between siblings and between island-based women and their emigrant children. The situation of children born to Martiniquans in the metropole, some of whom I have taught in classes on the Caribbean at the University of Paris-St. Denis, is yet more complex. For most of them, Martinique will never be more than a distant place of origin, known largely through their parents' reminiscences and the occasional vacation visit.

58. Playing the (metropolitan) horses through the PMU and the various games offered by the national lottery have become a major activity in Martinique, for women as well as men and for all social classes. In 1994, Martiniquans over the age of fifteen gambled *on the average* U.S. $1,200 on these state-run games (RFO evening news, 7/24/95, and Vennat 1995).

59. Glissant had already caught the imagery in *Malemort* (1975:180):

> But when the ship's on strike, within two days time you won't find bread or potatoes or apple juice or lentils or rice or salt-cod or salt and probably not sugar nor milk in cans nor milk in bottles nor anything at all nothing in the whole place and in just two days not a clove of garlic not a single onion.
> But there'll be *onyon-pays*.
> Which *onyon-pays*?
> "*Onyon-pays*, Which *onyon-pays*, *Onyon-pays*," "*Onyon-pays*, Which *onyon-pays*, *Onyon-pays*," they sang in a sweet, rhythmic chant.

60. Scholars have been largely complicitous. A rich and pervasive worldview is conceptually marginalized by labeling it "magic and superstition," and then, when it's time for a chapter on these subjects in, for example, the heavily illustrated *Grande Encylopédie de la Caraibe* (edited by a historian at the Université des Antilles-Guyane), twenty-three of its twenty-four illustrations depict Haiti (Ebroïn 1990).

61. In June 1996, Alpha told me that the play had also been successfully performed in 1990 in the commune of Ducos.

62. As one of my last acts before completing this book, I determined to go to France to search for a likeness of Médard in the boxes of unclassified photos

of prisoners held by the archives at Aix-en-Provence. But a letter from the head of the archives dissuaded me, stating that "since the photos are not classified, the files are not consultable" (Le conservateur général, F. Durand-Evrard, letter dated 7 August 1996).

63. According to the *Historial*, around noon on 24 May 1925, Zizine and Des Étages arrived in Ducos from Fort-de-France with a photographer, whom they had brought to document the barbed wire and machine-gun in front of the *mairie*. One of Eugène Aubéry's men "interfered with the photographer saying picture-taking was prohibited. . . . Zizine insisted it was allowed but was told 'we don't want any of that around here,' after which the photographer was roughed up by the gendarmes. . . . The socialists claim that at that point Police Commissioner Labalette told gendarme Roquette, 'Now's the time,' and the gendarme said, 'I'm firing, I'm firing,' and shot his gun before turning back to the chief to report 'the two of them [Zizine and Des Étages] are faces-to-the-ground'" (Celma 1981:355). Mauvois quotes Zizine as having told the gendarmes, "We are in the days of the Republic. He has every right to take pictures" (1990:94).

64. I had for years assumed that this was a conscious artistic choice by Alpha and Placoly, for among those people they interviewed in preparing the script was Philibert Larcher, who would have told them in no uncertain terms that Médard's sentencing was in fact for theft. Nevertheless, in June 1996 when I shared some of my post-1985 information on Médard with Alpha for the first time, he acted as if the idea that Médard had been officially sentenced for theft, and not for having made the statue, was something he'd never heard before.

65. In fact, the last shipment of "Congos" seems to have landed on either 6 or 7 August 1862 (David 1973:128; David 1978:56).

66. I do not know why, though some characters in the play speak Creole, Médard and Marie-Thérèse only speak a flowery French. José Alpha, when I asked him in 1996, had no explanation (and playwright Vincent Placoly is dead).

67. According to Alpha, Médard made this particular yellow piano in such a way that when the keys are struck, the hammers hit bottle caps that are nailed along a wooden bar to produce music.

68. Alpha described these various commissions to me in June 1996.

69. Alpha is an artist and impresario, not a scholar. Nevertheless, I should probably put on record that those "facts" that he and Placoly did not invent came largely (and without acknowledgment) from my 1985 article. Indeed, when Alpha, at my behest, again recounted a version of the making of the 1990 play (in June 1996), he did not mention my article at all but rather insisted on the original research he and his team had done as background. He had also forgotten by this time that Marie-Thérèse, Médard's mother, was born in Martinique and that he had Africanized her solely for dramatic purposes in the play (as he'd told me in 1990). Such, I suppose, is Memory—like her daughter History, a radical reconstruction and selection and rearrangement of events, places, and people out of the past.

70. My own initial experiences with the archives, though earlier, were not different. "Monsieur," wrote Liliane Chauleau, Director of the Departmental Archives of Martinique,

> Regarding your research on ARIBOT Médard I have the honor to inform you that, following your request . . . we have on your behalf systematically scrutinized the Official Journal of Martinique which provides, trimester by trimester, the list of all those appearing before the criminal courts and the nature of their crimes. But in these lists the name of Aribot Médard never appears.
>
> It seems unlikely that further information will be forthcoming about this affair. But we shall continue to turn the archives inside out, and if any details should appear, I shall not fail to communicate them to you. . . . (Letter of 16 August 1983)
>
> Monsieur—As a follow-up to my letter of 16 August, I have the honor to inform you of the current status of the research which we are conducting on your behalf (see attachments). Our investigation has focused on the Official Journal of Martinique and on the contemporary press: beginning in 1941–1942, we have worked backwards all the way to 1930. As I indicated to you previously, the Official Journal lists under the rubric "court sessions" the names and sentences of all appearing before it. We indeed found one person sentenced to forced labor in 1931. But there was no mention of the name Aribot Médard. Please accept, Monsieur, the expression of my distinguished salutations. . . . (Letter of 26 August 1983)

The several pages of attachments list in detail each newspaper examined, with dates, as well as every session of the criminal courts (with dates and page numbers for each) for every trimester between 1930 and 1942, the whole meticulously typed out for my benefit.

71. Michel-Rolph Trouillot, who was studying with me during the period I was developing my ideas about history-making (by Saramakas, but also by rural Martiniquans relating to Médard), has now written a sensitive work about the ways history more generally is made. His summary of how silences enter the process of historical production is worth quoting: "Silences enter the process of historical production at four crucial moments: the moment of fact creation (the making of *sources*); the moment of fact assembly (the making of *archives*); the moment of fact retrieval (the making of *narratives*); and the moment of retrospective significance (the making of *history* in the final instance)" (1995:26).

72. The editors of the *Cahiers*, in the "historians' disclaimer" mentioned earlier, had suggested this "magical belief" as being at the base of the "legend" of Médard's sentencing (Briand-Monplaisir and Alpha 1990:113).

73. Emilien and Merlande, of course, simply keep the statue in their house, next to their television set, as any regular of The Sunbeam could have told *France-Antilles*.

74. Médard's house at Anse Caffard is certainly better known. And the bust was not known at all, except to local fishermen, until I chose it for the cover of *Caribbean Review* in 1985.

As this book goes to press in June 1997, a project has been set in motion (with funds provided by the Office National des Forêts, the Direction Régionale des Affaires Culturelles, the Direction Régionale de l'Environnement, the Conseil Général, the Office du Tourisme, and the European Economic Community) to convert Médard's decaying house into an official "historic site." Metropolitan workers from a company called "Antilles Patrimoine Historique" are now repairing and repainting. And they have told me that a large parking lot and souvenir shop are in the works. When I asked what they knew of the story of Médard, they said, "He killed a white officer, didn't he? And they sent him to the *bagne*, where he was taught some carpentry. That's how he knew enough to build this house."

Meanwhile, what may be Martinique's largest supermarket has distributed a touristic guide which, next to a photo of Médard's house, notes, "It is surrounded by mystery" and asks, "Is it the house of the devil?" (*Corascope* 1997:5) And the French publishing giant Hachette has brought out a guide to Martinique (*Une Semaine* 1997), which provides the latest twist in the postcarding of Médard's house, by confusing one of the island's legendary ex-prisoners with another. In its section on the spectacular 1902 eruption of the Mont Pelée volcano, which wiped out Saint-Pierre, a city of some 30,000 people, the guide tells us that "Louis Cyparis, the sole survivor, had been locked up in an underground dungeon following a drunken brawl, and could therefore be said to owe his survival to rum!" (1997:98). And it counsels tourists that, when in Diamant, they should be sure to catch "the cute, miniature, and colorful wooden house given to Cyparis, lone survivor of the catastrophe of Saint-Pierre, who is said to have lived out his days there after having exhibited his burn scars all across the United States under the Big Top of the Barnum circus" (1997:62).

75. In his hallucinatory novel *Malemort* (1975), Glissant insists on this continuing subterranean stream of resistance and defiance amidst what otherwise appears to be "the complete success of colonialism" in Martinique. As Juris Silenieks summarizes, the agents of these obscure memories "are evoked in a vision of . . . 'the fallen risen' whose lineage extends back to the Maroon and continues in the rebel, boycotter, union striker and nonconformist who throughout Martinican history have defied the order of the slave owner, the colonizer, the oppressor, the exploiter. They have been persecuted and massacred, but they have always risen from death and dust to continue their relentless struggle for dignity and justice. In silent rage they wreak destruction as they rampage through the master's mansion, the sugar factory, the modern department store. They are felled by the bullets of the ancient *maréchaussée*, local militia, or modern gendarmes. Dead, their bodies fade into the earth to arise from it later in a different historical setting" (1984:123-124). In the more officially political realm, too, there are counterveiling tendencies to the dominant trend. For example, in Sainte-Anne—home of Martinique's Club Med—the *mairie* and other public sites have, for the past year or two, been contestationally festooned with the green-black-red flags of an independent Martinique. And in neighboring Rivière-Pilote—where the other day, at a large meeting of the Cercle Frantz Fanon, Sally and I once

again stated publicly (to the usual general mirth and disbelief) that the day Martinique has its own passports to issue, we intend to be first in line—Marie-Jeanne's Mouvement Indépendantiste Martiniquais still holds sway. Nevertheless, today's prevailing currents seem to flow in other directions.

76. A *conteur* gives a similar pronunciation in Laurent and Césaire 1976:236. Nora had told me, also, that Médard sometimes referred to the statue as *King David* (*le "rwa David"*). When Nora asked Médard the price, he said "110 francs. Give me the ten now and the other hundred whenever you want" (110 francs equalled roughly 22 cents U.S.).

77. After my 1986 conversation with Nora confirmed that I had misunderstood the king's identity, I published the revised story alongside a photo of the historic Béhanzin (R. Price 1990b:19–20)—but I kept quiet about it in Martinique, even when I met Alpha at Baj Strobel's in 1990. Meanwhile, Alpha, using the information in the 1985 *Caribbean Review* article, had popularized the *Roi des Indes* label. Everyone Alpha talked to about this "masterpiece," as well as the thousands of people who read his article in the *Cahiers du Patrimoine* or the more popular *France-Antilles* version, as well as Thierry Coco (the leader of the group that remodeled Médard's Anse Caffard house and the person who eventually received the king as a gift from Nora for "safe keeping"), now referred to it as *Le Roi des Indes*. Indeed, in 1996 when I asked Nora where his king was, he said that Thierry Coco, *conseiller municipal* of Diamant, had "taken away *Le Roi des Indes*." The power of print, the power of hierarchy. And the power of Médard's sculptural genius to continue to encourage multiple, rich interpretations—*King Béhanzin, King David, King of the Indies*.

Source Notes

p. xii　"her detailed chapter on Martiniquan political life": Celma 1981.

p. xiii　"his own historical essay": Abénon 1982.

p. xiii　"*France-Antilles Magazine* says": Rabussier 1993a:48 and 1993b:48.

p. xiii　"the editors of the *Cahiers* . . . add": Briand-Monplaisir and Alpha 1990:113.

p. xiii　"The first relatively reliable . . . census": see de Lépine 1980:27.

p. xiv　"Collini, for example, writes": Collini 1995:3.

p. 5　"Aimé Césaire's soaring words": Césaire 1955:15–16, 19–20.

p. 5　"as historian Cécile Celma puts it": Celma 1981:358.

p. 6　"The *békés*, as de Lépine reminds us": de Lépine 1980:14, 26, 31. See also Petit Jean Roget 1981:124–25.

p. 6　"Vast *béké* fortunes": Mauvois 1990:47–48, Parry and Sherlock 1971:251.

p. 7　"When on 5 February 1923": Mauvois 1990:50–51.

p. 7　"A few days later": Mauvois 1990:69–70, de Lépine 1980:196.

p. 7　"Slapped, kicked in the behind": cited in Mauvois 1990:55.

p. 8　"a formal duel": Mauvois 1990:55–56; see also Darsières 1996:15.

p. 8　"In the several capacities he has occupied": Archives d'Outre-mer, Dossier Gov. Richard, EEII 8002, EEII 435(17), EEII 1228(2).

p. 8　"I am in Martinique": *Le Matin* (1923), cited in Mauvois 1990:75.

p. 8　"There was a time": *Le Paix* (26 avril 1923), cited in Mauvois 1990:76.

p. 9　"There are two parties here": Archives d'Outre-mer, Richard's Comment on "*Rapport de Boulmer*," No. 43, dated 27 *fév* 1924, Affaires Politiques, carton 3201.

p. 9　"I will leave Martinique": cited in Mauvois 1990:91, without further source.

p. 9　"he pinned the medal of the *Légion d'honneur*": Mauvois 1990:91.

p. 9　"the man of the *békés*" who "helped 'arrange' the election": Celma 1981:349.

p. 10　"By early 1925": Mauvois 1990:105.

p. 10　"protest with indignation": cited in Mauvois 1990:109.

p. 10　"Hesse took it upon himself": cable of 20 April 1925, cited in Mauvois 1990:110.

p. 10　"Hesse reiterated": cable of Hesse, dated 21 May, cited in Mauvois 1990:113.

p. 11　"I am delighted": interview with Fernand Clerc in *Le Français* (28 August 1902), cited in Mauvois 1990:24; see also Darsière 1996:255, 274.

p. 12　"The only real question": cited in Mauvois 1990:74.

p. 12　"He is, indeed, so *sauvage*": Report of Pégourier, dated 28 May 1925 (see p. 39).

p. 12   "all voting must be overseen by the mayor": cited in Celma 1981:349.

p. 12   "almost all were later appealed": cited in Celma 1981:350.

p. 13   "Frossard cabled": *Paris-Soir* (29 April 1925).

p. 13   "Frossard's colleague Charles Lussy added": *Paris-Soir* (29 April 1925).

p. 13   "In a later dispatch, Frossard gave some particulars": *Paris-Soir* (20 May 1925).

p. 15   "two rows . . .": Marc Larcher 1954[1901], cited in Maran 1986:212.

p. 17   "Nonetheless, the governor already had at his disposition": Celma 1981:351.

p. 17   "Richard was operating in an atmosphere charged with paranoia": Archives d'Outre-mer, Letter of J. Turiaf, 28 April, Affaires Politiques, carton 317.

p. 18   "The governor meticulously annotated each photo by hand": Archives d'Outre-mer, Affaires Politiques, carton 317.

p. 18   "Other sources": Celma 1981:353; for similar practices, see Mauvois 1990:84–85.

p. 19   "in a handwritten report to Governor Richard, dated that very afternoon": Archives d'Outre-mer, Affaires Politiques, carton 317.

p. 20   "Inspector General Pégourier sent off a cable to the Minister of the Colonies": cited in Celma 1981:354, Mauvois 1990:111.

p. 21   "two of the candidates on the socialist list . . . sent a letter": Archives d'Outre-mer, Letter dated 18 May 1925, Affaires Politiques, carton 317.

p. 21   "a confidential letter": Archives d'Outre-mer, Affaires Politiques, carton 317.

p. 21   "I have but one regret": Letter of 30 May 1925, pp. 12–13, Archives d'Outre-mer, Affaires Politiques, carton 317.

p. 22   "a front-page editorial devoted to the 3 May elections": *l'Aurore* (9 mai 1925).

p. 25   Unless otherwise specified, all documents for this "gauche/droite" section (except for newspapers, which require no further footnoting) may be found in the Archives d'Outre-mer, located in Paris when I consulted them in 1985 and 1986; they have since been moved to Aix-en-Provence.

p. 25   "[Gendarmerie Nationale: 24 May]": Affaires Politiques, carton 317.

p. 26   "[Telegram from Giscon to Inspector Pégourier, sent 14:20 from Diamant, while voting still in progress]": Quoted in a report "*A.S. des événements dont la Martinique vient d'être le théâtre*," by l'Inspecteur des Colonies Pégourier, chargé de Mission à la Martinique, to Monsieur le Ministre des Colonies (Direction du Contrôle) (Direction Politique) (Direction du Personnel), 28 May 1925. Affaires Politiques, carton 317, no 4.

p. 30   "[Telegram: Gendarmerie Diamant]": Affaires Politiques, carton 317.

p. 30   "[Coded cable, gov richard]": Affaires Politiques, carton 317.

p. 32   "[cable to Sénateur Lémery]": Affaires Politiques, carton 317.

p. 33   "[coded cable from Inspector General]": Affaires Politiques, carton 777.

p. 34 "[Inspector of Colonies Pégourier to Minister of the Colonies Hesse, Report on the recent events for which Martinique served as the theater, dated 28 May 1925]": Report previously cited. Affaires Politiques, carton 317, no 4.

p. 35 "[coded cable from Gov Richard]": Affaires Politiques, carton 777.

p. 35 "[Letter from 'V.(?) Brochard']": Affaires Politiques, carton 317.

p. 36 "[Gov Richard to Minister of the Colonies, Report on 24 May Elections, dated 30 May 1925]": Affaires Politiques, carton 317.

p. 41 "[Gov Richard to Minister of the Colonies]": Affaires Politiques, carton 777.

p. 42 "[Inspector General Le Conte]": Affaires Politiques, carton 3201.

p. 42 "[Inspector of Colonies to Minister of the Colonies]": Report by Pégourier, previously cited. Affaires Politiques, carton 317, no 4.

p. 44 "[Gov Richard to Minister Hesse]": cited in Mauvois 1990:121.

p. 44 "[Minister Hesse to Gov Richard]": cited in Mauvois 1990:122.

p. 45 "[Gov Richard to Minister Hesse]": cited in Mauvois 1990:123.

p. 45 "[Gov Richard to Minister, Comments on M. Laperge's Report]": I neglected to copy this verbatim in the archives (Affaires Politiques, carton 3201, no. 27) and quote instead from Mauvois 1990:125.

p. 46 "[Attorney General Beaudu, Martinique, to Minister of the Colonies]": Affaires Politiques, carton 317.

p. 48 "[Gov's Office to Minister, cable dated 31 August 1925, on the sentencing of the ten Diamant 'agitators']": Affaires Politiques, carton 317.

p. 48 "[Inspector General Le Conte, at end of mission]": I have seen only Le Conte's (interim?) report on the municipal elections, cited above, so I quote here directly from Celma 1981:328.

p. 48 "[Gov Richard, cable dated 24 May 1925]": Affaires Politiques, carton 317.

p. 48 "[Gov Richard, coded cable]": Affaires Politiques, carton 777.

p. 60 "While in Suriname . . . the often-heroic ways these Afro-Americans envisioned their collective past": R. Price 1983, 1990a.

p. 60 "The French are very good at these sort of thing": Walcott 1987:75.

p. 63 "as Douglas Hall has written": 1962:309.

p. 63 "though slaves were legally property, masters were constantly calling upon them to act in human ways": Mintz and Price 1992[1976]:25.

p. 63 "Jamaica serves as a setting for one famous version": Phillippo 1843:252, cited in Mintz and Price 1992[1976]:39.

p. 79 "as historian Gordon Wright tells us": Wright 1983:143, 149.

p. 79 "they would be kept under penal supervision": Wright 1983:145.

p. 81 "Pierre writes": Pierre 1982:48–49.

p. 87   "Michelot concludes": Michelot 1981:86–87.

p. 87   "Another former convict, René Belbenoit, wrote": Belbenoit 1941:250–51.

p. 87   "journalist Albert Londres wrote": Londres 1933:186, cited in Pierre 1982:73.

p. 87   "A former prison doctor wrote": Emmanuel Hernette, cited in Pierre 1982:73.

p. 87   "An official French publication . . . audience explained": *Report* 1946:11.

p. 87   "'*Relégués*,' writes Alex Miles": Miles 1988:59.

p. 87   "the mortality rate was even higher": Pierre 1982:312.

p. 87   "Belbenoit claimed that during this period": Belbenoit 1941:252.

p. 88   "As Pierre writes": Pierre 1982:47, see also p. 192.

p. 88   "During the whole history of the *bagne*": Michelot 1981:84.

p. 88   "As Peter Redfield writes": Redfield 1995:175.

p. 88   "Overall, Africans and their descendants made up": Pierre 1982:41.

p. 89   "Captain Rosier . . . wrote": cited in Michelot 1981:40–41.

p. 90   "Incorrigibles were placed in special 'hot cells'": for this and other ship-board information in this paragraph, see Belbenoit 1949:30–33, Le Clère 1979:113–16, Findlay 1970: 7–9, Seaton 1951:19–20, and Michelot 1981: 38–40.

p. 90   "We debarked at Saint-Laurent": cited in Michelot 1981:43.

p. 92   "Only 25 percent of convicts survived for twenty years": Le Clère 1979:23.

p. 92   "Doctor Louis Rousseau . . . concluded that": 1930, cited in Pierre 1982:141 without page reference.

p. 92   "In the *bagne*, everything was dictated by texts": Pierre 1982:101, 103–105.

p. 93   "a vast room . . . with desks for different specialists": Michelot 1981:54.

p. 93   "As one author described the generic scene": Niles 1928:43–44.

p. 94   "but at least one eyewitness claims": Belbenoit 1941:252.

p. 94   "This new dossier": Michelot 1981:54.

p. 94   "Suriname journalist D.G.A. Findlay": Findlay 1970:33–34.

p. 96   "The prisoner population of Saint-Jean": sources for this paragraph include Le Clère 1979:37; Michelot 1981:61, 252; Pierre 1982:73; and Seaton 1951:115, 125.

p. 96   "'Saint-Jean, . . .' writes one specialist": Donet-Vincent 1992:26.

p. 96   "A former guard's account": cited in Michelot 1981:53.

p. 98   "In 1936 at Saint-Jean-du-Maroni": Le Clère 1979:201.

p. 98   "other famous 'queens' of the day": Pierre 1982:125.

p. 98   "a former theatrical director, the *relégué* Mayol": Pierre 1982:125.

p. 98   "Europeans placed in one large room": Michelot 1981:79–81, see also p. 239.

p. 98   "the administration set up the Camp des Malgaches": Pierre 1982:75.

p. 98   "Michelot noted dryly": Michelot 1981:79.

p. 98   "the early-twentieth-century specifications for daily food rations were officially differentiated by race": Pierre 1982:103–04.

p. 98   "Although it is generally agreed": Pierre 1982:90.

p. 98   "As one of his *relégué* contemporaries testified": cited in Michelot 1981:251.

p. 99   "A former *relégué* told Michelot": cited in Michelot 1981:250, 108–109.

p. 99   "routinely punished by 'complete withholding of food'": Pierre 1982:105.

p. 100 "The maximum sentence that the Disciplinary Commission was permitted to pronounce was thirty days per offense": Michelot 1981:177.

p. 100 "Prison doctor Rousseau described": Rousseau 1930:142-143.

p. 100 "I have known of men": Seaton 1951:35–36; see also pp. 79, 193–194.

p. 105 "with some writers estimating": see, for example, Michelot 1981:125.

p. 106 "22,750 escapes were recorded for a total of 15,995 men": Michelot 1981:86.

p. 106 "In 1940, 472 (of 2,312 *relégués*) escaped": *Report* 1946:14.

p. 106 "the extreme case of one *relégué* who escaped nine times": Michelot 1981:193.

p. 106 "Pierre writes of another escapee": Pierre 1982:202.

p. 106 "but not, normally, on the offshore Iles du Salut": Michelot 268–289.

p. 107 "thirty or so Arab turnkeys": Charles Péan, cited in Michelot 1981:169.

p. 107 "Sometimes, large-scale chases were organized": Pierre 1982:223.

p. 107 "four particularly fierce North Africans": Michelot 1981:154.

p. 107 "Another account suggests": Pierre 1982:235.

p. 108 "The rupture of shipping traffic caused": Donet-Vincent 1992:126.

p. 108 "Even the official French embassy publication": *Report* 1946:12.

p. 108 "V. Garcia, reminisced": cited in Michelot 1981:248–49, 253–54.

p. 108 "Mortality, which had been running at 5 percent annually": Michelot 1981:325, Donet-Vincent 1992:132.

p. 108 "between 1940 and 1943": Pierre 1982:294–95.

p. 108 "With Camus's arrival": Pierre 1982:294.

p. 108 "the Vichyist 'Work, Family, Fatherland' decrees": Donet-Vincent 1992:128.

p. 109 "between 1940 and 1943": Donet-Vincent 1992:128–29.

p. 109 "the widespread underground market": Donet-Vincent 1992:132.

p. 109 "These remaining men": Epailly 1994:125, Donet-Vincent 1992:135.

p. 109 "Those *relégués* still alive at this point": Le Clère 1979:277.

p. 109 "and the final ones . . . leaving Guyane in 1952–1953": Michelot 1981:326–27.

p. 125 "'Your story,' wrote . . . H. Stuart Hughes": letter dated 24 July 1989.

p. 139 "what Glissant identified ten years later as a 'spectacular' case": 1981:103–106.

p. 140 "a fundamental 'critique'": Taussig 1980:10.

p. 140 "'Sensitivity to envy,' as Taussig found in Colombia": 1987:393–394.

p. 146 "what Césaire has called 'miraculous arms'": Césaire 1946.

p. 146 "with such literary verve": see, for example, Zobel 1974; Chamoiseau 1990, 1994; Confiant 1993; and I. Césaire 1994.

p. 147 "Zobel's *Diab'-la* . . . describes the evening return of the bus:": 1946:42–44.

p. 148 "Our surveys found that well over 90 percent": R. Price 1964.

p. 150 "Patrick Chamoiseau caught the spirit of this kind of grocery": 1990:134–135.

p. 153 "on some sort of fault line": Geertz 1995:65.

p. 153 "one of the half-dozen such rumshop/stores": R. Price 1985b.

p. 155 "the theatre was about us" Walcott 1970:7, 22–23.

p. 158 "Walcott's 'alphabet of the emaciated'": 1973:16–22.

p. 158 "Describing small-town life in Trinidad": Lovelace 1988:25–26.

p. 158 "the extended gallery of characters": Naipaul 1971[1959].

p. 159 "Raphaël Confiant provides a recent Martiniquan illustration": 1994b:79, 116, 131, 132, 203, 249, 150–51, 252, 305, 379.

p. 160 "He ran up against a man named Oscar": Wilson 1974:94–5.

p. 160 "Wilson writes, 'I began taking notes'": 1974:xii.

p. 160 "to study local knowledge of health and sickness": Littlewood 1993:xi.

p. 161 "anthropologist Lawrence Fisher argued that": 1985:247.

p. 161 "what Albert Memmi called the colonialist hoax": 1965:88.

p. 162 "what Herskovits . . . labeled 'socialized ambivalence'": 1971[1937]:299.

p. 162 "what Du Bois . . . had called 'double-consciousness'": 1969[1903]:45.

p. 163 "dynamited by alcohol": Césaire 1956[1939]:26.

p. 163 "A schoolteacher . . . recorded the relevant parts": Oscar n.d.:48–49.

p. 164 "As Walcott wrote . . . 'These dead, these derelicts'": 1973:22.

p. 164 "Or as Lovelace replayed it, 'These are our celebrities'": 1988:25.

p. 165 "as Simon Gikandi wrote of novelist Sam Selvon": Gikandi 1992:117–118.

p. 165 "In *A Brighter Sun*, Selvon had reported": 1971[1952]:17.

p. 166 "A character in one of Paule Marshall's novels explains": 1969:130.

p. 166 "the vitriolic queries of V. S. Naipaul": 1969[1962]:29.

p. 166 "the pointed asides of Édouard Glissant": 1981:277; 1990:86; see also 1996:223.

p. 166 "Aimé Césaire's allusions to": 1956[1939]:48.

p. 166 "the stark conclusions of Derek Walcott": 1974:4.

p. 166 "or Orlando Patterson": 1982:258.

p. 167 "two Barbadian schoolboys in the 1930s": Lamming 1953:51–52.

p. 168 "Lamming has reflected on changes—and continuities": 1995:21–22.

p. 168 "the perspective of Westminster": Walcott 1973:70.

p. 168 "Carpentier, in the famous formulation": 1964[1949]:12-13.

p. 168 "Lamming reminds us": 1992[1960]:77 (see also Gikandi 1992:58).

p. 169 "Wilson Harris has criticized": 1981:24–25, 28–29.

p. 169 "Glissant, who conjures up the need": 1981:132, 159; see also 1996:115.

p. 169 "Walcott's advice is complementary": 1989:6; 1970:5; 1974:2.

p. 169 "which one recent student has dubbed the 'Isle of Intellectuals'": Taylor n.d.

p. 169 "a higher concentration of diplomas per square kilometer": Lepape 1993.

p. 169 "Walcott . . . describes his own literary 'discipleship'": 1970:12.

p. 170 "Our History, or more precisely our histories, are shipwrecked": Bernabé, Chamoiseau and Confiant 1993[1989]:36–38.

p. 171 "From my experience in Saramaka": R. Price 1983, 1990a.

p. 171 "I was able to write with assurance that": R. Price 1985a:28.

p. 174 "Patrick Chamoiseau and Raphaël Confiant have, between them, written": for example, Bernabé, Chamoiseau, and Confiant 1993[1989]; Chamoiseau 1986, 1988a, 1988b, 1990, 1992, 1994; Chamoiseau and Confiant 1991; Confiant 1986, 1988, 1991, 1993, 1994, 1995.

p. 174 "Neither Europeans nor Africans nor Asians . . . but Creoles": Bernabé, Chamoiseau, and Confiant 1993[1989]:13, 27.

p. 174 "Moreover, the French Antillean plantation is depicted as a relatively 'gentle' institution": see, for example, Chamoiseau and Confiant 1991:35–41.

p. 174 "As for maroons": Bernabé, Chamoiseau, and Confiant 1993[1989]:30, Chamoiseau, and Confiant 1991:34, 39.

p. 174 "on the margins of general processes": Chamoiseau 1992:107, 142.

p. 175 "secure in their secret dignity": Chamoiseau and Confiant 1991:61.

p. 175 "Among the most docile of slaves": Chamoiseau and Confiant 1991:56–64.

p. 175 "as Françoise Vergès has argued": 1995:81.

p. 175 "As literary critic Richard Burton has argued": 1993:23.

p. 176 "the kind of 'patrimonialization' of which Walcott wrote": 1970:7.

p. 176 "we tried to stick as close as possible to historical reality": in Thomas 1994.

p. 177 "In contrast to his African homeland": Chapelle 1995.

p. 177 "Or, as the film's director put it": in Thomas 1994:36.

p. 179 "a mini-village made up of rural cabins": Staszewski 1993:48–50.

p. 180 "the traditional society we have forgotten": E. H-H. 1992:44–45.

p. 180 "Celebration of the *patrimoine* permeates the press": see Cottias 1992.

p. 180 "nostalgia for the present": Jameson 1991:279–96.

p. 182 "French [jazz] fans": *International Herald Tribune* (January 9, 1987):7.

p. 182 "Two decades ago Glissant argued": 1981:213.

p. 183 "Richard Burton, writing in Glissant's wake": 1993:7–8.

p. 186 "ALL DAY LONG THE TOWN OF ANSES D'ARLET WAS ABUZZ": *France-Antilles* (20 December 1995):12.

p. 188 "to depict the places, the events, and the people of Martinique": Alpha, personal communication June 26, 1996.

p. 189 "In a review of that work, Sally and I noted": R. and S. Price 1995b:139–40.

p. 194 "the advertisements reported from 1995 Barbados": Potter 1996:3.

p. 194 "An outsider's view—from the latest *Guide Hachette*": Mathieu 1992:92–93.

p. 198 "Meanwhile, *France-Antilles*": E. J. S. 1996.

p. 199 "Glissant . . . paved the way in an angry passage": 1981:103–106.

p. 199 "A '*Voyant*' Takes Advantage of His Clients": *France-Antilles* (29 June 1989):2

p. 200 "Abuse of Power": *France-Antilles* (22 July 1989):2

p. 201 "The *Quimboiseur* Took Advantage": *France-Antilles* (12 February 1991):2.

p. 201 "The Perverted Healer": *France-Antilles* (26 October 1993):2.

p. 202 "a clipping from *France-Antilles*": (April 28, 1990):[page number missing from clipping].

p. 208 "Alpha and another colleague had published an article": Briand-Monplaisir and Alpha 1990.

p. 208 "The first response to this article": Editors 1990.

p. 209 "The weekend magazine of *France-Antilles* . . . presented a two-part, illustrated article": Rabussier 1993a, 1993b.

p. 212 "In a reflection on collective memory in Martinique": Jolivet 1987: 306.

p. 213 "José Alpha had illustrated what he called—following my 1985 article—*Le Roi des Indes*": Briand-Monplaisir and Alpha 1990:111–112.

p. 215 "one that Glissant . . . had already prefigured":1981:18, 496.

p. 217 "The Poet observes": Walcott 1990:227–228.

p. 217 "writing (somewhere between exhaustion and ennui)": Geertz 1995:65.

p. 217 "to struggle against a single History": Glissant 1981:159.

Illustration Credits

p. 27   The bust of Colonel Coppens. Photo by Martha Cooper.

p. 29   Uncaptioned: street map. Redrawn by Sondra Jarvis from sketch map in Report of Pégourier dated 28 May 1925.

p. 30   Machine-gun in front of *mairie*. Photo by Fernand Clerc. Archives d'Outre-mer, Affaires Politiques, carton 317.

p. 33   Charles Zizine and Louis Des Étages. Mauvois 1990: facing p. 81.

p. 47   In front of the *mairie*. Photo by Fernand Clerc. Archives d'Outre-mer, Affaires Politiques, carton 317.

p. 49   Election-day reinforcements, May 1925. Photo by Fernand Clerc. Archives d'Outre-mer, Affaires Politiques, carton 317.

p. 50   "House of the Fisherman—or of the Convict," ca. 1983. Postcard: Editions Pumas-Montpeyroux. Photo by Marcel Astruc.

p. 52   Uncaptioned: Maps drafted by Sondra Jarvis.

p. 53   Julien and Tina, 1983. Photo by Richard or Sally Price.

p. 55   "The tiny house." Photos by Richard or Sally Price.

p. 56   Charlemagne (Emilien) Larcher, in front of The Sunbeam, 1983. Photo by Richard or Sally Price.

p. 57   ". . . among the rum bottles . . . a painted wooden statue." Photo by Martha Cooper, 1986.

p. 57   Ador's house, 1962. Photo by Richard Price.

p. 58   Uncaptioned. Médard's colonel. Photo by Martha Cooper, 1986.

p. 59   "We . . . photographed him from various angles." Photos by Richard or Sally Price.

p. 66   The entrance to Médard's cave, 1996. Photos by Richard Price.

p. 68   Entrance to the "Transat." Postcard: Imp. Phot. Neurdein et Cie. Paris.

p. 69   ". . . the great ships he'd see passing out at sea." Photo by Richard or Sally Price.

p. 70   "Whenever there was a military parade." Photo by Richard Price.

p. 77   Detail of one of Médard's ships. Photo by Richard or Sally Price.

p. 78   Entrance to the *quartier-disciplinaire*. Photo by Rodolphe Hammadi, 1994, © CNMHS/SPADEM.

p. 81   Section V (detail). Archives d'Outre-mer.

p. 89   *On board the* La Martinière, by Francis Lagrange. Musée Départemental Franconie, Cayenne.

p. 90   *Debarking on the Maroni from the* La Martinière, by Francis Lagrange. Lagrange and Murray 1961, facing p. 52.

p. 91   "Médard built his own *La Martinière*." Photo by Kenneth Bilby, 1984. Courtesy of Claude Polony.

p. 93   The geography of the *bagne*. Map drafted by Sondra Jarvis.

p. 95 "Soon, we crossed a *pousse.*" *La pousse*, by Francis Lagrange. Musée Départemental Franconie, Cayenne.

p. 97 *Settling a Score*, by Francis Lagrange. Musée Départemental Franconie, Cayenne.

p. 99 *Hauling Timber*, by Francis Lagrange. Musée Départemental Franconie, Cayenne.

p. 102 Médard's *registre matricule*. Archives d'Outre-mer.

p. 111 Uncaptioned. Postcard: Anses d'Arlet. Editions La Case à Rhum.

p. 114 ". . . pulling from his sack a fantastical bust of a king." Photos by Richard Price.

p. 116 Médard's lived-in house at Anse Caffard, ca. 1970. Photo by Claude Breteau.

p. 117 "He'd play the piano for us." Photo by Richard or Sally Price.

p. 118 ". . . he built himself his very last house." Photo by Richard or Sally Price.

p. 119 Plaster plates by Médard Aribot. Photos by Richard or Sally Price.

p. 120 Uncaptioned. Top, Mayoro, Trinidad, 1968, photo by Richard Price; center, postcard, Martinique, courtesy Loïs Hayot; bottom, Petite Anse, 1962, photo by Richard Price.

p. 122 Médard's House at Anse Caffard, 1983. Photo by Richard or Sally Price.

p. 122 Médard's House at Anse Caffard, 1986. Photo by Martha Cooper.

p. 123 Reconstructed house, ca. 1988. Postcard. Photo by André Exbrayat.

p. 123 A painter at work, 1995. Photo by Richard Price.

p. 124 "Rocher du Diamant" cover from the *Guide Gallimard, Martinique*. Illustration © 1994 by H. Galeron. By permission of Gallimard.

p. 127 "Last night . . . made a fifth. . . ." Ballpoint on onionskin, 1962.

p. 128 "At four o'clock, I left the land behind with Emilien . . ." Photo by Richard Price.

p. 129 "We dropped our nets in the sea." Photo by Richard Price.

p. 130 Wedding picture. Photo by Richard Price.

p. 131 Emilien with the newly painted *Notre Dame*. Photo by Richard Price.

p. 132 Guilos (left) finishing a large bamboo *nasse*. Photo by Richard Price.

p. 133 Guilos with his *nasse*. Photo by Richard Price.

p. 134 Setting a net to dry. Photo by Richard Price.

p. 136 Amédée, Anno Henry, R.P., and Amédée's redoubtable brother Amélius, 1962. Photographer unknown.

p. 137 Two young fishermen—Hernoud and Hippolyte—clown for the camera. Photo by Richard Price.

p. 138 Amédée and his sister Laurence. Photo by Richard Price.

p. 139 Midday meal at the Nauds. Photo by Richard Price.

References

Abénon, L. 1982. De la colonie à la dépendance départmementale (1870-1981). In *Histoire des Antilles et de la Guyane*. Edited by Pierre Pluchon. Toulouse: Privat, 413–439.

Adélaïde-Merlande, Jacques. 1994. *Histoire générale des Antilles et des Guyanes: Des Précolombiens à nos jours*. Paris: Editions Caribéennes / L'Harmattan.

Bébel-Gisler, Dany. 1994. *Léonora: The Buried Story of Guadeloupe*. Charlottesville: University Press of Virginia. [French original, 1985].

Belbenoit, René. 1941. *Hell on Trial*. New York: Blue Ribbon Books.

———. 1949. *Dry Guillotine*. New York: Bantam [orig. 1938: New York, E.P. Dutton].

Bernabé, Jean, Patrick Chamoiseau, and Raphaël Confiant. 1993[1989]. *Éloge de la créolité*. Paris: Gallimard.

Bilby, Kenneth M. 1990. The remaking of the Aluku: Culture, politics, and maroon ethnicity in French South America. Unpublished Ph.D. dissertation, Johns Hopkins University.

Brathwaite, Kamau. 1993. *Roots*. Ann Arbor: University of Michigan Press.

Briand-Monplaisir, Zélie, and José Alpha. 1990. La maison du bagnard: une histoire pas comme les autres. *Les Cahiers du Patrimoine* 7 and 8:109–112.

Bruner, Edward M. 1996. Tourism in the Balinese borderzone. In *Displacement, Diaspora, and Geographies of Identity*. Edited by Smadar Lavie and Ted Swedenburg. Durham: Duke University Press, 158–179.

Buffon, Alain. 1981. Le système bancaire aux Antilles. In *Historial Antillais*. Vol. 6, edited by Roland Suvélor. Pointe-à-Pitre: Société Dajani, 80–115.

Burton, Richard. 1993. *Ki Moun Nou Ye?* The Idea of Difference in Contemporary French West Indian Thought. *New West Indian Guide* 67:5–32.

Carpentier, Alejo. 1964[1949]. "Prólogo." *El reino de este mundo*. Montevideo, Uruguay: ARCA.

Celma, Cécile. 1981. La vie politique en Martinique des années 1910–1939. In *Historial Antillais*. Vol. 5, edited by Roland Suvélor, Fort-de-France: Société Dajani, 317–359.

Césaire, Aimé. 1956[1939]. *Cahier d'un retour au pays natal*. Paris: Présence Africaine.

———. 1946. *Les armes miraculeuses*. Paris: Gallimard.

———. 1955. *Discours sur le colonialisme*. Paris: Présence Africaine.

———. 1963. *La tragédie du Roi Christophe*. Paris: Présence Africaine.

———. n.d. Discours prononcé à Genève devant le Comité "Genève et le monde noir," cited in Hector Elisabeth, Fondements réciproques de la personnalité et de la dynamique socio-culturelle aux Antilles françaises. In *Historial Antillais*. Vol. 1, edited by Jean-Luc Bonniol. Pointe-à-Pitre: Société Dajani, 1981. 305–318.

Césaire, Ina. 1981. Littérature orale et contes. In *Historial Antillais*. Vol. 1, edited by Jean-Luc Bonniol. Pointe-à-Pitre: Société Dajani, 479–490.

———. 1985. *Mémoires d'isles: Maman N. et Maman F.* Paris: Éditions Caribéennes.

———. 1994. *Zonzon tête carrée.* Monaco: Editions du Rocher.

Chamoiseau, Patrick. 1986. *Chronique des sept misères.* Paris: Gallimard.

———. 1988a. *Au temps de l'antan: Contes du pays Martinique.* Paris: Hatier.

———. 1988b. *Solibo magnifique.* Paris: Gallimard.

———. 1990. *Antan d'enfance.* Paris: Hatier.

———. 1992. *Texaco.* Paris: Gallimard.

———. 1994. *Chemin-d'école.* Paris: Gallimard.

Chamoiseau, Patrick, and Raphaël Confiant. 1991. *Lettres créoles: tracées antillaises et continentales de la littérature.* Paris: Hatier.

Chapelle, David. 1995. Dieu, l'exil, l'amour et la mort: Béhanzin. *France-Antilles* (30 March): 7.

Clark, Vévé. 1994. Performing the memory of difference in Afro-Caribbean dance: Katherine Dunham's choreography, 1938–87. In *History & Memory in African-American Culture.* Edited by Geneviève Fabre and Robert O'Meally. New York: Oxford University Press, 188–204.

Collini, Stefan. 1995. "The Heritage and the Truth: How Should Historians Respond to the Explosion of Popular Interest in 'Pastifying'?" *TLS* (March 10): 3–4.

Confiant, Raphaël. 1986. *"Kòd yanm."* Fort-de-France: Éditions K. D. P.

———. 1988. *Le nègre et l'amiral.* Paris: Grasset.

———. 1991. *Eau de café.* Paris: Grasset.

———. 1993. *Ravines du devant-jour.* Paris: Gallimard.

———. 1994a. *Commandeur du sucre.* Paris: Écriture.

———. 1994b. *L'allée des soupirs.* Paris: Grasset.

———. 1995. *La savane des pétrifications.* Paris: Mille et Une Nuits.

Constant, Fred. 1988. *La retraite des flambeaux: société et politique en Martinique.* Paris: Editions Caribéennes.

Corascope. 1997. *Corascope 97: Un autre regard sur la Martinique.* Nanterre: Burke Communication.

Cottias, Myriam. 1992. Société sans mémoire, société sans histoire: le patrimoine désincarné. In *Encyclopedia Universalis*, 263–265.

Darsières, Camille. 1996. *Joseph Lagrosillière: Socialiste colonial. Les années pures*

(1872–1919). Fort-de-France: Éditions Désormeaux.

Dash, J. Michael. 1994. Exile and recent literature. In *A History of Literature in the Caribbean*. Vol. 1, *Hispanic and Francophone Regions*, edited by A. James Arnold. Amsterdam: John Benjamins, 451–461.

David, Bernard. 1973. *Les origines de la population martiniquaise du fil des ans (1635–1902)*. Mémoire no. 3. Fort-de-France: Société d'Histoire de la Martinique.

———. 1978. Coolies, Congos et Chinois. In *Le mémorial martiniquais*. Edited by Philippe Godard. Vol. 3. Nouméa, New Caledonia: Société des Éditions du Mémorial, 44–59.

Dibangu, Manu. 1994. *Three Kilos of Coffee* (In collaboration with Danielle Rouard). Chicago: University of Chicago Press [French orig. 1989].

Donet-Vincent, Danielle. 1992. *La fin du bagne (1923–1953)*. Rennes: Éditions Ouest-France.

Du Bois, W. E. B. 1969[1903]. *The Souls of Black Folk*. New York: New American Library.

Dunand, Marcel. n.d. *De la prison au bagne*. Manuscript, 169 pp. [written 1935]. Cayenne.

Ebroïn, Ary. 1990. Magie et superstition. In *La Grande Encyclopédie de la Caraibe*. Vol. 1, *Arts et Traditions*, edited by Danielle Bégot. Italy: Sonoli, 166–177.

"Editors". 1990. P.S. *Cahiers du Patrimoine* 7 and 8:113.

E. H-H. 1992. Le premier éco musée de Martinique. *France-Antilles Magazine* (28 November–4 December): 44–45.

E. J. S. 1996. Anses d'Arlets: Le marché itinérant. *France-Antilles* (12 March): 9.

Epailly, Eugène. 1994. *Francis Lagrange: Bagnard, Faussaire Génial*. [No place, no publisher—apparently self-published in Guyane].

Errington, Frederick and Deborah Gewertz. 1996. The Individuation of Tradition in a Papua New Guinea Modernity. *American Anthropologist* 98:114–126.

Fanon, Frantz. 1952. *Peau noire, masques blancs*. Paris: Seuil.

Fernández Retamar, Roberto. 1989. *Caliban and Other Essays*. Minneapolis: University of Minnesota Press.

Findlay, D.G.A. 1970. *De geschiedenis van het bagno van Frans Guyana (overdrukken uit "De West")*. Paramaribo: Drukkerij De West.

Fisher, Lawrence E. 1985. *Colonial Madness: Mental Health in the Barbadian Social Order*. New Brunswick, NJ: Rutgers University Press.

France Telecom. 1994. *Les pages jaunes, les pages blanches*. Martinique: France Telecom.

Geertz, Clifford. 1995. *After the Fact: Two Countries, Four Decades, One Anthropologist*. Cambridge: Harvard University Press.

Gikandi, Simon. 1992. *Writing in Limbo: Modernism and Caribbean Literature*. Ithaca, NY: Cornell University Press.

Glissant, Édouard. 1975. *Malemort*. Paris: Seuil.

———. 1981. *Le discours antillais*. Paris: Seuil.

———. 1990. *Poétique de la relation*. Paris: Gallimard.

———. 1996. *Faulkner, Mississippi*. Paris: Stock.

González, José Luis. 1980. *El país de cuatro pisos y otros ensayos*. San Juan, PR: Huracán.

Guide Gallimard. 1994. *Martinique*. Paris: Gallimard.

Hall, Douglas. 1962. Slaves and Slavery in the British West Indies. *Social and Economic Studies* 11:305–318.

Harpin, Serge. 1995. *La pêche à la Martinique. Dictionnaire encyclopédique des technologies créoles (créole-français)*. Fort-de-France: AMEP.

Harris, Wilson. 1981. *Explorations: A Selection of Talks and Articles 1966–1981*. Mandelstrup, Denmark: Dangaroo Press.

Herskovits, Melville J. 1971[1937]. *Life in a Haitian Valley*. Garden City, NY: Doubleday/Anchor.

Jameson, Fredric. 1991. *Postmodernism, or, the Cultural Logic of Late Capitalism*. Durham: Duke University Press.

Jolivet, Marie-José. 1987. La construction d'une mémoire historique à la Martinique: du schoelchérisme au maronnisme. *Cahier d'Études africaines* 107–108:287–309.

———. 1990. Culture et bourgeoisie créoles: à partir des cas comparés de la Guyane et de la Martinique. *Ethnologie française* 20:49–61.

Kincaid, Jamaica. 1996. *The Autobiography of My Mother*. New York: Farrar Straus Giroux.

Krakovitch, Odile. 1990. Quelques dates, quelques chiffres, quelques lieux. In *Terres de Bagne*. Edited by Sylvie Clair. Aix-en-Provence: Centre des Archives d'Outre-mer, 39.

Lagrange, Francis, with William Murray. 1961. *F.Lag on Devil's Island*. New York: Doubleday.

Lamming, George. 1953. *In the Castle of My Skin*. New York: McGraw-Hill.

———. 1981[1958]. *Of Age and Innocence*. London: Allison & Busby.

———. 1992[1960]. *The Pleasures of Exile*. Ann Arbor: University of Michigan Press.

———. 1995. *Coming Coming Home: Conversations II*. St. Martin: House of Nehesi Publishers.

Larcher, Marc. 1954[1901]. *A travers la Martinique, ou les vacances de Gérard*. Paris: Les Presses Artisanes.

Lasserre, Guy. 1961. *La Guadeloupe: Étude géographique*. Bordeaux: Union Française d'Impression.

Laurent, Joëlle, and Ina Césaire. 1976. *Contes de mort et de vie aux Antilles*. Paris: Nubia.

Le Clère, Marcel. 1979. *La vie quotidienne dans les bagnes*. 2d ed., revised. Orig. 1973. Paris: Hachette.

Lepape, P. 1993. La mosaïque universelle. *Le Monde des livres* (10 December).

de Lépine, Édouard. 1977. Autour des sénatorials . . . Le GRS et les élections. *Tranchées* 1 (cited in Celma 1981:358).

———. 1980. *La crise de février 1935 à la Martinique*. Paris: L'Harmattan.

Littlewood, Roland. 1993. *Pathology and Identity: The Work of Mother Earth in Trinidad*. Cambridge: Cambridge University Press.

Londres, Albert. 1923. *Au bagne*. Paris: Albin Michel.

Lovelace, Earl. 1988. *A Brief Conversion and Other Stories*. Oxford: Heinemann International.

Lucrèce, André. 1994. *Société et modernité: Essai d'interprétation de la société martiniquaise*. Case Pilote, Martinique: L'Autre mer.

Lucrèce, J. 1932. *Histoire de la Martinique. Cours Supérieur et Complémentaire des Écoles Primaires*. Paris: Presses Universitaires de France.

Maran, Jean-Claude. 1986. Le Diamant. In *Histoire des Communes Antilles-Guyane*. Edited by Jacques Adelaïde-Merlande. Vol. 2. Italy: Pressplay, 199–212.

Marshall, Paule. 1969. *The Chosen Place, the Timeless People*. New York: Harcourt, Brace & World.

Mathieu, Betty. 1992. *À la Martinique* (Guides Visa Hachette). Paris: Hachette.

Mauvois, Georges B. 1990. *Louis des Étages (1873–1925): Itinéraire d'un homme politique martiniquais*. Paris: Karthala.

Memmi, Albert. 1965. *The Colonizer and the Colonized*. New York: Orion.

Michelot, Jean-Claude. 1981. *La guillotine sèche: Histoire du bagne de Cayenne*. Paris: Fayard.

Miles, Alexander. 1988. *Devil's Island: Colony of the Damned*. Berkeley: Ten Speed Press.

Miller, Daniel. 1994. *Modernity, an Ethnographic Approach: Dualism and Mass Consumption in Trinidad*. Oxford: Berg.

Mintz, Sidney W. 1966. The Caribbean as a Socio-Cultural Area. *Cahiers d'Histoire Mondiale* 9:912–937.

———. 1996. Enduring Substances, Trying Theories: The Caribbean Region as *Oikoumenê*. *Journal of the Royal Anthropological Institute* 2:289–311.

Mintz, Sidney W., and Richard Price. 1992[1976]. *The Birth of African-American Culture*. Boston: Beacon Press.

Morrison, Toni. 1987. *Beloved*. New York: New American Library.

Naipaul, V.S. 1971[1959]. Man-man. In *Miguel Street*. Harmondsworth, Middlesex: Penguin, 38–44.

———. 1969[1962]. *The Middle Passage*. Harmondsworth, England: Penguin.

Niles, Blair. 1928. *Condemned to Devil's Island: The Biography of an Unknown Convict*. New York: Grosset & Dunlap.

Oliven, Ruben. 1996. *Tradition Matters: Modern Gaúcho Identity in Brazil*. New York: Columbia University Press.

Ortiz, Fernando. 1940. *Contrapunteo cubano del tabaco y el azucar*. Havana: Consejo Nacional de Cultura.

Oscar, Albert. n.d. *Devant moi la mort. . . .* Fort-de-France: Désormeaux.

Parépou, Alfred. 1987[1885]. *Atipa (roman guyanais)*. Paris: L'Harmattan.

Parry, J.H., and Philip Sherlock. 1971. *A Short History of the West Indies*. 3d ed. New York: St. Martin's.

Patterson, Orlando. 1982. Recent Studies on Caribbean Slavery and the Atlantic Slave Trade. *Latin American Research Review* 17: 251–275.

Péan, Charles. 1924. *Terre de bagne*. Paris: Fischbacher.

Petit, M. L. Félix-Théodose, and Jean Camille Petit. 1981. La vie des martiniquais pendant la Grande Guerre. In *Historial Antillais*. Vol. 5, edited by Roland Suvélor. Pointe-à-Pitre: Société Dajani, 27–69.

Petit Jean Roget, Bernard. 1981. Aperçu sur l'évolution économique de la Martinique au début du xxème siècle. In *Historial Antillais*. Vol. 5, edited by Roland Suvélor. Fort-de-France: Société Dajani, 113–153.

Pierre, Michel. 1982. *La terre de la grande punition: Histoire des bagnes de Guyane*. Paris: Ramsay.

———. 1990. Guyane: La terre de la grande punition. In *Terres de Bagne*. Edited by Sylvie Clair. Aix-en-Provence: Centre des Archives d'Outre-mer, 41–42.

Phillippo, James M. 1843. *Jamaica: Its Past and Present State*. London: John Snow.

Potter, Robert B. 1996. The "New Tourism," Postmodernity and the Culture and History of the Caribbean. *Caribbean Studies Newsletter* 23(1):3–4.

Price, Richard. 1964. Magie et pêche à la Martinique. *L'Homme* 4:84–113.

———. 1965. Trial Marriage in the Andes. *Ethnology* 4:310–322.

———. 1966a. Caribbean Fishing and Fisherman: A Historical Sketch. *American Anthropologist* 68:1363–1383.

———. 1966b. Fishing Rites and Recipes in a Martiniquan Village. *Caribbean Studies* 6(1):3–24.

———. 1983. *First-Time: The Historical Vision of an Afro-American People*. Baltimore:

Johns Hopkins University Press.

——. 1985a. An Absence of Ruins? Seeking Caribbean Historical Consciousness. *Caribbean Review* 14(3):24–29, 45.

——. 1985b. The Dark Complete World of a Caribbean Store: A Note on the World-System. *Review* 11:215–219.

——. 1990a. *Alabi's World*. Baltimore: Johns Hopkins University Press.

——. 1990b. *Ethnographic History, Caribbean Pasts*. College Park: Department of Portuguese and Spanish, University of Maryland.

——. 1995. Duas variantes de relações raciais no Caribe. *Estudos Afro-Asiáticos* 28:185–202.

Price, Richard, and Sally Price. 1992. *Equatoria*. New York: Routledge.

——. 1993. "Based Where We Ought To Be": Two Anthropologists Abandon the Comforts of an Academic Home for a Fisherman's Cottage in Martinique. *Chronicle of Higher Education* (August 11): B3–B4.

——. 1994. Ethnicity in a Museum Case: France's Show-Window in the Americas. *Museum Anthropology* 18(2):3–15.

——. 1995a. *Enigma Variations*. Cambridge: Harvard University Press.

——. 1995b. Sancocho. *New West Indian Guide* 69:127–141.

——. 1996. Museums, ethnicity, and nation-building: Reflections from the French Caribbean. In *Ethnicity in the Caribbean: Essays in Honor of Harry Hoetink*. Edited by Gert Oostindie. London: Macmillan, 81–105.

——. 1997. Shadowboxing in the Mangrove. *Cultural Anthropology* 12:3–36.

Price, Sally. 1995. Experience Wedded in the Mind and Muscles. *American Anthropologist* 97:368–369.

Rabussier, Dominique. 1993a. Médard Aribot, artiste ou bagnard? (1). *France-Antilles Magazine* (14–20 August): 48–49.

——. 1993b. Médard Aribot, artiste ou bagnard? (2). *France-Antilles Magazine* (21–27 August): 48–49.

Redfield, Peter W. 1995. Space in the tropics: Developing French Guiana, penal colony to launch site. Unpublished Ph.D. dissertation, University of California at Berkeley.

Report. 1946. *Report from Overseas France. French Guiana: Liquidation of the Penal Colony*. New York: French Press and Information Service.

Rousseau, Louis. 1930. *Un médecin au bagne*. Paris: Armand Fleury.

Samuel, Raphael. 1994. *Theatres of Memory*. Vol 1, *Past and Present in Contemporary Culture*. London: Verso.

Schuler, Monica. 1980. *"Alas, Alas, Kongo": A Social History of Indentured African*

Immigration into Jamaica, 1841–1865. Baltimore: Johns Hopkins University Press.

Seaton, George John. 1951. *Isle of the Damned: Twenty Years in the Penal Colony of French Guiana.* New York: Farrar, Straus and Young.

Selvon, Sam. 1971[1952]. *A Brighter Sun.* London: Longman.

Silenieks, Juris. 1984. The maroon figure in Caribbean Francophone prose. In *Voices from Under: Black Narrative in Latin America and the Caribbean.* Edited by William Luis. Westport, CT: Garland, 115–125.

———. 1994. Toward *créolité*: Postnegritude developments. In *A History of Literature in the Caribbean.* Vol. 1, *Hispanic and Francophone Regions*, edited by A. James Arnold. Amsterdam: John Benjamins, 517–525.

Simmons, Sally. 1966. A study of mating relations in a fishing village in Martinique. Unpublished B.A. thesis, Department of Anthropology, Radcliffe College.

Staszewski, Gérard. 1993. Images et couleurs d'un village d'antan. *France-Antilles Magazine* (6-12 March): 48–50.

Stewart, John O. 1989. *Drinkers, Drummers, and Decent Folk: Ethnographic Narratives of Village Trinidad.* Albany: State University Press of New York.

Taussig, Michael. 1980. *The Devil and Commodity Fetishism in South America.* Chapel Hill: University of North Carolina Press.

———. 1987. *Shamanism, Colonialism, and the Wild Man: A Study in Terror and Healing.* Chicago: University of Chicago Press.

Taylor, Lucien. n.d. Isle of intellectuals. Doctoral dissertation in preparation, Department of Anthropology, University of California at Berkeley.

Thelwell, Michael. 1980. *The Harder They Come.* New York: Grove.

Thomas, François. 1994. Guy Deslauriers . . . la passion du cinéma. *France-Antilles Magazine* (22–28 October): 36–37.

Trouillot, Michel-Rolph. 1995. *Silencing the Past: Power and the Production of History.* Boston: Beacon Press.

Une Semaine. 1997. *Une Semaine en Martinique.* Paris: Hachette Tourisme (Marco Polo).

Vennat, Francis. 1995. *Tableaux Economiques Régionaux Martinique.* Fort-de-France: INSEE.

Vergès, Françoise. 1995. Métissage, discours masculin et déni de la mère. In *Penser la créolité.* Edited by Maryse Condé and Madeleine Cottenet-Hage. Paris: Karthala, 69–83.

Walcott, Derek. 1970. What the twilight says: An overture. In *Dream on Monkey Mountain and Other Plays.* New York: Farrar, Straus and Giroux, 3–40.

———. 1973. *Another Life.* New York: Farrar, Straus and Giroux.

———. 1974. The muse of history. In *Is Massa Day Dead?* Edited by Orde Coombs. New York: Anchor, 1–27.

———. 1986[1979]. The Schooner *Flight*. In *Collected Poems*, 1948–1984. New York: Farrar, Straus and Giroux, 345–361.

———. 1986[1979]. The Sea Is History. In *Collected Poems*, 1948–1984. New York: Farrar, Straus and Giroux, 364–367.

———. 1987. French Colonial. "Vers de Société." *The Arkansas Testament*. New York: Farrar, Straus and Giroux, 75–76.

———. 1989. History in E.K. Brathwaite and Derek Walcott: Panel Discussion. *The Common Wealth of Letters Newsletter* (Yale University) 1(1):3–14.

———. 1990. *Omeros*. New York: Farrar, Straus and Giroux.

Walmsley, Anne. 1992. *The Caribbean Artists Movement, 1966–1972*. London: New Beacon Books.

Wilson, Peter J. 1974. *Oscar: An Inquiry into the Nature of Sanity*. New York: Random House.

Winkler, Anthony C. 1987 *The Lunatic*. Kingston: Kingston Publishers.

Wright, Gordon. 1983. *Between the Guillotine and Liberty: Two Centuries of the Crime Problem in France*. New York: Oxford University Press.

Zobel, Joseph. 1946. *Diab'-la*. Paris: Nouvelles Éditions Latines.

———. 1974. *La rue Cases-Nègres*. Paris: Présence Africaine.

Joséphine, 1996

Remerciements

Given that the off-again, on-again research that has found its way into this book began, in a real sense, with my arrival in Martinique thirty-five years ago, my debts are hardly possible to remember, much less to enumerate systematically.

To the best of my knowledge, direct financial support for my fieldwork has been limited to a small grant from the National Science Foundation and the Milton Fund of Harvard University (1962), a pre-doctoral fellowship from the U.S. Public Health Service (1963), a small research budget from the dean's office at Johns Hopkins University in the early 1980s, and support for final fact-checking from the College of William and Mary. However, I also used the "writing up" of this project as at least partial justification for fellowship applications to the Stanford Humanities Center, the Shelby Cullom Davis Center for Historical Studies (Princeton), and the Rockefeller Fellows Program at the University of Florida where (in 1989–1990, 1992, and 1994, respectively) I ended up working, happily and productively—each time for one or another then-pressing reason—on an entirely different book. I thank all three institutions for their understanding, and their patience.

My debts in Martinique are innumerable but include, specifically for this project: Emilien and Merlande Larcher, the Naud family that hosted us in the 1960s, Tina Larcher, Julien Privat, Liliane Larcher, Georges Radinez, Ernest Larcher, Julien Erdual, Génor Naud, Clairville Naud, Amélius Naud, Philibert Larcher, Frazius Canton, Dinette Louisy, Cécile Senzamba, Albert Andrieu, Hubert Andrieu, Nora Angély, Armand Ribier, Amédée Larcher, Lusianna Larcher, Ti Louis Larcher, Hubert Larcher, St.-Oïde Marie-Angélique, José Alpha, Michèle Baj Strobel, Axionas Sénart, Gérard Sénart, Sisi Mathurin Larcher, Marie-Claire Joseph-Julien, Donatien Colombe, Olga Delbois, Michel Delbois, Cécile Celma, Claude Bellune and the rest of the staff of the Bibliothèque Schoelcher, Liliane Chauleau, Véronique and Yannick Tarrieu, Jeremy Hobday, Jeannie England, and Loïs Hayot. And all the fishermen and others in Petite Anse whose names may not appear here but who've helped in one way or another—everyone I spoke to once or more, however fleetingly, about Médard.

In Guyane, I received help on this project from Ken Bilby, Alex Miles, Anne-Marie Bruleaux, Anne-Claude Clovis, and Peter Redfield. In France, a number of people deserve thanks: Mademoiselle Menier (to whom Bob Forster provided my introduction), Sylvie Clair and the staff of the Archives d'Outre-mer, Ed Marcus for his photos of the original colonel, and Kristin Couper for many and varied kindnesses. In France and in Guyane, over many years, Diane Vernon helped with archival detective work and other varied intelligence and support.

In the early 1990s, during several visits, Niko Price played a decisive role in convincing me, finally, to write ethnographically about Martinique.

For a number of fine photos, I want to thank professional photographer Martha Cooper, who spent a couple of days with us in Martinique in 1986.

For photographic permissions, I wish to acknowledge: the Bibliothèque Nationale, the Direction des Archives de France (CAOM), the Mission du Patrimoine Photographique (Ministère de la Culture-France), The Musée Départemental Franconie (Guyane), The Caisse Nationale des Monuments Historiques et des Sites, Rafael Duharte Jiménez (Casa del Caribe, Santiago de Cuba), André Exbrayat, Serge Harpin (AMEP), Editions Case à Rhum, Loïs Hayot, and Georges Mauvois, and, for drafting the maps, Sondra Jarvis.

Some of these materials have been published, in different form, in *Caribbean Review* (R. Price 1985a), *Review* (R. Price 1985b), *Cultural Anthropology* (R. and S. Price 1997), R. Price 1990b, and R. and S. Price 1996.

For providing unusually sensitive, detailed, and constructive critiques of the manuscript—comments that really made a difference—I am very grateful to Ken Bilby, Leah Price, Peter Redfield, and Kevin Yelvington, and for additional helpful comments to Abdollah Dashti and the members of my 1996 Ethnographic History seminar at William and Mary.

Deb Chasman has been an editor extraordinaire, ever sensitive, responsive, and upbeat, and it has been a consistent pleasure working with the rest of the Beacon staff. I am grateful to book artist Scott-Martin Kosofsky for respecting my initial design concept while carrying it, with flair, in imaginative new directions.

Sally Price's recent attention to scholarly acknowledgments of wives (S. Price 1995:368) surely renders discretion the better part of valor here. As I hope the pages of this book make clear, our personal and professional journey continues very much *à deux*.